A Fleet History of the San Francisco Municipal Railway

Paul Bignardi

A Fleet History of the San Francisco Municipal Railway
Copyright and Information

A Fleet History of the San Francisco Municipal Railway

Copyright © 2019 by Paul Bignardi
First Edition

All rights reserved. No part of this book may be reproduced in any form or by any electronic or mechanical means, except for brief excerpts of information or brief quotations used in reviews, without the written consent of the author.

Muni, the Muni "Worm" logo and the O' Shaughnessy logo are registered trademarks of the Municipal Transportation Agency of the City and County of San Francisco (SFMTA). They are used in this book with the permission of the SFMTA.

This edition is published by RRB Books.

Printed in the United States of America by IngramSpark.

Library of Congress Control Number: 2099332211

ISBN: 978-1-73357-670-3

Book layout and cover design by Paul Bignardi

A Fleet History of the San Francisco Municipal Railway
Dedication

DEDICATION

This book is dedicated to the thousands of people
who have worked for the San Francisco Municipal Railway (Muni)
and the San Francisco Municipal Transportation Agency (SFMTA) in the past,
those who currently work at Muni and the SFMTA,
and those who will work at Muni and SFMTA in the future.

A Fleet History of the San Francisco Municipal Railway
Acknowledgements

ACKNOWLEGMENTS

Creation of a large history book like this one requires help from many people whose names do not appear on the cover. Without the assistance of the following people, the rich story of the first century of vehicle fleet history of the San Francisco Municipal Railway (Muni) could never have been completed.

In 1981 and 1982 the volumes <u>The Peoples Railway</u> by Anthony Perles and <u>Inside Muni</u> by John McKane and Anthony Perles were published by Interurban Press. These landmark books were extensively relied upon for material used in this book. Yes the books contained some errors, but they were great pieces of work and have served as encyclopedias of information for almost decades. Those books followed the first major volume that must be acknowledged, <u>White Front Cars of San Francisco,</u> by Charles Smallwood, published in 1971 (reprinted in 1978). Also printed by Interurban Press, the book told the story of the Market Street Railway up to the point of its acquisition by Muni in 1944. These three books, supplemented by more recent publications including, <u>Tours of Discovery</u> by Anthony Perles, <u>The Cable Car in America</u> by George Hilton, <u>San Francisco's F-Line</u> by Peter Ehrlich, <u>San Francisco's Century of Streetcars</u> by by Fred A. Stindt, and <u>The First Century of the Municipal Railway</u> by Grant Ute provided large amounts of information that appears in this book.

Building upon that significant base of information to fill in the events of the past 35+ years was the primary task. Foremost among support and assistance were Jeremy Menzies (SFMTA photographer) and Katy Guyon (Photographer Archivist) who helped me find, save, and use dozens of photos located in the SFMTA photo archives. Close behind their effort was Emiliano Echeverria, a retired Muni employee, transit and history professional, and author of multiple books on San Francisco transit history. He provided photos, editing work, and support that was invaluable. Also focused on historic accuracy were Tony Marquardt, who provided valuable information on streetcars and cable cars, and Jerry McGovern, the SFMTA librarian who helped research agency records and documents. Many photographs were provided by Matthew C. Lee currently of the SFMTA Transit Division, who allowed use of several dozen photographs of recent Muni equipment. Additional photos and information were provided by Val Lupiz of SFMTA (Muni), Ron Downing of Golden Gate Transit, Kevin Mueller, L.C Carlson and Jack Demnyan. Photos, or the approval to use online photos, were sent from museums around the nation that currently have historical Muni vehicles in their collections, the Market Street Railway Museum and from the San Francisco Public Library. At the 11th hour unexpected assistance was received from Phillip A. Wright, son of Arnold Gridley, who allowed photos to be taken of original California Street cable cars he owns in storage, which were motorized by his father, including Jones Street Shuttle Cable Car #60.

Editing and proofreading of the finished document was performed by Eileen Housteau, Art Curtis, Terri Dien, and others who are not named here. Special mention goes to two people who provided extraordinary contributions: Rick Laubscher of the Market Street Railway Museum, and Art Curtis, retired Chief Inspector at Muni in the 1980s. Both carefully edited the draft manuscript. Rick also provided the foreword on the next page. Finally, a thank you and acknowledgement to my wife Terri Dien for her support in this effort.

      Paul Bignardi
      December 2018

A Fleet History of the San Francisco Municipal Railway
Foreword

FOREWORD

Of America's myriad transit systems, San Francisco's Municipal Railway (Muni) is unique. When its first streetcar lines opened, on Geary Street in 1912, it was the very first big city transit operation owned by the people themselves: a public utility, offering riders an alternative to for-profit transit companies that dominated the city's politics at the time. Well-managed and methodical in its expansion, Muni opened up whole new neighborhoods to development with investments in tunnels and rights-of-way, and eventually absorbed its private competitors to provide unified service throughout the city.

Muni is also unique in the variety of equipment it has operated over its century-plus of service. No other agency runs cable cars, historic streetcars, light rail vehicles, electric trolley buses, diesel-electric hybrid buses, and biodiesel buses all at the same time.

Paul Bignardi has captured the history of Muni's diverse fleet in this valuable volume. This is a much-needed update to the historical record of Muni's fleet, which hasn't been documented so closely since the 1980s. His research has been meticulous and the coverage is thorough. All transit fans, and San Franciscans in particular, will enjoy his work.

    Rick Laubscher
    President - Market Street Railway Museum
    November 2018

A Fleet History of the San Francisco Municipal Railway
Table of Contents

Section 1: Introduction and History   1

Section 2: Streetcars and Light Rail Vehicles   9

Section 3: Buses   47

Section 4: Trolley Buses   81

Section 5: Cable Cars   95

Section 6: Divisions, Yards, Barns and Work Cars   135

Section 7: Figures and Graphics   159

Bibliography and Photo Credits   197

A Fleet History of the San Francisco Municipal Railway
Section 1: Introduction and History

A Fleet History of the San Francisco Municipal Railway
Section 1: Introduction and History

A Fleet History of the San Francisco Municipal Railway
Section 1: Introduction and History

INTRODUCTION

In 2012 the San Francisco Municipal Railway, popularly known as "Muni", celebrated its Centennial anniversary. Muni, which has been a part of the larger San Francisco Municipal Transportation Agency (SFMTA) since 1999, is one of the largest transit agencies in the United States. Muni operates over 1,000 transit vehicles and carries over 700,000 daily passengers. It is also unique transit as it operates five modes of transit equipment: motor buses, trolley buses, light rail vehicles (LRVs), historic streetcars, and cable cars. Muni is the last transit operator in the world to use cable cars, it is one of only five transit operators in the United States to use trolley buses, and it operates the largest and most diverse historic streetcar fleet of any transit operator in the world.

The last thorough compilation of Muni transit equipment information was done nearly 40 years ago in 1981. The twin volumes titled The People's Railway and Inside Muni were complete agency history books that were giant in scope and detailed in information content. They continue to serve as excellent reference manuals, and this book is not an attempt to recreate either volume. However, a passage of over three decades of time represents multiple generations of transit vehicles, and the many stories that accompany each vehicle. This book is a new volume to document the Muni story that continues to unfold on the streets of San Francisco every day, especially as the agency enters into its second century of transit service.

HISTORY

SFMTA can trace its public origins back to multiple city agencies, including the San Francisco Department of Public Works and the San Francisco Police Department, but the transit service side of the modern agency traces its public origins back to the San Francisco Municipal Railway, or "Muni", which was established in 1912 as a unit of the San Francisco Department of Public Works. The name and image of Muni is so strong that almost two decades after the SFMTA was established, Muni is still often used as a name for the larger agency. Although Muni has always been a public agency, it also has an extensive private background due to its acquisition of three privately owned transit systems. Via lineage through the acquired Market Street Railway (MSRy) and its predecessor companies, Muni can trace its privately held origins back almost to the Gold Rush. Although Muni is world famous today for the operation of cable cars, these unique transit vehicles only became a part of Muni after the merger with MSRy in 1944.

Muni's story begins in earnest after passage of Proposition 1, a bond measure for $1.90 million dollars, in a special election on December 30, 1909 with 31,151 "yes" votes, vs. 11,704 "no" votes. The funds were used to build a streetcar route that mostly followed the former cable car route of the Geary Street, Park and Ocean Railroad. The new service became Muni Route 'A' with commencement of operations on December 28, 1912. At the time Muni began service San Francisco was still recovering from the 1906 Earthquake and had a population of 416,912 (1910 census). Muni was the first public transit agency in a large American city, as transit was mostly a private enterprise operation across the United States, and would continue to be so until after World War II. Transit in 1912 meant streetcars. The cable car, which had been invented in San Francisco 40 years earlier in 1873, had almost disappeared from the scene, except in a few places like San Francisco, because it could not compete in performance or economics with the electric streetcar. Due to politics, San Francisco still had one operational horse car transit line which ended service in 1913, and transit buses were in their infancy and rarely seen in most places.

A Fleet History of the San Francisco Municipal Railway
Section 1: Introduction and History

Sharing the streets of San Francisco with Muni in 1912 were the streetcars and cable cars of the large and powerful United Railroads (URR), which would be renamed (for a second time) as the Market Street Railway (MSRy) in 1921, the cable cars of the California Street Cable Railroad (CAL), and the small Presidio & Ferries Railroad (P&FRR) (streetcar routes). All other private transit companies had been consolidated into the URR by 1902. The three private companies, and all of their predecessors operated via "franchises". These were contracts between the private transit operators and the city government to provide transit service on a for profit basis for a fixed period of time (50 years was a common length) on clearly identified streets in exchange for a fee paid to the City of San Francisco. The P&FRR franchise was about to expire, so in fall 1913, the City bought the assets of the Union Street line for $312,333.

Intercity transit service (service beyond the borders of San Francisco) was mostly provided by the Southern Pacific Railroad (SPRR) and subsidiary companies with connections to the North Bay (Northwestern Pacific RR) (1907-1969); via ferry boat service, the East Bay (SPRR) (1862-1938), and later the Interuban Electric Railway (IERR) (1938-1941); via ferry boats and later trains on the Bay Bridge, and the Peninsula and South Bay; via steam trains of the mainline SPRR Peninsula line (1863-current). The Peninsula route continues to be served by Caltrain in 2018, but the other routes have either been taken over by other public transit service, are abandoned, or were converted to roads. Only in the East Bay, where the Key System operated from 1903-1960, was a sizable private transit agency present to compete with SPRR. In 1960 the Key System morphed to become the Alameda-Contra Costa Transit District, or AC Transit.

During the first ten years of existence, Muni commenced on an aggressive expansion program, which included the purchase of the aforementioned Presidio and Ferries Railroad, and an intensive capital construction campaign led by San Francisco City Engineer Michael Maurice (M.M.) O'Shaughnessy. Although he did not directly manage Muni, O'Shaughnessy was the driving force behind many of its noteworthy accomplishments, which included building new streetcar lines following the construction of the Stockton Street Tunnel (1914), the Dolores Park Serpentine (1917), and the Twin Peaks Tunnel (1918). At the time of its opening in 1918, the Twin Peaks Tunnel was the longest streetcar tunnel in the world. During the same time Muni achieved access to new tracks on Market Street parallel to URR tracks, making Market Street one of the few streets with four streetcar tracks in the world. This was the beginning of the "Roar of the Four" era. Later, the Sunset Tunnel (Duboce Tunnel) opened in 1926. From inception through World War I in 1918, Muni had a farebox recovery of 100% or more, and through the 1920's farebox recovery exceeded 90% annually. Muni began its first bus service in the Sunset District in 1917, and gradually additional routes were added, but buses were only a small part of Muni operations into the 1930s.

The time period between the early 1920s and World War II were two decades where the newer and expanding Muni and the older, but still powerful and vibrant MSRy shared the City and actively competed for passengers. MSRy was rejuvenated from the harsh management of the URR days following a reorganization in 1921 and the implementation of the Byllesby management system in 1925. Simultaneously between 1920-1933 the MSRy engaged in an aggressive program to build new streetcars in-house at their Elkton Shops facility. Over 250 were produced, usually pairing new wooden bodies with recycled hardware from older cars. The cars were built at the rate of a new car about every 2-3 weeks. In 1926 MSRy introduced "The White Front" car concept, which required MSRy streetcars to be painted with "white fronts" to increase visibility. The concept became a patented safety measure and was a successful early example of agency branding.

A Fleet History of the San Francisco Municipal Railway
Section 1: Introduction and History

The new paint scheme was a contrast to the understated silver or gray and red colors found on Muni vehicles. Most buildings were painted green with large MSRy logos to show their presence across San Francisco. In 1931, the MSRy obtained a 25 year extension on its franchises (several had expired in 1929) to operate transit in San Francisco, but by the early 1930s the transit landscape in San Francisco was slowly changing.

In 1931 San Francisco voters approved a new City Charter by passing Proposition 1. The new charter replaced the Board of Public Works with a Department of Public Works for most functions, and a Public Utilities Commission (SFPUC) for public utilities, including Muni, Hetch Hetchy and the S.F. Airport. It also removed direct control of these agencies from M.M. O'Shaughnessy, and exposed the real costs of Muni operations for all to see. In an effort to operate in the black, which magically Muni started doing in 1934 after a decade in the red, actions such as deferred maintenance, postponement of new equipment purchases, and other economic measures became the normal in operations.

After the late 1920s both agencies saw ridership levels decrease due to the Great Depression and competition with private automobiles. In the 1930s as economic conditions remained stagnant, Muni continued to grow, while MSRy, burdened with several lower performing ridership routes, struggled financially, and sank into decline. An effort to allow one-man streetcar operation by MSRy was successful starting in 1934, but by 1938 San Francisco reinstituted requirements for two-man car operations, which had a large negative financial impact. Initial efforts to achieve a public buyout of the MSRy were rejected by voters in 1925, 1938, 1942 and 1943. In 1938 MSRY increased its fare to 7c and made transfers free, while Muni remained 5c, plus 2c for transfers. This seemingly small change actually resulted in many passengers moving away from MSRy to Muni. In 1935 the ridership split between the two agencies was roughly 70% MSRy and 30% Muni. By 1944 they were about even.

The 1940s was the decade of greatest change in the history of Muni. In December 1941 the United States entered World War II, which changed San Francisco forever. Ridership on all transit service increased to record levels as gasoline was rationed and San Francisco became a key port city for the war effort in the Pacific Theater. Although ridership increased revenues, the heavy use along with deferred maintenance wore the transit fleets down at both agencies. By this time Muni's oldest streetcars were nearing 30 years in service, and MSRy had active cars with nearly 40 years of service time. Earlier in 1941 Muni introduced its first trolley bus route, the R-Howard. MSRy had begun trolley bus service on Route 33 a few years earlier in 1935. This new mode would become very important after World War II.

In the middle of World War II, on May 16, 1944, San Franciscans approved Charter Measure 1 authorizing expenditure of $7.5 million dollars to buy out MSRy. The vote was 198,621 "yes", and 84,078 "no". A little over four months later on September 29, 1944, the two agencies officially merged ending the MSRy as operating entity after over 50 years of existance as MSRy reincarnated (1921-1944), United RRs (1902-1921) and MSRy (1893-1902). Service links via acquired lines dated back to 1851. Muni more than doubled in size overnight acquiring 440 streetcars, 154 buses, 9 trolley buses, 48 cable cars of equipment, and several dozen work cars and non-revenue rubber tired vehicles (cars and trucks). Also acquired were 14 divisions or barns, 197 miles of streetcar tracks, including a line that extended from the San Francisco - Daly City border to San Mateo 14 miles to the south, and 6 miles of narrow gauge track. The 1944 merger is when Muni acquired its first cable cars on the Powell - Mason and Washington - Jackson lines formerly owned by MSRy.

A Fleet History of the San Francisco Municipal Railway
Section 1: Introduction and History

Muni at the time of the merger consisted of 2 divisions, plus a leased bus division, and owned 75 miles of streetcar tracks. Muni also owned 238 streetcars, 107 buses, 9 trolley buses, and 0 cable cars. The MSRy workforce of about 1,700 also merged with the Muni staff of 1,500 to create a new agency of 3,200, which swelled to almost 4,500 with new war time hires. In 1945 the workforce included 800 women. Labor issues were worked out, and the new Muni moved forward, but in light of the realities of the size of the two entities at the time of the merger, a question that often is still asked today is, "who absorbed who?"

The merger also saw the end of the "White Front" Car era, as the City Charter didn't allow for the patent payments, and so Muni quickly painted the MSRy equipment with a menagerie of colors to remove the white fronts on streetcars. Some were completely repainted in Muni's blue and yellow colors, but others received blue or yellow fronts while the bodies remained green, some had partial blue fronts, and so on. In 1946 Muni addressed the vehicle appearance issue by adoption of green and cream colors and a "Wings" design, which many consider Muni's finest paint scheme.

The end of World War II in August 1945 ushered in a time of major change at Muni. The year of 1945 was the most profitable year in Muni history with a farebox recovery of 123%, while Muni's peak ridership year was 1946 when it carried 326 million passengers, although farebox recovery was lower than in 1945. Mayor Roger Lapham who had led the charge to buy out the MSRy in 1944 moved to implement more changes at Muni. In fall 1947 Proposition 1, a bond measure for $20 million dollars, was approved by voters, and with the application of those funds Muni transformed from a transit agency focused on streetcar operations to a transit agency focused on bus and trolley bus operations in less than a decade. Marmion Mills, a consultant and a former Army Colonel in World War I - who later worked for Yellow Bus and National City Lines, was hired to lead the transformation. Hundreds of old streetcars were scrapped, tracks were removed, and hundreds of buses and trolley buses replaced them. The fleet vehicles arrived in new colors of green and cream, with most sporting the "Wings" design. However, the streetcars through the Twin Peaks Tunnel were spared, and in an ironic twist, in the midst of scrapping old streetcars, Muni finally acquired its first Presidents' Conference Committee (PCC) cars in 1948. In 1952 a second streetcar order included purchase of Car #1040, the last U.S. made PCC car. In 1946 work began to remove the outer tracks on Market Street. By 1948 the "Roar of the Four" era was over.

Mills and Mayor Roger Lapham also planned for buses to replace cable cars, which they saw as obsolete and expensive to operate. However, the cable cars survived due to the efforts of many people, including socialite Friedel Klussmann, who led a grass-roots effort in opposition. The passage of Proposition 10 in November 1947 saved the cable cars. Ironically, the same ballot included the aforementioned Proposition 1 to fund purchase of new buses and trolley buses, and Proposition 2, which approved bonds to complete the purchase of the MSRy. In January 1952 Muni acquired the California Street Cable Railroad, the last private transit operator in San Francisco following its bankruptcy. The cost was $132,758. For a brief time Muni operated five cable car lines. Although the former MSRy cable car lines were supposedly protected after 1947, the Cal Cable lines were not, and in 1954-1957 a consolidation occurred. When it was over lines that existed on O'Farrell, and Jones Streets were removed or significantly cut back, the California Street line was shortened, and only three cable cable car lines remained. However, ultimately the iconic image of cable cars won out, and they were declared a National Historic Landmark in 1964.

A Fleet History of the San Francisco Municipal Railway
Section 1: Introduction and History

By the early 1950s, aside from early BART planning, transportation planning in the Bay Area was primarily focused on plans for cars and freeways. Simultaneously, transit costs were rising faster than revenues and cost was a major concern for transit managers. Athough Muni enjoyed solid ridership in the era, times were lean. In 1953 Muni operated at a profit from the farebox for the last time, and voters rejected a bond measure that included funding for new buses. In desperation, Muni turned to Mack Trucks and leased 450 Mack buses that arrived in 1955-1960 to replace worn out buses purchased in the 1930s and 1940s. After legislation of "one man streetcar" operation was approved in 1954, the pre-World War II era streetcars were retired by 1958. Two years earlier, in December 1956, Muni ended streetcar service on the B-Geary and C-California lines. The end result was by late 1958 Muni operated an all PCC fleet on only five streetcar lines: J, K, L, M and N. All other transit service was provided by buses, trolleybuses, or the surviving cable cars.

The 1960s began with a flourish. After years of planning BART was approved with a 61.2% yes vote overall in November, 1962. A 60% "yes" vote was needed for passage following approval of a bill by the California Legislature that lowered the amount from a 2/3 majority. On the ballot in San Francisco as Proposition A, it received 166,539 "yes" votes and 80,967 "no" votes, or 66.9% "yes" vote overall. The measure actually failed in Contra Costa County with only a 54.4% "yes" vote, but was carried by San Francisco and Alameda County voters, so the three county plan was approved. The vision of a Market Street Subway first drafted by Bion J. Arnold in a 1913 report was set to become a reality. A few years later in twin conflicting actions, the San Francisco Board of Supervisors voted against further freeway construction in fall 1965 and spring 1966 on 6-5 votes, but in fall 1966 voters failed to approve Proposition B which would have built a subway under Geary Boulevard and other transit improvements. The vote was 143,135 "yes" and 104,251 "no", or 57.9% yes, when a 66.67% "yes" vote was required for passage. BART construction under Market Street began in 1967 while Muni operated PCC streetcars on a 2.5 minute schedule frequency on the surface. While BART charged forward, Muni didn't develop a solid operations or fleet plan for Muni subway service until the early 1970s. In the midst of a turbulent decade, in 1967 Muni adopted a new logo and color scheme of maroon and gold, known informally as the "Cable Car Livery" or the "Ribbon" logo.

During the same time period, at the national level Congress approved the law to create the Urban Mass Transit Administration (UMTA) in 1964. UMTA became the Federal Transit Administration (FTA) in 1978. The 1964 legislation also included guaranteed federal funding assistance to purchase transit equipment. The last item transformed the process of getting new transit vehicles more than any legislation before or since. Following approval of the UMTA legislation Muni delayed plans to buy new buses in the mid-1960s so they could utilize the new funding set up, and over 300 General Motors "New Look" buses began to arrive in 1969.

The 1970s were also a busy decade. In 1973 the Board of Supervisors approved a "Transit First" policy, to reaffirm a commitment to public transit. Muni debuted a stored value "Fast Pass", in May 1974. In the mid-1970s the 1950 era trolley bus fleet was replaced, and the new vehicles were the first to wear the Muni "Worm" logo and the new Muni colors of "Sunset Glow" and "California Poppy Gold" developed by the Walter Landor design firm.

BART construction was mostly complete by 1971, and BART opened under Market Street and Mission Street in early 1973. Muni Metro construction lagged, but demolition of the West Portal tunnel facade to allow for a new station, and stations at Church and Castro Streets previewed forthcoming changes.

A Fleet History of the San Francisco Municipal Railway
Section 1: Introduction and History

The first Muni light rail vehicles (LRVs), which became known as the Boeing cars, were delivered in 1978. In preparation for the modern LRV cars, the Metro Divison (later renamed Green Division) was built on the site of the former Ocean Division bus yard and the decrepit Elkton Shops complex adjacent to the Balboa Park BART station. Green Division opened in 1977. Muni subway service began slowly, and the venerable PCC surface fleet was replaced by subway service in phases between 1979-1982.

The 1980s were a decade of surprises at Muni. In 1982 the Cable Car system was forced to shutdown with little notice for a major capital reconstruction due to safety and operations issues. The $60 million cost to rebuild the system was daunting, but with extensive federal funding assistance, the system was rebuilt and opened again in 1984. While the cable cars were out of action, the S.F. Historic Trolley Festival was organized in summer 1983, and was a great success. The Trolley Festival returned in the summers of 1984-1987 to great fanfare, even after the cable cars returned to service. The outcome was the festival became the genesis for the F-Line historic streetcar route that began in 1996. On October 17, 1989 the Loma Prieta Earthquake heavily damaged San Francisco, and led to removal of the Embarcadero and Central Freeways. The opening of the Embarcadero dramatically improved the extension of the the F-Line to Fisherman's Wharf.

The past two and a half decades saw Muni to be as busy in fleet related issues as any previous era. During this time Muni acquired its first articulated buses (1990), new LRV trains (1997), a fleet of restored PCC streetcars (1991), a fleet of restored "Peter Witt" streetcars from Milan, Italy (1998), its first articulated trolley bus (2002), its first low-floor and hybrid buses (2006) and more historic streetcars (2002 and 2008). The new F-Line opened on Market Street in 1996 and was expanded in 2001. An extension to the LRV J-line route opened in 1993, and Muni's first totally new rail line in 75 years, the T-Third line, opened in 2007.

In 1993 voters approved Proposition M with a vote of 72,090 "yes" and 65,925 "no", and Muni was removed from the SFPUC, and a separate Publc Transit Commission (PTC) was created. In 1999 voters acted again by passing Proposition E with a vote of 110,079 "yes" and 70,113 "no", to merge Muni (and the PTC) with the San Francisco Department of Parking and Traffic (SFDPT) and create the San Francisco Municipal Transportation Agency (SFMTA). Voters approved two measures to fund transit. Proposition B, a 1/2 c sales tax, was approved in 1989 with a vote of 107,017 "yes" and 55,997 "no", and Proposition K, an extension of the Proposition B 1/2 c sales tax was approved in 2003 by a vote of, 142,104 "yes" and 47,879 "no". The sales tax revenue has generated several million dollars for Muni. All-door boarding was implemented systemwide in 2013, and the stored value regional transit Clipper Card replaced the Fast Pass in 2014.

An extension of the T-Line, known as the Central Subway, is due to open in 2020. A new generation of LRV cars, known as LRV4 cars, built by Siemens, began to arrive in 2017. Within a decade Muni is supposed to operate over 200 LRV4 cars and the Breda cars are due to be retired. Over 400 new buses and trolley buses entered into service during the past few years or will enter service by 2021 to replace older transit equipment. Finally plans are in development to transition the Muni rubber tired fleet to an all-electric fleet, and early planning is underway to rebuild Potrero, Presidio and Kirkland transit divisions by 2030.

Over 2,000 transit vehicles have worn the Muni name or logo since 1912. This fleet history tells quite a story of over a century of operations by the San Francisco Municipal Railway - or Muni - in the City by the Bay.

A Fleet History of the San Francisco Municipal Railway
Section 2: Streetcars and Light Rail Vehicles

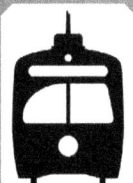

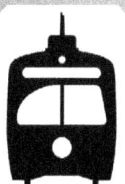

A Fleet History of the San Francisco Municipal Railway
Section 2: Streetcars and Light Rail Vehicles

A Fleet History of the San Francisco Municipal Railway
Section 2: Streetcars and Light Rail Vehicles

The San Francisco Municipal Railway (Muni), which is currently the largest division of the The San Francisco Municipal Transportation Agency (SFMTA), began operations on December 28, 1912. Muni was originally a unit of the San Francisco Department of Public Works, which also included the Water Department. The first Muni streetcar line, named Route 'A', was partially built along the expired franchise route of the Geary Street, Park and Ocean Railway, which had been acquired by the City of San Francisco using funds from a bond approved by voters in December 1909. From the outset in 1912, Muni routes were designated with letters to lessen confusion with the older Market Street Railway (MSRy) routes, which were designated with numbers.

During the next 20 years the Muni streetcar network grew until it numbered 13 lines in 1932, and it grew again to 34 lines following the merger with the MSRy in 1944 (11 Muni + 23 MSRy). Equipment was diverse and produced both locally and by companies located all across the United States. In 1939 Muni purchased five "Magic Carpet" streetcars, which were similar to a Presidents' Conference Committee Car (PCC), but with enough differences to deny use of that title. They were known locally as "Magic Carpet" streetcars for their smooth ride. After World War II Muni acquired its first true PCC streetcars in 1948, and purchased more PCC streetcars in 1952, which included Car #1040, the last PCC produced in the United States.

However, in the dozen years following World War II, a massive transformation to transit service using motor buses and trolley buses that coincided with the scrapping of hundreds of old and mostly worn out streetcars, and the removal of miles of streetcar tracks, decreased the number of Muni rail lines to only five: J, K, L, M and N by the end of 1956. Following adoption of single operator streetcar operations in 1954, the last "original era" streetcars were retired in 1958. Additional secondhand PCC streetcars were acquired in 1957, 1962, and 1974, and the system continued with mostly minor changes through the 1960s and into the 1970s.

The pending arrival of the first light rail vehicles (LRVs) in the late 1970s and the opening of the Market Street Subway (built as part of BART) ushered in a new era in rail operations at Muni. In 1977 the new Metro rail division (later renamed Green Division) opened on the site of the historic old rail division (Elkton Shops). The M Line was extended to Green Division in 1979, and an expansion for the J Line from the Outer Mission District through the Glen Park neighborhood to the new Green Division opened in 1982. By 1982 LRV's replaced all PCC streetcars in regular service.

In the past 35 years rail transit has continued to perform a vital role in Muni operations due to the importance and performance of the Twin Peaks Tunnel / Market Street Subway, and worsening surface congestion that slows buses, trolley buses and rail in non-exclusive right of way throughout San Francisco. The aforementioned M and J Line extensions were built, a second and third generation of LRVs entered service in the 1990s, and the wonderfully improbable, but very uniquely San Franciscan historic streetcar service began operations on Market Street and later on the Embarcadero between 1996 and 2001. In 2007, the new 'T' line opened on 3rd Street along with a second rail division named Metro East.

In 2017 the fourth generation of LRV entered service, construction continued on the extension of the 'T' line, (known as Central Subway), that is due to open in 2020, and multiple conceptual new rail extensions and system upgrades are in the planning stages for possible future implementation.

A Fleet History of the San Francisco Municipal Railway
Section 2: Streetcars and Light Rail Vehicles

No. 1	Years	Seats	Length / Width / Height / Weight	Model	Manufacturer
1-20	1912-1951	48	47'1" / 8'6" / 11'9" / 50,000	Type A	W. L. Holman Car Co. San Francisco, CA

Type 'A' streetcars were the first model of streetcar at Muni. The cost of each car was $7,700. These were built by the W. L. Holman Company of San Francisco, and were often referred to as "Arnold" cars, because the design followed recommendations made by consultant Bion J. Arnold. Upon delivery all were painted in a light gray color with red trim and highlights. When Muni started service on December 28, 1912, all of the streetcars in service were Type 'A' streetcars. All were scrapped in 1951, except Car #1, which was placed in storage. The average scrap price was $350. In 1962 to celebrate the 50th anniversary of Muni, Car #1 received a superficial restoration and operated in limited special service. Since 1962 Car #1 has been refurbished or restored multiple times, with the lastest work being a complete overhaul prior to the Muni Centennial in 2012. In 2018 Car #1 continues to operate in special service, and occasionally on the F-Line.

Car #1 at Geneva Division in a late 1940s view showing the green and cream "wings" paint scheme

Car #1 repainted gray with red trim for Muni 50th anniversary in 1962

A Fleet History of the San Francisco Municipal Railway
Section 2: Streetcars and Light Rail Vehicles

Car #1 in 2017 - a few years after a restoration prior to the Muni Centennial in 2012.

No. 2	Years	Seats	Length / Width / Height / Weight	Model	Manufacturer
21-43	1913-1951	48	47'1" / 8'6" / 11'9" / 50,000	Type A	Union Iron Works, San Francisco, CA

This group of streetcars was the second order of the "Type A" model. Since Holman had difficulties completing the original contract, the Union Iron Works filled this order. All were retired and scrapped by 1951

A Fleet History of the San Francisco Municipal Railway
Section 2: Streetcars and Light Rail Vehicles

No. 3 301-329	Years 1913-1922	Seats 26	Length / Width / Height / Weight 26'10" / 8' 8.5" / N/A / 20,300	Model Type G	Manufacturer Hammond Car Company San Francisco, CA

Car #315 - Only known photo in Muni archives of this car type with Muni markings. Photo taken after an accident in 1921

The "Type G" streetcars were built in 1895-1898 for the Market Street Railway (first company - later became part of United RRs). Muni came to own these cars when it acquired the Presidio & Ferries RR (P&FRR) in 1913. The P&FRR acquired the streetcars from the United Railroads after the 1906 Earthquake for conversion of the Union Street line from cable cars to electric streetcars. The streetcars, featuring a California Car design, were the oldest streetcars to operate at Muni. All but five were sold in 1922 for $125 each. The remaining cars were converted to work cars. Four were scrapped in 1940 and 1946, although the remains of one wound up at the Western Railway Museum in the 1960s, where it continues to await rebuild and restoration 50+ years later.

No. 4 44-168	Years 1914-1958	Seats 50	Length / Width / Height / Weight 47'1" / 9'2.5" / 12'3" / 48,000	Model Type B	Manufacturer Jewett Car Company Newark, OH

Muni "Type B" streetcars were known as "Iron Monsters", "Box Cars" or "Battleships". The cost when delivered was $7,100 per unit. These were some of the most durable and heavily used streetcars in San Francisco history. All from this group except Car #130 and Car #162 were retired and scrapped by 1958. "Type B" streetcars had open end sections flanking a closed middle section (California Car style). In the 1920s open end sections were enclosed to protect passengers from the foggy and cool weather of San Francisco. In 2002 Car #162 was purchased from the Orange Empire Railway Museum for $70,000 and returned to San Francisco. In 2018 Cars #130 and #162 are part of the historic fleet and operate at times on the E and F-Lines and in special service.

A Fleet History of the San Francisco Municipal Railway
Section 2: Streetcars and Light Rail Vehicles

"Type B" Iron Monster streetcar Car #72 in a 1943 photo - with the end sections enclosed, except at the doors, and the Muni adopted paint scheme of blue and yellow that was used for streetcars starting in 1939

Car #130 ended passenger service in 1958, but was retained by Muni and converted to a work car. In 1983 Muni craftsmen restored Car #130 for passenger service in preparation of the first Streetcar Festival. It has been used in F line service and for charters for over 35 years. This photo was taken on a charter in 2013

Car #162 at Orange Empire Museum in Perris, CA in the 1970s (left), and restored in S.F. in 2013 (right). In 2018 Car #162 returned to Muni after an extensive repair by Carlos Guzman, Inc. of Signal Hill, CA following an accident in early 2014. Unfortunately other problems were found with the car and by late 2018 it was still undergoing repairs and was not in service

A Fleet History of the San Francisco Municipal Railway
Section 2: Streetcars and Light Rail Vehicles

No. 5	Years	Seats	Length / Width / Height / Weight	Model	Manufacturer
351-370	1922-1948	32	29'10" / 8' 6" / 11'2" / 26,000	Type J	American Car Company, Philadelphia, PA

"Type J" streetcars were small vehicles known as "dinkies", and were unusual with center loading doors. These cars were most commonly used on the E-Union Street line. Each unit cost $11,500 when delivered painted gray with red trim in 1922. The prototype for the "Type J" car is was Car #371, which is listed in some Muni history documents as a separate model, J-1. At the time of delivery in 1921 it was numbered as Car #200, but was renumbered at a later date. It was scrapped in 1948. All of the "Type J" model streetcars were scrapped by 1948. Scrap value in 1948 was $150 per car. None exist in 2018.

A Fleet History of the San Francisco Municipal Railway
Section 2: Streetcars and Light Rail Vehicles

No. 6	Years	Seats	Length / Width / Height / Weight	Model	Manufacturer
169-188	1923-1958	50	47'1" / 9'2.5" / 12'2" / 51,000	Type K	Bethlehem Steel, San Francisco, CA

The Muni "Type K" streetcars were also nicknamed "Battleships", "Box Cars" or "Iron Monsters". These cars were built locally in San Francisco and were fully enclosed unlike some of their predecessors. Each unit cost $16,500 when they were delivered in summer 1923. They operated into the 1950s before being scrapped in 1958. In 2017 two survive; Car #171 is owned by the Orange Empire Museum in Perris, California, and Car #178 is owned by the Western Railway Museum in Suisun City, CA.

Car #178 (left photo) in its original gray paint with red trim is shown in a front view on Masonic Avenue. Car #182 (above photo) is shown about 1940 when it wore the blue and yellow paint colors that came after the gray and red scheme and before the green and cream "Wings" paint scheme

A Fleet History of the San Francisco Municipal Railway
Section 2: Streetcars and Light Rail Vehicles

Car #178 in 2017 at the Western Railway Museum, Suisun City, CA

No. 7	Years	Seats	Length / Width / Height / Weight	Model	Manufacturer
189-213	1926-1958	50	47'1" / 9'2" / 12'2" / 51,000	Type L	St. Louis Car Company, St. Louis, MO

"Type L" cars were built to the same specifications as the "Type K" cars and were delivered and entered service in 1926-1928. They cost slightly more than their predecessors at $19,200 per unit. They also had the unique nickname of "The Big Valves" due to the cars having a different air brake valve than the 'A', 'B' and 'K' types. All were retired by 1958 and scrapped. None of these cars exist in 2018.

A Fleet History of the San Francisco Municipal Railway
Section 2: Streetcars and Light Rail Vehicles

No. 8	Years	Seats	Length / Width / Height / Weight	Model	Manufacturer
1001-1005	1939-1959	60	50' 5" / 9' 0" / 10' 1" / 39,100	Type C	St. Louis Car Company, St. Louis, MO

"Type C" (also referred to as "Type HP") streetcars were known as "Magic Carpet" cars. They were nearly identical to the Presidents' Conference Committee (PCC) cars, but had some differences to avoid S.F. City Charter issues with patent royalties. One unique feature was the use of a combined power/brake Cinestron controller that was the source of their other nickname; "One-Arm Bandits". They cost $22,136 each and arrived in Muni's new blue and yellow paint colors. All were converted to one-man operation in 1955. All were retired in the late 1950s and scrapped except for Car #1003 which is preserved at the Western Railway Museum in Suisun City, CA.

Car #1003 in 2017 at the Western Railway Museum in Suisun City, CA

A Fleet History of the San Francisco Municipal Railway
Section 2: Streetcars and Light Rail Vehicles

On September 29, 1944 the S.F. Municipal Railway (Muni) merged with the privately owned Market Street Railway (MSRy) following voter approval of Charter Measure 1 to purchase the MSRy at a cost of $7.5 million dollars. All property owned by MSRy became Muni property and the MSRy ceased to exist. Former MSRy vehicles used in revenue service by Muni are listed here with an "M" prefix to their number to designate they were ex-MSRy cars that became Muni cars via the merger. Most of these cars only briefly operated in Muni service before they were retired.

No. 9	Years	Seats	Length / Width / Height / Weight	Model	Manufacturer
M101-M180	1944-1949	46	47' 0" / 9' 2" / ?? / 48,600	N/A	Jewett Car Company Newark, OH

A total of 80 streetcars of this type, built in 1911 for the MSRy, came to Muni after the merger. Thirty-six were renumbered as "400" series cars, because Muni already had a "100" series of streetcar. The upper photo shows the model in its MSRy appearance in the 1920s, while the lower photo shows this type of car in Muni service shortly after World War II. All 80 streetcars in this series were retired and scrapped by 1949.

A Fleet History of the San Francisco Municipal Railway
Section 2: Streetcars and Light Rail Vehicles

No. 10	Years	Seats	Length / Width / Height / Weight	Model	Manufacturer
M201-M265	1944-1950	50	47' 0" / 9'2" / ?? / 50,200	NA	American Car Company, St. Louis, MO

This design was known as a "California Comfort Car", and was seen with minor differences throughout the Muni and MSRy fleets prior to the arrival of PCC cars. All 65 streetcars, built in 1913, came to Muni after the merger, but only 26 were renumbered as "600" series cars. The renumbering occurred, because Muni already had a "200" series of streetcars. As evidenced by Car #696, all of the streetcars in this group were scrapped by 1950 as part of the large late 1940s Muni conversion from streetcar to bus and trolleybus.

No. 11	Years	Seats	Length / Width / Height / Weight	Model	Manufacturer
M266-M305	1944-1949	44	47' 0" / 9'3" / ?? / 38,900-43,000	N/A	Elkton Shops, MSRy, San Francisco, CA

A total of 257 "California Comfort Car" type streetcars were built by MSRy locally in their Elkton Shops Facility (current site of Muni Green Division) between 1920-1933 using the "200" series car as a template. All came to Muni after the 1944 merger. They were built in two groups that overlapped one another in delivery dates. The first group of 40 (#266-#305) received new trucks (wheel assemblies), while the second group received rehabilitated trucks removed from older streetcars that were retired and scrapped. A slightly smaller seating capacity was also present on the first group of cars which entered service in two sub-units. The first sub-unit was built in 1920-1921 and the second sub-unit was built in late 1924-1925. Between 1945-1950 all cars in the group were retired, stripped for parts and scrapped.

A Fleet History of the San Francisco Municipal Railway
Section 2: Streetcars and Light Rail Vehicles

No. 12	Years	Seats	Length / Width / Height / Weight	Model	Manufacturer
M778-M994	1944-1950	50	47'0" / 9'3" / ?? / 38,900-45,300	N/A	Elkton Shops, MSRy San Francisco, CA

The second group of MSRy built "California Comfort Car" type streetcars, numbering 217 vehicles (#778-#994), were built at Elkton Shops, also in two sub-units. The first 31 cars were built in 1923-1924, and the remainder were built between 1926-1933. At the time of the 1944 merger an S.F. PUC assessment assigned each of the 257 cars a value of approximately $16,000, meaning the entire fleet was valued at approximately $4.0M in 1944. Some cars were repainted with the new Muni green and cream "Wings" paint scheme after 1946, but by 1950 almost all of the streetcars in this second group were also scrapped as Muni moved toward a motor bus and trolley bus centered fleet. Their scrap value ranged from approximately $75-$200, which means Muni received less than $50,000 in value for the entire fleet. The only cars to escape being scrapped were Car #974 and #798. Car #974 was saved by the Bay Area Electric Railroad Association (now Western Railway Museum), but was destroyed in an arson fire in Stockton in the 1950s. Information on Car #798 is on the next page.

A Fleet History of the San Francisco Municipal Railway
Section 2: Streetcars and Light Rail Vehicles

Artist graphic of a restored Car #798 and a photo in storage in 2017

"Elkton Shops" Car #798 is the only surviving streetcar from the local production of 257 streetcars. It entered MSRy service on April 7, 1924, came over to Muni in the 1944 merger, and was retired by Muni on July 7, 1946. Car #798 was sold as surplus in 1946 at a value of $75 to a private party. It served as an office at a scrap yard, and then was moved Columbia, CA where it was a jewelry store. Later a larger building was built around it. In the early 1980s as that building was slated for demolition, a group of rail fans banded together to buy the car from its owner and it returned to San Francisco in 1985. In 1990 Muni spent $300,000 to have the body completely rebuilt by inmates at the Dueul Vocational Institute in Tracy, CA, but then the project was stopped and has remained inactive since that time. In 2018 Car #798 is in storage at Cameron Beach Yard. It has been identified to receive funds to complete the unfinished restoration and return to operation in the near future likely in service on the E and F lines.

No. 13	Years	Seats	Length / Width / Height / Weight	Model	Manufacturer
M735-M736	1944-1946	40	43' 9" / 8' 11" / ?? / 41,490	N/A	J.G. Brill Philadelphia, PA

Car # 735 on Geneva Ave. - 1936

In 1935 MSRy purchased several cars secondhand from the Williamsport Railway in Williamsport, PA. including these two cars built by the J.G. Brill Co. in 1916 that were converted from two man to one man operation a few years later. MSRy used them briefly while one man operation was legal in 1935-1937, but then placed them into storage. Muni never used them and sold them for scrap in 1946.

A Fleet History of the San Francisco Municipal Railway
Section 2: Streetcars and Light Rail Vehicles

No. 14	Years	Seats	Length / Width / Height / Weight	Model	Manufacturer
M601 (578)	1944-	26	26' 10" / 8' 8.5"/ N/A / 20,300	N/A	Hammond Car Company, San Francisco, CA

Car #578 in 2017

Car # 578 is a streetcar with a unique history. It was built in 1896 for the original Market Street Railway as part of a group of over 100 streetcars, but was converted to a work car in 1906 following the San Francisco Earthquake as larger streetcars entered the service fleet of United RRs (successor to the original Market Street Railway). Upon conversion it was renumbered as Car #0601. A group of streetcars from the same batch of cars as #0601 were sold by United RRs to the Presidio & Ferries RR (P&FRR) in 1907 and numbered #1-#29. This sub-group was acquired by Muni when it bought the P&FRR in 1913. These cars were dubbed as "Type G" streetcars, renumbered #301-329 by Muni, and operated in service until 1922. Five cars of this group became work cars that continued in service until the last was retired in 1946.

Meanwhile, Car #0601 remained as part of the United RRs and later MSRy fleet until the merger in 1944, when it arrived as part of a fleet of 30 work cars of many different types that also became Muni property. Most of these work cars were scrapped by 1950, but in 2018 two remain at Muni (Car #0304, and Car #0601). Car #0304 is still in service as a work car, but Car #0601 (a sand car used to haul sand to be placed on tracks to improve traction), followed a different fate. First it was used along with a new White transit bus to advocate public support for the 1947 bond measure that transformed Muni by replacing hundreds of old streetcars with new buses and trolley buses. A few years later it was restored to its original first MSRy passenger car appearance by Muni craftsmen in 1956 for the 50th anniversary of the 1906 Earthquake. Upon restoration, it received its original number and became Car #578 again. Although technically it was rebuilt 60 years ago, with its 1896 date of origin, Car #578 is currently the oldest active streetcar in the Muni historic fleet, and is one of the oldest operating streetcars in the world. It is estimated to be comprised of over 95% original parts and materials. It has received ongoing renovation work during the past several decades to allow it to remain in service. In 2018 it operates as the center of attention in its bright yellow paint in special service or on the F-line.

A Fleet History of the San Francisco Municipal Railway
Section 2: Streetcars and Light Rail Vehicles

No. 15	Years	Seats	Length / Width / Height / Weight	Model	Manufacturer
M740-M749	1944-1946	40	41' 0" / 8' 8" / N/A / 42,050	N/A	St. Louis Car Company, St. Louis, MO

In 1936 MSRY purchased 20 cars from the East St. Louis & Suburban Railway. Originally built by St. Louis Car Company in 1918, these cars were placed into storage after the 1939 World's Fair. In "The White Front Cars of San Francisco", all 20 cars are listed as being scrapped at Elkton Shops in 1941, but Cars #740-#749 appear in the 1947 edition of "Rolling Stock of the Munciipal Railway" - with retirement dates of 1945 and 1946, so it appears likely they were owned by Muni, but were in storage and were never used in active service.

No. 16	Years	Seats	Length / Width / Height / Weight	Model	Manufacturer
M1225-M1238	1944-1949	46	48' 1" / 9' 6" / ?? / 56,100	N/A	Laclede Car Company
M1241-M1244	1944-1948	46	48' 1" / 9' 6" / ?? /		St. Louis, MO

This group of streetcars that came to Muni from MSRy were a heavier "interurban" style rarely seen in San Francisco. Built in 1903, they primarily operated on MSRy Routes 12, 14 in San Francisco, and Route 40 which ran from the 5th and Market Street to Mission Street and then out Mission Street to Daly City. At Daly City they continued south parallel to the old SPRR Peninsula route through South San Francisco, San Bruno, Millbrae and Burlingame to a downtown San Mateo terminal. They served this route from 1903 until Route 40 was abandoned south of Daly City on January 15, 1949. Car #1244 burned in Millbrae in 1947 and the other cars were scrapped between 1947 and 1949. None exist in 2018. The left photo shows a car in Muni blue and yellow, ca. 1945, while the right photo shows a streetcar in the Muni green and cream "Wings" paint scheme at Leipsic Junction, ca. 1948, which was near the location of the current South San Francisco BART station.

A Fleet History of the San Francisco Municipal Railway
Section 2: Streetcars and Light Rail Vehicles

No. 17	Years	Seats	Length / Width / Height / Weight	Model	Manufacturer
San Francisco	1944-1948	26	37' 0" / 9' 8" / ?? / 38,300	N/A	St. Louis Car Company, St. Louis, MO

The "San Francisco" was built in 1901 as Interurban Car #61 for the San Mateo Electric Railway, which was absorbed into URR in 1902. It was rebuilt in 1904 as the "San Francisco", a luxury private charter car. In 1921 it was painted white and became an MSRy school car offering tours and safety education to children in S.F. The tours ended with the start of World War II, but the car came over to Muni as part of the merger. Muni offered it for charters again, but then placed it in storage at the Geneva Car House. In 1951 Muni management ordered it scrapped and it was sold for $400. After time as a hot dog stand and in storage on a ranch in Penngrove, CA it was acquired by the Western Railway Museum in Suisun City, CA in 1980. It was placed on wheels and an undercarriage of another streetcar. In 2018 it is non-operable and remains at the Western Railway Museum.

No. 18	Years	Seats	Length / Width / Height / Weight	Model	Manufacturer
M1553, M1572, M1583, M1595, M1599, M1715, M1716, M1722, M1731	1944-1949	44	45' 4" / 9' 2" / ?? / 54,400	N/A	St. Louis Car Company, St. Louis, MO

A total of nine cars out of an original order of 200 cars of this type, initiallly ordered in 1906-07 after the San Francisco Earthquake, came to Muni following the merger. Cars #1715, #1716 and #1722, which were rebuilt in 1918, were joined by six more cars. Only Car #1553, was repainted in the green and cream "Wings" paint scheme. This small group was also scrapped, with the last car going to the wrecker in 1949.

A Fleet History of the San Francisco Municipal Railway
Section 2: Streetcars and Light Rail Vehicles

No. 19 M778 (II)	Years 1944-1948	Seats 44	Length / Width / Height / Weight 47' 0" / 9' 3" / ?? / 38,900	Model N/A	Manufacturer Elkton Shops, MSRy San Francisco, CA

This single car was built at Elkton Shops as Car #1424 and served for several years as the streetcar on Grand Avenue between Leipsic Junction (about 1/4 mile south of South S.F. BART station) and the industrial area (east of U.S. 101) in South San Francisco. The South S.F. line was abandoned in 1938. Car #1424 was rebuilt by MSRy in the late 1930s, renumbered to #778 in 1939, and was on the roster in 1944. It was scrapped in 1948.

No. 20 1006-1015	Years 1948-1982	Seats 59	Length / Width / Height / Weight 50' 5" / 9' 0" / 10' 0" / 40,020	Model Type D	Manufacturer St. Louis Car Company St. Louis, MO

The "Type D" streetcars (aka "BIG TENS' or "TORPEDOES") were the first PCC's at Muni. They were built as "two-man" cars in Job Order #1667, and were delivered in 1948 at a cost of $27,500 each. These cars were "double-end" cars with operator controls at both ends so they didn't need a loop to turnaround, but were converted to "single-end one-man" cars in 1954. They were nicknamed "Big Tens" or "Torpedoes", because they were longer than the next group of PCC cars. Car #1008 was the test car for the Muni Metro Subway in the late 1970s before the new light rail vehicles (LRVs) arrived in San Francisco. After 30+ years of service, they were retired as Muni entered into the light rail vehicle (LRV) era in 1982. Cars #1012 and #1013 were scrapped, Car #1008 was converted to a work car, and Car #1014 was sent on permanent loan to a museum in Sydney, Australia. The remaining six cars were placed into storage, and later restored for F-Line service with three entering service in 1995, and the other three, plus Car #1008 entering service in 2012-2013.

A Fleet History of the San Francisco Municipal Railway
Section 2: Streetcars and Light Rail Vehicles

No. 21	Years	Seats	Length / Width / Height / Weight	Model	Manufacturer
1016-1040	1952-1982	58	46' 5 1/2"/ 9' 0" / 10' 3" / 37,600	N/A	St. Louis Car Company, St. Louis, MO

Car #1016 in 2017.

The second group of PCC streetcars (aka "BABY TENS") procured by Muni were smaller and were built as "single-end" cars with operator controls only on one end. They were Job Order #1675 and were delivered in 1951-52 at a cost of $37,750 each. Four feet shorter than the "Big Tens" (note door locations and number of windows), they were nicknamed "Baby Tens". Similar to their older and larger "Big Ten" predecessors, they operated for 30+ years before being retired in 1982. Most were sold and several no longer exist. In 2018 Muni owns six cars from this series. The cars are in storage. Car #1040, the last PCC built in the U.S. in 1952, has been restored and is in service on the F-Line. Car #1016, the first in the series has been restored and is at the Western Railway Museum in Suisun City, CA.

No. 22	Years	Seats	Length / Width / Height / Weight	Model	Manufacturer
1101-1166	1957-1982	53	46' 0" / 9' 0" / 10' 1/4" / 36,420	N/A	St. Louis Car Company, St. Louis, MO

Back view of a single end PCC streetcar.

The third group of PCC streetcars to arrive at Muni came "second-hand" from St. Louis Public Service (transit agency). Built in 1946 as Job Order #1655 these "single-end" streetcars were obtained via a lease-purchase agreement at a cost of $7,400 each in 1957. Retired in 1982, most were sold, but Muni saved twelve cars and placed them into storage. At the end of 2018 five cars were due to be scrapped leaving seven in storage. Car#1153 is preserved at the Western Railway Museum in Suisun City, CA, Car #1159 is at the Oregon Electric Railway Museum, and Car #1155 is at the Seashore Railway Museum in Maine.

A Fleet History of the San Francisco Municipal Railway
Section 2: Streetcars and Light Rail Vehicles

No. 23	Years	Seats	Length / Width / Height / Weight	Model	Manufacturer
1167-1170	1962-1982	53	46' 0" / 9' 0" / 11' 2" / 36,400	N/A	St. Louis Car Company, St. Louis, MO

This group of four "single-end" PCC streetcars built in 1947 were also obtained second-hand from St. Louis Public Service via another lease-purchase agreement in 1962. Each car cost $6,800. Shown at Geneva Division after being painted in the Muni green and cream "wings" paint colors, these cars operated until 1982. Muni currently owns Car #1168, which is in storage waiting a possible restoration.

No. 24	Years	Seats	Length / Width / Height / Weight	Model	Manufacturer
1180-1190	1974-1979	50	46' 5" / 8' 4" / 10' 3" / 37,500	N/A	St. Louis Car Company, St. Louis, MO

In the early 1970s Muni needed more streetcars, because BART construction slowed service on Market Street, so this group of "single-end" PCC streetcars was acquired "third-hand" from the Toronto Transit Commission (TTC) to help the tired and aging Muni PCC fleet. Muni paid $1,000 per unit. They were built in 1946-47 as part of Job Order #1650 for the Kansas City Public Service (transit), and the the TTC purchased them from Kansas City Public Service (transit) in 1957. They were the last of 115 PCC steetcars Muni purchased (81 purchased used), and were the only PCCs to receive the maroon and gold Muni paint colors. Their wheels needed to be regauged because Toronto used a non-standard rail gauge. They also had a different door safety mechanism that frustrated operators. They were retired in 1979. Three have been scrapped. The fourth one, Car #1190, was returned to Kansas City and became Car #551 (original number). It is located at River Market in Kansas City.

A Fleet History of the San Francisco Municipal Railway
Section 2: Streetcars and Light Rail Vehicles

No. 25, 26	Years	Seats	Length / Width / Height / Weight	Model	Manufacturer
1201-1299	1977-1996	68	71' 0" / 8' 10" / 11' 4" / 67,000	USSLRV	Boeing-Vertol
1301-1329	1993-2001	68	71' 0" / 8' 10" / 11' 4" / 67,000	USSLRV	Morton, PA

The Boeing-Vertol United States Standard Light Rail Vehicle (USSLRV) was an attempt to create a new PCC streetcar for America, but only San Francisco and Boston purchased these vehicles. Known as "Boeings", their sleek appearance was offset by many design and operations problems. In two separate purchases Muni acquired 130 of these vehicles at a cost of $310,000 per unit for the first series (100 cars) and $715,000 per unit for the second series (30 cars). The second series of cars were rejected by MBTA in Boston before Muni acquired them. All 130 were delivered wearing Muni's new "Landor" Sunset Glow and Poppy Gold paint scheme and the "Muni worm" logo. They were 50% longer and about 75% heavier than the PCCs, and were built with an articulated joint in the middle of the car. They were most frequently operated as single or 2-car units, but during their first decade of service were regularly coupled into 4-car units at West Portal to operate in the Market Street Subway. The San Francisco Boeings were designed with the unique feature of movable stairs for high platform subway operation under Market Street and low platform street operations. In 1996 they started to be replaced by newer Breda LRVs, and the last Boeing was retired in 2003. Car #1213 is preserved by the Oregon Electric Railway and Car #1258 is preserved at the Western Railway Museum. Muni kept two Boeings in storage until 2016 when it was finally decided not to restore them. When no museums were interested in taking them for preservation, they were scrapped.

A Fleet History of the San Francisco Municipal Railway
Section 2: Streetcars and Light Rail Vehicles

No. 27	Years	Seats	Length / Width / Height / Weight	Model	Manufacturer
1400-1424	1997-	60	75' 0" / 9' 0" / 11' 5" / 79,000	LRV2	Breda Construzioni-
1425-1451	1998-	60	75' 0" / 9' 0" / 11' 5" / 79,000	LRV2	Ferrovarie (Breda Co.)
1452-1474	1999-	60	75' 0" / 9' 0" / 11' 5" / 79,000	LRV2	Pistoia, Italy /
1475-1481	2000-	60	75' 0" / 9' 0" / 11' 5" / 79,000	LRV3	South S.F., CA
1482-1508	2001-	60	75' 0" / 9' 0" / 11' 5" / 79,000	LRV3	
1509-1524	2002-	60	75' 0" / 9' 0" / 11' 5" / 79,000	LRV3	
1525-1550	2003-	60	75' 0" / 9' 0" / 11' 5" / 79,000	LRV3	

The "LRV2" series of vehicles, built by Italian manufacturer Breda Construzioni Ferrovarie (Breda Company), and known informally as "Breda Cars", or simply "Bredas", began to arrive and enter service in 1997. The new LRVs, which were painted in the retro Muni silver-gray with red trim paint scheme, continued to arrive in small numbers between 1997-1999 as "LRV2" units, and between 2000-2003 as "LRV3" units, until a total of 151 vehicles were delivered. Although produced by Breda, the LRVs, each of which cost $1.8 million dollars, were fabricated at a plant in South San Francisco to meet "Buy America" requirements. These were the longest and heaviest streetcar / LRV in Muni history. Generally they have operated as single car or 2-car units, although rarely they have operated as 3-car units. Overall performance was much better than their predecessor Boeings. As the Siemens "LR4" series is phased in at Muni, plans are in place to keep the Bredas in service until 2022.

A Fleet History of the San Francisco Municipal Railway
Section 2: Streetcars and Light Rail Vehicles

No. 28	Years	Seats	Length / Width / Height / Weight	Model	Manufacturer
	2017 -	60	75' 0" / 8' 8" / 11' 6" / 78,770	LRV4 S200SF	Siemens Corporation Sacramento, CA

The "LRV4" series of light rail vehicles began to arrive in 2017, and future deliveries of the same vehicles, with minor upgrades, are scheduled to continue beyond 2025. Muni has ordered 215 units of this vehicle, and has options for an additional 45 units. The "LRV4" units are a version of the S200 LRV vehicle, which is also in use on the LRV system in Calgary, Canada. The "LRV4" vehicles are built by Siemens USA, a subsidiary of the larger Siemens Corporation, which is a world wide company based in Germany. The "LRV4" units are being produced at a facility in Sacramento, CA. Each unit of the first series of delivery (2017-2018) cost $3.4 million dollars. The Siemens cars are very similar in appearance to the older Breda cars, and wear a slightly different version of the retro silver-gray and red trim. The two series of vehicles will share subway and surface light rail operations assignments until 2022 when the older Breda cars are scheduled for a gradual replacement by Siemens cars as more vehicles enter service.

A Fleet History of the San Francisco Municipal Railway
Section 2: Streetcars and Light Rail Vehicles

| No. 29
1007, 1010
1015 | Years
1995- | Seats
60 | Length / Width / Height / Weight
50' 5" / 9' 0" / 10' 0" / 40,020 | Model
N/A | Manufacturer
St. Louis Car Company
St. Louis, MO

Rebuilt By
Morrison-Knudsen
Hornell, NY |

"BIG TENS" or "TORPEDOES" - Act II - Three Muni PCC streetcars from the "Big Ten" or "Torpedo" series, originally purchased in 1948 were restored at a cost of $1.5 million per unit in preparation of the opening of the new "F-Line" historic streetcar service on Market Street in 1995. The "Torpedoes" were restored as "double-end" cars with controls at both ends - 40 years after being converted from "double-end" to "single-end" cars in 1955. Along with other PCC streetcars that were restored for service, these vehicles were painted in tribute colors and design schemes used by other cities in the U.S, Canada and Mexico that operated PCC streetcars at one time. These cars were painted as follows:
    Car #1007: S.F. Muni - silver and red (Breda cars), then repainted to
              Philadelphia Suburban (Philadelphia, PA) - maroon & cream "Red Arrow Lines" - 1950s,
    Car #1010: S.F. Muni - blue and gold (pre MSRy merger) - 1940s,
    Car #1015: Illinois Terminal RR (St. Louis, MO) - green and white - 1950s

A Fleet History of the San Francisco Municipal Railway
Section 2: Streetcars and Light Rail Vehicles

No. 30	Years	Seats	Length / Width / Height / Weight	Model	Manufacturer
1050, 1051, 1052, 1053, 1054, 1055, 1056, 1057, 1058, 1059, 1060, 1061, 1062, 1063	1995-	47	46' 8 1/4"/ 8' 4" / 10' 3" / 37,990	N/A	St. Louis Car Company St. Louis, MO Rebuilt By Morrison-Knudsen Hornell, NY (1995-1996) Brookville Equip. Company Brookville, PA (2016-2018)

"PHILADELPHIA PCCS" - This group of 14 PCC streetcars were built in 1948 for the Philadelphia Transportation Corporation (later part of the Southeastern Pennsylvania Transportation Authority (SEPTA)), where they operated until 1989. Muni purchased 16 cars in 1992 at a cost of $12,000 each and had 14 restored at a cost of $1.5 million per unit. These cars, plus three restored S.F. PCC "Torpedoes", were the core fleet of the new "F-Line" historic streetcar service on Market Street in 1995. This group of streetcars were painted in tribute colors used in other cities in the U.S., Canada and Mexico that operated PCC streetcars. In 2016 all cars in this group began to be sent for a second rebuild by the Brookville Equipment Corporation at a cost of $2.12 million for each unit. At the end of 2018 Car #1057 and Car #1058 were still under rebuild, but all other cars had been completed. This group of cars were painted as follows:

- Car #1050: S.F Muni - green & cream - 1950s (1st rebuild),St. Louis - red & cream 1940s (2nd rebuild),
- Car #1051: S.F. Muni - modified green & cream - 1960s 1970s (designated the Harvey Milk streetcar),
- Car #1052: Los Angeles, CA - "LA Railways-yellow cars" - yellow & gold - 1940s,
- Car #1053: Brooklyn, NY - light gray & green - 1940s,
- Car #1054: Philadelphia Transit Commission (Phila, PA) - wrecked in 2003 - retired, scrapped in 2018,
- Car #1055: Philadelphia, PA - green, cream & red - 1950s,
- Car #1056: Kansas City, MO/KN - cream & black - 1950s,
- Car #1057: Cincinnati, OH - yellow with green stripes - 1940s,
- Car #1058: Chicago, IL - pale green, cream & orange - 1940s,
- Car #1059: Boston, MA - orange, cream & silver - 1940s,
- Car #1060: Philadelphia, PA - silver, blue & cream - 1930s,
- Car #1061: Los Angeles, CA - "Pacific Electric Red Cars" - red, orange & gray - 1950s,
- Car #1062: Louisville, KY - green, cream & black 1950s (1st rebuild), Pittsburgh, PA - red, cream & black 1950s (2nd rebuild)
- Car #1063: Baltimore, MD - yellow & gray - 1950s

A Fleet History of the San Francisco Municipal Railway
Section 2: Streetcars and Light Rail Vehicles

No. 31	Years	Seats	Length / Width / Height / Weight	Model	Manufacturer
1807, 1811, 1814, 1815, 1818, 1834, 1856, 1859, 1888, 1893, 1895	1998-	30	45' 7" / 7' 9" / 12' 2" / 33,000	Peter Witt	Carminati & Toselli Milan, Italy Refurbished SFMTA San Francisco, CA

A total of eleven "Peter Witt" cars (first introduced in Cleveland, OH) that were built in 1928 in Milan, Italy, and which operated in Milan for 60+ years were acquired by Muni in 1998 to augment the F-Line streetcar fleet. Car #1834 arrived earlier to participate in the Streetcar Festival, and its performance led to efforts to obtain more Milan streetcars. Each car cost $30,000 and the entire fleet received modifications by Muni staff at the Green Division before entering service. Cars #1807 and #1811 wear the original 1928 white and yellow paint scheme. Cars #1818 and #1888 wear the 1930s-1970s two-tone green paint scheme. Cars #1814, #1815, #1834, #8156 and #1859, #1893 and #1895 wear the 1970s to present orange paint scheme.

A Fleet History of the San Francisco Municipal Railway
Section 2: Streetcars and Light Rail Vehicles

No. 32	Years	Seats	Length / Width / Height / Weight	Model	Manufacturer
1070, 1071, 1072, 1073, 1074, 1075, 1076, 1077, 1078, 1079, 1080	2007/08-	54	46' 5" / 9' 0" / 10' 2" / 37,000	N/A	St. Louis Car Company, St. Louis, MO Rebuilt Brookville Equip. Company Brookville, PA

"MINNEAPOLIS - NEWARK PCCS" - This group of 11 PCC were built in 1946 for "Twin Cities Rapid Transit" in Minneapolis, MN where they operated until they were sold to "Public Service Coordinated Transport" in Newark, NJ in 1954. Newark operated the PCC streetcars until 2001, and after retirement, sold the vehicles to Muni in 2004 for $15,000 each. Muni operated some of them briefly in 2004-06, but then this group was sent to Brookville Equipment Company in Brookville, PA to be rewired and receive other rehabilitation that varied by vehicle, but averaged about $700,000 per car. All re-entered service in 2007-2008. All are single-end cars. The streetcars in this group were painted as follows:

- Car #1070: Newark, NJ - blue/gray & blue/white - w/ red wheels - 1950s
- Car #1071: Minneapolis-St. Paul, MN - yellow & green - 1950s
- Car #1072: Mexico City, Mexico - cream, orange & green - 1950s
- Car #1073: El Paso, TX & Juarez, Mexico - light green, white & red - 1960s
- Car #1074: Toronto, Canada - maroon & cream - 1950s
- Car #1075: Cleveland, OH - brown, tan & orange - 1940s
- Car #1076: Washington, DC - teal, white, light green & orange - 1950s
- Car #1077: Birmingham, AL - dark green, red & cream - 1940s
- Car #1078: San Diego, CA - pale green, brown & cream - 1940s
- Car #1079: Detroit, MI - tan & red - 1950s
- Car #1080: Los Angeles, CA - "National City" - light green, orange, yellow & white - 1950s

A Fleet History of the San Francisco Municipal Railway
Section 2: Streetcars and Light Rail Vehicles

No. 33	Years	Seats	Length / Width / Height / Weight	Model	Manufacturer
1006, 1008, 1009, 1011,	2012/13-	60	50' 5" / 9' 0" / 10' 0" / 40,020	N/A	St. Louis Car Company St. Louis, MO
1040		58	46' 5 1/2" / 9' 0" / 10' 0" / 37,600	N/A	Rebuilt Brookville Equip. Company Brookville, PA

"TORPEDOES II" and a "BABY TEN" - This group of five San Francisco PCC cars consisting of four "Torpedo" streetcars designed for "double-end" operations and one "single-end" streetcar, Car #1040. Car #1008 was the last PCC in regular Muni service on the N-Line in 1982 before all service was provided by Boeing cars, and Car #1040 was the last PCC made In the U.S.A. All were sent to Brookville Equipment Company for restoration in 2009-2010. The "Torpedoes" were built in 1948 and Car #1040 was built in 1952. This group of cars were the second part of an $18.7 million dollar contract to rewire and upgrade the "Minneapolis-Newark Cars" that were acquired in 2004. The cost to restore each of these streetcar was approximately $2.0-$2.5 million dollars per vehicle depending upon their condition at the time of restoration. The rebuilt streetcars entered service in 2012-2013. The streetcars in this group were painted as follows:
    Car #1006: S.F. Muni - green & cream "wings" - 1950s
    Car #1008: S.F. Muni - green & cream "wings" - 1950s
    Car #1009: Dallas, TX - red, cream & silver - 1940s
    Car #1011: S.F., CA - "Fantasy" - Market Street Railway - green, white & yellow "zip" - 1940s
    Car #1040: S.F. Muni - green & cream "wings" - 1950s

S. F. Municipal Railway
PCC #1040
The last PCC streetcar manufactured in the U.S.A. in 1952

A Fleet History of the San Francisco Municipal Railway
Section 2: Streetcars and Light Rail Vehicles

S.F. Municipal Railway PCC Streetcar # 1009 - unrestored and in heavily damaged condition in 2008 (left) and restored and painted in tribute colors of Dallas Terminal Railway Company in 2013 (right)

No. 34	Years	Seats	Length / Width / Height / Weight	Model	Manufacturer
1012, 1013	2018-	58	50' 5" / 9' 0" / 10' 0" / 49,000	N/A	St. Louis Car Company, St. Louis, MO
					Rebuilt By Brookville Equip. Company Brookville, PA

SEPTA / Philadelphia Suburban Transportation Company (Red Arrow)#18 at Shore Line Trolley Museum - on its way to Brookville for a rebuild to return to S.F. as Muni # 1012 - 2017

"SHORE LINE MUSEUM TORPEDOES" and "PHILADELPHIA PCCS II" - SFMTA acquired two double-end cars in 2017 from the Shore Line Museum in East Haven, CT., numbered #18 and #21, that were built for Philadelphia Red Arrow service in 1949. They cost $84,500 each. Although they used PCC bodies, they had non-PCC trucks and controls. SFMTA also sent non-operating Cable Car #28 (formerly #528) to the Museum as part of the deal. Muni planned to spend about $2.5 million per car to rehabilitate them for E-Line service, using all PCC type equipment, so they are "true" PCCs, and renumber them as #1012 and #1013 to acknowledge two double-end "Torpedoes" with those numbers that were scrapped in the 1980s. However as of late 2018 higher cost estimates for the restoration work have stalled the project. Two other former Philadelphia cars, #2133 and #2147 are being retained, most likely as parts cars.

A Fleet History of the San Francisco Municipal Railway
Section 2: Streetcars and Light Rail Vehicles

No. 35	Years	Seats	Length / Width / Height / Weight	Model	Manufacturer
1026, 1027, 1028, 1033, 1034, 1039	Non-Op	58	46' 5 1/2" / 9' 0" / 10' 3" / 37,600	N/A	St. Louis Car Company St. Louis, MO

Car # 1034 - 2016

"BABY TENS II" - Orignally, this group consisted of ten PCC streetcars from a larger group of 25 PCC streetcars procured by Muni in 1951-1952 that were retired and placed into storage in 1982. They were built as "single-end cars" and were nicknamed "Baby Tens". Car #1040, the last PCC built in the U.S., has been restored and is in service on the F-Line. In 2018 three of these cars were due to be disposed of, while six remain in storage awaiting a future restoration, or to be used as parts cars for the existing PCC fleet.

No. 36	Years	Seats	Length / Width / Height / Weight	Model	Manufacturer
1103, 1115, 1128, 1130, 1146, 1150, 1158, 1159, 1160, 1164, 1168	Non-Op	59	46' 0" / 9' 0" / 10' 1/4"/ 36,420	N/A	St. Louis Car Company St. Louis, MO

"ST. LOUIS CARS II" also known as "THE 1100s" - This group of PCC streetcars that were built in 1946-1947 as Job Order #1655. They were obtained second-hand from St. Louis Public Service (transit agency) via lease agreements in 1957 and 1962, and were purchased for $7,000 each in 1964. They operated until retired in 1982. In 2003 the Market St. Railway non-profit group bought Cars #1106 and #1140 from private owners. Muni owns 16 unrestored cars from this group, but in late 2018 plans are in place to scrap five cars considered in poor shape. Of the remaining 11 cars, seven remain in storage: #1103, #1115, #1128 (aka #1704), #1130, #1158, #1160 and #1168. These will either be restored in the future, or used as parts cars to support the existing PCC fleet. Four are loaned to other museums; Car #1146-Clearlake, IA, Car #1150-LaGrande, CA, Car #1159-Brooks, OR, Car #1164- St. Louis, MO.

A Fleet History of the San Francisco Municipal Railway
Section 2: Streetcars and Light Rail Vehicles

No. 37	Years	Seats	Length / Width / Height / Weight	Model	Manufacturer
1023, 1031, 1038, 1054	Non Op.	58	46' 5 1/2" / 9' 0" / 10' 3" / 37,600	N/A	St. Louis Car Company St. Louis, MO
1064, 1106, 1108, 1125, 1139, 1140,	Non Op.	59	46' 0" / 9' 0" / 10' 1/4" / 36,400	N/A	
4008, 4009	Non-Op.	46	46'5" / 8' 4" / 10' 0" / 37,400	N/A	

Pittsburgh (PATH) Car #4009 in storage - 2018

"DISPOSITION FLEET" - The term "disposition" is used to classify surplus items that are to be disposed of so they are no longer property of the owner. In this situation, it applies to several non-operable historic streetcars that were made available for sale, donation, or were scrapped. In 2018, at a time when storage locations of some equipment were changed, SFMTA made the decision to dispose of the non-operable streetcars listed below via SFMTA Board Resolution 10.5 on May 8, 2018.

"BABY TENS II" - At the end of 2018 three of the nine "Baby Ten" streetcars that were retired by Muni in 1982, and which were placed in storage for 35 years: Cars # 1023, #1031 and #1038 are due to be scrapped. Usable parts are to be removed for later use prior to the disposal of the streetcars.

"ST. LOUIS CARS II" also known as "THE 1100s" - Twelve of "The 1100" series of cars that were in this group of PCC streetcars were retired by Muni in 1982 and placed in storage. Five of these cars: #1106, #1108, #1125, #1139, and #1140 are scheduled to be scrapped due to being in poor condition. Usable parts are to be removed for later use on other cars prior to the disposal of the streetcars.

"A PHILADELPHIA CAR" & "PITTSBURGH CARS" - This group of three streetcars included one from the Southeastern Pennsylvania Transportation Authority (SEPTA #2121), which was renumbered as #1054. It was acquired by Muni along with 14 others in 1992 at a cost of $12,000 each and renovated for service. It had been non-operable since it was severely damaged in a 2003 accident. The other two cars were from the Port Authority of Allegheny County (Pittsburgh) (#4008,#4009 - formerly #1709 and #1700) prior to a rebuild with "modern" components) that were acquired in 2001 at a cost of $5,000 each. Although complete, the Pittsburgh cars had non-compatible features to Muni service and were deemed surplus. At the end of 2018 the streetcars were waiting to be disposed of - via sale or donation, or to be scrapped.

A Fleet History of the San Francisco Municipal Railway
Section 2: Streetcars and Light Rail Vehicles

No. 38 "WHEELS OF THE WORLD" - This mixed group of 19 vehicles is comprised of streetcars from around the world. Some were part of a fleet that was retired, while others were part of a fleet that remains in service in their countries of origin. Some descriptions of this group include the "Milan Cars", but those are listed separately in this book. Each of the Wheels of the World vehicles is summarized separately.

No. 38-1	Years	Seats	Length / Width / Height / Weight	Model	City / Country
106	Non Op.	N/A			Mosccow, Russia

This streetcar was built in 1912 in Russia and served in Moscow until 1960. It was moved to Orel and remained in service until 1978. It was a gift from the former Soviet Union to San Francisco in January, 1987 and operated in the 1987 Trolley Festival. It currently is stored at the Cameron Beach Yard adjacent to the Green Division and awaits restoration. In 2017 SFMTA made an initial determination not to include Car #106 in long-range future historic streetcar plans. It may be donated to a museum in the future.

Car # 106 in 1992 Streetcar Centennial Parade on Market St. (left) and in storage in 2017 (right)

No. 38-2	Years	Seats	Length / Width / Height / Weight	Model	City / Country
151	Non Op.	N/A		N/A	Osaka, Japan

This streetcar was built in 1927 and operated in Osaka, Japan until 1988. It was acquired via donation from Osaka, Japan, which was a sister city to San Francisco. The photos show it with plastic covering removed at the Marin Yard in 2018. Currently it is in storage and has been selected as one of the double-end cars to be restored starting in 2019. Upon completion plans are to use it in E-Line service on the Embarcadero.

A Fleet History of the San Francisco Municipal Railway
Section 2: Streetcars and Light Rail Vehicles

No. 38-3	Years	Seats	Length / Width / Height / Weight	Model	City / Country
189	Non Op.	23	30' 6" / 7' 10" / 11' 5" / 28,000	N/A	Oporto, Portugal Compo Carris de Ferro de Porto Shops

Car #189 is a rare single truck streetcar (4 wheels on one frame which contacts the rails - instead of the common two truck design). It was built in Portugal in 1929 following plans of a small American streetcar made by the J. G. Brill Company of Philadelphia, PA. It operated in service for over 50 years in Oporto, Portugal before being declared as surplus, and then being leased for the 1983 Trolley Festival. In 1984 Muni purchased Car #189 for $5,000. It operated in all four Trolley Festivals, but was in need of major structural repairs by 1987. A restoration started in 2002, but other priorities put the work on hold. In 2018 Car #189 was identified as one of a group of a half-dozen old streetcars scheduled to begin restoration again in 2019.

Car #189 artist rendition left and in storage in 2018

No. 38-4-5	Years	Seats	Length / Width / Height / Weight	Model	City / Country
228	1987-	44	42' 0" / 8' 2" / 11' 6" / 20,000	N/A	Blackpool, UK
233	2015-	44	42' 0" / 8' 2" / 11' 6" / 20,000	N/A	English Electric Preston, Lancashire

Following the success of Blackpool Car #226, known as the "Boat Car" in the 1983 and 1984 Trolley Festivals, Car #228 was donated by Blackpool Transport prior to the 1985 Trolley Festival. Almost 30 years later the opportunity arose to obtain another "Boat Car", and the Market Street Railway with additional private funding purchased #233 for $20,000 in 2013. Both cars were built in 1934 for the seaside resort town of Blackpool, England, and operated there until the 1970s. Curently both are used in special service and F-Line service. The "Boat Cars" are two very popular streetcars in the historic fleet.

A Fleet History of the San Francisco Municipal Railway
Section 2: Streetcars and Light Rail Vehicles

No. 38-6	Years	Seats	Length / Width / Height / Weight	Model	City / Country
351	Non Op.	44	41' 5" / 7' 0" / 11' 3" / 36,680	N/A	Johnstown, PA St. Louis Car Co. St. Louis, MO

Car #351 was built in 1926 and operated in Johnstown, PA until 1960. It was purchased by a private party in Sonoma County, CA, and moved to the west coast. In 1988 Car #351 was acquired by the Market Street Railway at a cost of $5,000 and moved to San Francisco. In 2018 Car #351 was identified as one of a group of a half dozen old streetcars scheduled to begin restoration in 2019. It is currently in storage at Cameron Beach Yard.

Car # 351 artist rendition above and in storage in 2017

No. 38-7	Years	Seats	Length / Width / Height / Weight	Model	City / Country
496	1987-	52	47' 10" / 9' 0" / 10' 7" / 37,900	W2	Melbourne, Australia
586	Non Op.	52	47' 10" / 9' 0" / 10' 7" / 37,900	W2	Moore Comapny Melbourne, Australia

A Melbourne W2 class streetcar was leased from the Western Railway Museum for the early Trolley Festivals, and it proved to be very popular. In 1987 Muni and Market Street Railway purchased Car #496 and Car #586, both of which were Melbourne W2 model streetcars, at a cost of under $20,000 for each car. A unique feature of W2 cars are their "reverse California Car design" - featuring closed ends with a semi-open middle section. Since 1987 Car #496 has generally been available for special service or work on the F-Line, while Car #586 has mainly served as a "parts car". Currently there are no plans to restore Car #586.

A Fleet History of the San Francisco Municipal Railway
Section 2: Streetcars and Light Rail Vehicles

No. 38-8	Years	Seats	Length / Width / Height / Weight	Model	City / Country
578-J	Non Op.	36	44' 9" / 8' 2" / 10' 1" / 32,000	N/A	Kobe/Hiroshima, Japan
					Fujinagata Zosen Co.
					Osaka, Japan

This streetcar was built in Osaka, Japan in 1927 for the Kobe City Railways. It operated in Kobe receiving modest upgrades, such as electric doors and a public address system until 1971 when it was sold to Hiroshima Electric Railways, and operated in its second city until it was acquired in time for the 1986 Trolley Festival. Following the 1987 Trolley Festival it was removed from service for some work, including the installation of a hand brake, but has not been used in service for over 30 years. The unusual vehicle number of 578-J is to help distinguish this streetcar from Car # 578 (aka 578-S), Muni's oldest streetcar.

No. 38-9	Years	Seats	Length / Width / Height / Weight	Model	City / Country
737	2005-	35	45' 7" / 7' 9" / 10' 1" / 36,300	N/A	Brussels, Belgium
					La Brugeoise
					Brugge, Belgium

Streetcar #737, built in 1951, was acquired by the Market Street Railway and Muni in 2004 at a cost of $25,000 following retirement from service in Brussels, Belgium. It is a unique car that used U.S. PCC technology adapted to Europe after World War II, at a time when the PCC was in decline in America. When it was rehabilitated at Muni for San Francisco service, the color scheme from Zurich, Switzerland, which operated similar streetcars, was selected at the request of Mayor Gavin Newsom instead of keeping its Brussels paint scheme. Currently it still is wearing Zurich colors and operates in special service and on the F-Line.

A Fleet History of the San Francisco Municipal Railway
Section 2: Streetcars and Light Rail Vehicles

No. 38-10-11	Years	Seats	Length / Width / Height / Weight	Model	City / Country
913	Non Op.	54	47' 8" / 8' 7" / 11' 6" / 42,200	N/A	New Orleans, LA
952	1998-	54	47' 8" / 8' 7" / 11' 6" / 42,200	N//A	Perley-Thomas Co. High Point, NC

Streetcars # 913 and # 952 were both built in 1923 for service in New Orleans, LA. They are both the type and model of streetcar made famous by the Tennessee Williams play, _A Streetcar Named Desire._ Car #952 came to Muni after it was retired from service in New Orleans via a lease agreement made between Mayor Willie Brown of San Francisco and Mayor Marc Morial of New Orleans. The agreement also included Muni sending retired California Cable Car #59 to New Orleans. Car # 913 was purchased for $200,000 from the Orange Empire Museum in Perris, CA in 2005 after the museum acquired it from New Orleans in 1964. Car #952 is used in special service and on F-Line service. Car # 913 is one of six old streetcars scheduled to begin restoration in 2019.

Car #913 in storage in 2017.

No. 38-12	Years	Seats	Length / Width / Height / Weight	Model	City / Country
916	Non Op.	52	46' 6" / 9' 0" / 10' 4" / 38,600	SW6	Melbourne, Australia Tramways Board Melbourne, Australia

A third Melbourne streetcar, #916, built in 1946 was acquired by Muni following a donation by the City of Melbourne in 2009. It is a more modern version (Model SW6) built in 1946 than its predecessors that were built in 1928. Like the W2 class, it also features a "reverse California Car design" with an open center with doors and closed ends. In 2018 it is in operational condition at Cameron Beach Yard adjacent to the SFMTA Green Divison, ready to enter revenue service as part of the historic fleet.

A Fleet History of the San Francisco Municipal Railway
Section 2: Streetcars and Light Rail Vehicles

No. 38-13	Years	Seats	Length / Width / Height / Weight	Model	City / Country
3557	Non Op.	31	46' 3" / 7' 3" / 10' 10" / 40,250	V6E	Hamburg, Germany Hamburger Hochbahn Aktiengesellschaft Hamburg, Germany

Streetcar # 3557 was obtained as a donation from Hamburg Germany by Streetcar buff Maurice Klebolt in 1979. Nicknamed, "The Red Baron", it was built in 1954 and operated in Hamburg until 1978. Car #3557 was used in the 1983-1987 Trolley Festivals, and was active until 1992, when it was removed from service due to exterior corrosion and a need to replace entrance doors. Currently it is in storage, although in 2018 it does not appear to be a candidate for restoration in the near future.

Artist graphic of a restored Car # 3557 and a photo in storage in 2017

No. 38-14-18	Years		Seats	Length / Width / Height / Weight	Model	City / Country
1	1912-1951	1962-	48	47'1" / 8'6" / 11'9" / 50,000	Type A	Holman Co. S.F., CA
578	1944-1956	1956-	26	26' 10" / 8' 8.5"/ N/A / 20,300	N/A	Hammond Co. S.F., CA
130	1914-1958	1971-	50	47'1" / 9'2.5" / 12'3" / 48,000	Type B	Jewett Car Co. Newark, OH
162	1914-1958	1986-	50	47'1" / 9'2.5" / 12'3" / 48,000	Type B	Jewett Car Co. Newark, OH
798	1944-1946	1985-	50	47' 0" / 8' 9" / 12' 2" / 39,895	N/A	Elkton Shops S.F., CA

Although they have appeared earlier in this section, this space is reserved for the local sub-group of older preserved (non PCC) San Francisco streetcars. Currently this group consists of five cars. Car #1, Muni's first streetcar, was received new in 1912, and has continuosly been owned by Muni. After a 1962 refresh it has been on the Muni roster as an operational car except when under repair or restoration. Car #578 is Muni's oldest streetcar (ca. 1896), and was a work car when acquired by Muni in 1944. After a restoration as a passenger car in 1956, it has been on the roster for over 60 years. Car #130, a Type B "Battleship" has been owned by Muni since 1914. In 1983 after serving as a work car for 25 years, it was restored as a passenger car for the first Trolley Festival, and has been active for 35 years. Car #162 was retired in 1958 and went to the Orange Empire Museum for 45 years, before being reacquired in 2003. Following a resotration, it joined the historic fleet in 2008. Finally, Car #798, the "Elkton Shops" Car, has been a non-operative part of the fleet since 1985, but is expected to join the active fleet in the near future.

46

A Fleet History of the San Francisco Municipal Railway
Section 3: Buses

A Fleet History of the San Francisco Municipal Railway
Section 3: Buses

A Fleet History of the San Francisco Municipal Railway
Section 3: Buses

The San Francisco Municipal Railway has operated over 50 different types and models of buses in its history, and in 2018, buses comprised both the largest fleet and carried the most passengers of the five modes of transit service at Muni. Originally buses began as transit vehicles on feeder routes to connect passengers to more heavily traveled streetcar lines, but after World War II this changed as rubber tired transit became dominant. A quirk, somewhat unique to Muni, was all early buses up to the acquisition of the Mack fleet in the mid-1950s included a zero (0) as the first digit of their fleet number. This was done to differentiate from otherwise identical numbers present in the rail fleet. The dominance of buses increased with the introduction of the articulated 60-foot long bus when vehicles of this type were first purchased by Muni in the 1980s. The bus continues to be the most versatile transit vehicle at Muni operating on both its busiest lines on Mission Street and Geary Boulevard, and on the lightest community circulator routes. The two largest changes to buses in recent times are the adoption of low-floor buses as standard during the past decade, and the introduction and adoption of hybrid buses that utilize complex powertrain systems that allow buses to operate using diesel fuel or electricity stored in batteries that is generated from buses using their brakes. The hybrid buses both pollute less and have better fuel economy than their non-hybrid predecessors.

No. 1	Years	Seats	Length	Model	Manufacturer
01-06	1918-1927	19	20' 5"	TDB	Meister & Sons Sacramento, CA

The second Superintendent of Muni, Fred Boeken, standing with Muni's first buses at the Geary Car House (now Presidio Division) - 1918

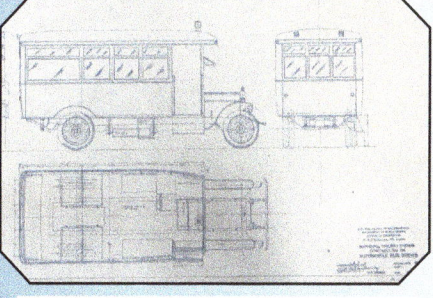

Bus #01-06 - blueprints - 1918

The small buses in the photo were the frst buses operated by Muni. They were comprised of a White Model TDB chassis, frame and motor paired to a wooden Brill body. All were painted gray with red trim to match the streetcars. Assembly was performed by A. Meister and & Sons in Sacramento, CA. The exact cost is unknown, but costs of similar buses support an estimated cost of about $4,000-$5,000 per unit. Bus #06 arrived a year later in 1919, and was the first transit vehicle to wear the Muni "SF" or "O' Shaughnessy" logo. Bus #03 was traded back to White as partial payment for a newer buses in 1925, and buses #01, #04 and #05 were traded back to White in 1927. Bus #02 was made into a tower truck and was still present at Muni in 1948. None of these vehicles are known to exist in 2018.

A Fleet History of the San Francisco Municipal Railway
Section 3: Buses

No. 2	Years	Seats	Length	Model	Manufacturer
07-09	1920-1930	18	?	20-45	White Motor Company Cleveland, OH

Photo not available

The second group of buses were similar to the first group, and were also traded in as partial payment on later buses, except Bus #07 was converted to a tower truck and existed at Muni as late as 1948. The White Model 20-45 was a very popular bus in its time. The cost of the buses when new is unknown, but a good assumption is they were about the same price as the first group of buses. At trade the two buses were valued at $1,117.50 each. Unfortunately, no photos exist in the Muni archives or in known private collections of these vehicles, which were painted in gray with red trim. Although White Model 20-45 buses have been preserved elsewhere, none of the Muni vehicles exist in 2018.

No. 3	Years	Seats	Length	Model	Manufacturer
010-012	1924-1929/31	25	?	50A	White Motor Company Cleveland, OH

The third type of bus acquired by Muni were White Model 50A vehicles which had a slightly longer body that could hold more passengers. Although the cost of these buses is no longer known, a similar Model 50A cost about $5,000 in 1924. All three were traded in to White or Fageol as partial payment on newer buses between 1929 and 1931. When #010 was traded in it had a value of $1,166.50 in 1929, but when Bus #012 was traded in it only had a value of $460 two years later. None of the Muni vehicles exist in 2018.

A Fleet History of the San Francisco Municipal Railway
Section 3: Buses

No. 4	Years	Seats	Length	Model	Manufacturer
013-015	1925-1933	29	25'	Z	Pierce Arrow Motor Company Buffalo, NY

Three "deluxe" Pierce-Arrow "Model Z" buses were purchased privately by real estate interests associated with the Westwood Highlands development, and then were leased to Muni to provide service on the 3-Monterey route. The exact cost is unknown, but Pierce-Arrow was advertising this type of bus at a cost of $5,850. With 29 seats these were the largest buses at Muni up to that time. All three were traded to White as partial payment on new buses in 1933, and none of the Westwood Highland / Muni buses exist in 2018.

No. 5	Years	Seats	Length	Model	Manufacturer
016-017	1927-1934	29	?	AB	Mack Trucks Inc. Allentown, PA

These two buses of the iconic "Model AB" design represented the first Mack buses to operate at Muni. The cost of the buses when new isn't known, but similar buses at that time cost around $5,500. They were traded in to White Motor Company for $200 in value for each bus on the purchase of new White buses in 1934. Neither of the two buses exist in 2018.

A Fleet History of the San Francisco Municipal Railway
Section 3: Buses

No. 6	Years	Seats	Length	Model	Manufacturer
018-019	1927-1937	29	?	Streetcar	Fageol Motors Oakland, CA

This group of two buses, known as "Safety Coaches", were built by the Fageol Motors across the bay in Oakland, CA. The cost when new is no longer known, but similar buses from Fageol cost about $7,000 each in the mid-1920s. Outfitted with rattan seats and a composite "wood and steel" body, they were traded in to White with a value of $200 each for new buses in 1937. Neither bus is known to exist in 2018.

No. 7	Years	Seats	Length	Model	Manufacturer
020-021	1927-1934	29	?	50B	White Motor Company Cleveland, OH

Photo not available

Buses #020 and #021, both White Motor Company Model 50B, were purchased in 1927. The original cost is no longer known, but similar White buses at that time were valued at about $7,500. Their value when traded back to White seven years later was $200 per bus. Neither bus exists in 2018.

No. 8	Years	Seats	Length	Model	Manufacturer
022-024	1927-1938	29	?	AB	Mack Trucks Inc. Allentown, PA

Photo not available

A second small group of Mack "Model AB" buses was obtained in 1927. As with other buses from this era the costs of the buses are unknown, but a similar Mack AB bus from around the same time cost about $7,000. They were traded in at a value of $175 each for the newer "Baby White" buses in 1938. Neither exist in 2018.

A Fleet History of the San Francisco Municipal Railway
Section 3: Buses

No. 9	Years	Seats	Length	Model	Manufacturer
025	1927-1938	29	?	105	Fageol Motors, Oakland, CA

> Photo not available

A single Fageol "Model 105" bus was acquired in 1927 and lasted over a decade until it was traded in for a value of $250 on new White buses in 1938. The cost at purchase is unknown, but it was probably around $8,000 based on the value of other Fageol buses sold during that time. The Fageol "Model 105" bought by Muni no longer exists in 2018.

No. 10	Years	Seats	Length	Model	Manufacturer
026	1929-1938	29	?	BK	Mack Trucks Inc., Allentown, PA

A single Mack "Model BK", possibly a demonstration model at the outset, arrived at Muni in 1929 and operated for almost a decade before it was traded in with a value of $225 in 1938. The cost when new isn't known, but was likely about $7,500. This bus was the first at Muni with a rear door. It no longer exists in 2018.

No. 11	Years	Seats	Length	Model	Manufacturer
027-029	1930-1938	28	?	160	Fageol Motors, Oakland, CA

> Photo not available

As the 1930s began Muni continued with a bus operations plan from the 1920s by acquiring new buses in very small numbers and using them for 7-10 years before trading them in as small payment on the cost of new buses. Little information exists about the these buses: no cost when new, (although similar Fageol buses cost about $8,000), no information on why these buses were chosen, and no photos exist. The buses were traded in when new White buses were acquired in 1938. None of these buses exist in 2018.

A Fleet History of the San Francisco Municipal Railway
Section 3: Buses

No. 12 030-031	Years 1931-1938	Seats 27	Length ?	Model 155-6	Manufacturer Fageol Motors Oakland, CA

Photo not available

These two Fageol "Model 155-6" buses started service in 1931. They were traded in for a value of $275 and $300 in 1938. The cost when new isn't known, but other other Fageol buses available at that time cost around $8,000. Neither are known to exist in 2018.

No. 13 032-033	Years 1933-1941	Seats 29	Length ?	Model 54	Manufacturer White Motor Company Cleveland, OH

The last buses with front engines at Muni were two White "Model 54" buses. Their original cost was $9,724. Although listed as being built by White, old Muni documentation states the steel bodies were done Wm. B. Gibson. These were the last new buses to be painted in the Muni gray and red colors for 70 years. Like their predecessors, they were traded in for partial value of $300 each on newer buses in 1941. Neither exist in 2018.

A Fleet History of the San Francisco Municipal Railway
Section 3: Buses

No. 14	Years	Seats	Length	Model	Manufacturer
034-036	1934-47	32	?	684	White Motor Company
037-038	1936-47				Cleveland, OH
039-040	1937-55				

This group of White "Model 684" buses represented a major change in bus design at Muni. They entered service as the largest buses operated by Muni, were the first buses with a rear engine and were the first buses to have both a front and a rear door. Buses #034-#036 were 16 inches shorter than the rest, and cost $9,855 in 1934. Buses #037 and #038 cost $10,278 in 1936, and buses #039-#040 cost $10,117 in 1937. These buses arrived painted in a unique orange and black color scheme. Buses #034-#037 were no longer at Muni in 1947, and the remaining three were no longer in service at Muni by 1955. None are believed to exist in 2018.

No. 15	Years	Seats	Length	Model	Manufacturer
041-050	1938-1975	32	30'	784	White Motor Company
051-062					Cleveland, OH

A second larger group of slightly more modern White "Model 784" buses entered service in 1938. The cost at purchase for the first four buses was $10,161 per unit, and the rest were $10,328 per unit. These were also colored orange and black until the post World War II adoption of green and cream "Wings" design. After larger White buses entered service in the late 1940's, this group was nicknamed the "Baby Whites." The last three buses were in regular service on the 39-Coit route until 1975, because Muni didn't have any small buses in its fleet. The last few units were painted in the maroon and gold color scheme in the late 1960s. The last bus from this fleet, Coach #42 was restored for the Muni Centennial in 2012 and in 2018 is used for special events.

A Fleet History of the San Francisco Municipal Railway
Section 3: Buses

Muni "Baby White" #042 - after restoration back to its original orange and black colors in 2012. At one time it was renumbered as #062, but was given its original number again in 2012.

No. 16 063-072	Years 1941-1955	Seats 26	Length 30' 0"	Model 26-S	Manufacturer ACF Brill Company Philadelphia, PA

A fleet of ten smaller "Model 26-S" buses built by American Car Foundry (ACF) arrived in Muni's new blue and yellow colors just before World War II and operated at Muni in the 1940s. The cost when new was $7,933 each. These buses were scrapped in 1954-55. None are believed to exist in 2018.

A Fleet History of the San Francisco Municipal Railway
Section 3: Buses

No. 17	Years	Seats	Length	Model	Manufacturer
073-074	1941-1955	31	32' 0"	31-S	ACF Brill Company Philadelphia, PA

Two larger "Model 31-S" buses built by American Car Foundry (ACF), and also painted in Muni blue and yellow colors, arrived along with the other ACF buses in early 1941. Each bus cost $9,969. In 1953 Bus #073 was scrapped, but the frame was used along with the body of Cable Car #62 to create Muni's first and only motorized Cable Car. It appears that Bus #074 was scrapped in 1954-55.

On September 29, 1944 the S.F. Municipal Railway (Muni) merged with the privately owned Market Street Railway (MSRy) following voter approval of Charter Measure 1 to purchase the MSRy at a cost of $7.5 million dollars. All property owned by MSRy became Muni property and the MSRy ceased to exist. Former MSRy vehicles used in revenue service by Muni are listed here with an "M" prefix to their number to designate they were ex-MSRy buses that became Muni buses via the merger. Most of these vehicles only briefly operated in Muni service before they were retired.

No. 18	Years	Seats	Length	Model	Manufacturer
M8	1944-1946	30	23' 9"	1932	Fageol Motors Oakland, CA

The Fageol Model 1932, MSRy Bus #8, was in storage at the time of the 1944 merger and was not used in Muni service. This was the remaining unit of two buses that had a Fageol chassis combined with a body from the California Motor Coach Company. It was retired and sold in 1946 for $110, and is not believed to exist in 2018.

A Fleet History of the San Francisco Municipal Railway
Section 3: Buses

No. 19	Years	Seats	Length	Model	Manufacturer
M21	1944-1946	17	14' 1"	T-26-C	Yellow Coach (General Motors) Pontiac, MI

Another bus in storage acquired by Muni in the 1944 merger was MSRy Bus #21, a Yellow Coach originally delivered in 1932. The small bus with only 17 seats had been removed from active service by MSRy and converted to a work vehicle. Outfitted with a strong magnet it drove along MSRy streetcar tracks picking up stray metal that could damage the wheels on active streetcars. There is no record it performed this duty at Muni. It was retired and sold in 1946 for $41, and does not exist in 2018.

No. 20	Years	Seats	Length	Model	Manufacturer
M25-M28	1944-1946	23	22' 9"	23R	Twin Coach Company Kent, OH

Originally built by Twin Coach for MSRy in 1937-38, this small group of buses briefly operated in Muni service before they were sold in early 1946. None exist in 2018.

A Fleet History of the San Francisco Municipal Railway
Section 3: Buses

No. 21	Years	Seats	Length	Model	Manufacturer
M30-M41	1944-1948	25	24' 2"	739	Yellow Coach (General Motors)
M60-M76	1944-1948	25	24' 2"	739	Pontiac, MI

MSRy #34 in 1939 - five years before it became part of Muni in the 1944 merger.

The Market Street Railway (MSRy) purchased many Yellow Coach buses, which were made by a division of General Motors in Pontiac, MI. The first group of a dozen and the second group of seventeen "Model 739" buses were built in 1939 and were delivered in MSRy colors of green and white. The second group cost $7,365 each when delivered new. Once they became the property of Muni only a few were repainted into the Muni colors of blue and yellow. All were sold by Muni in 1946 and 1948. None are believed to exist in 2018.

No. 22	Years	Seats	Length	Model	Manufacturer
M101-M120	1944-1948	36	30' 10"	731	Yellow Coach (General Motors) Pontiac, MI

Yellow Bus #104 wearing MSRy colors before the 1944 merger.

Twenty larger "Model 731" Yellow Coach buses were built for MSRy in 1939-40. Each bus cost $9,822. Following the 1944 merger these buses operated at Muni until all were sold in 1948. The sales price was $35 each. A few were repainted Muni colors of blue and yellow in the interim before being sold. None are believed to exist in 2018.

A Fleet History of the San Francisco Municipal Railway
Section 3: Buses

No. 23	Years	Seats	Length	Model	Manufacturer
M121-M122	1944-1955	36	30' 5"	TG-3601	Yellow Coach (GM)
M151-M159	1944-1955	36	30' 5"	TG-3601	Pontiac, MI
M160-M166	1944-1954	36	30' 5"	TG-3605	

Yellow Bus #157 wearing MSRy colors before the 1944 merger

Yellow Bus #157 wearing Muni colors after the 1944 merger

These three groups of Yellow Coach "Model TG3601" and "TG3605" buses were built in 1940 (121-122), 1941 (151-159) and 1942 (160-166). After the merger most of these three groups of buses were repainted in either Muni blue and yellow colors, or the subsequent green and cream "Wings" design. The first group was removed from service in 1949, and the second and third groups were retired in 1951. All were sold between 1951-1955. The second and third groups were used by MSRy to replace the Fillmore Street counter-balance cable cars, Castro Street cable cars and Sacramento-Clay Street cable cars in 1941-42 prior to their arrival at Muni. None are known to exist in 2018.

No. 24	Years	Seats	Length	Model	Manufacturer
M201-M207	1944-1953	32	28' 0"	TG-3201	Yellow Coach (General Motors) Pontiac, MI

Yellow Bus #203 wearing MSRy colors before the 1944 merger

This group of seven Yellow Coach "Model TG-3201" buses was delivered to MSRy in 1939, and after the merger they were repainted in the green and cream "Wings" design and operated at Muni unil 1953, when they were sold. Among their service highlights were trips on the 39-Coit to serve Coit Tower, which was usually the domain of the Baby Whites for over 30 years. None of these buses are believed to exist in 2018.

A Fleet History of the San Francisco Municipal Railway
Section 3: Buses

No. 25	Years	Seats	Length	Model	Manufacturer
M301-M311	1944-1955	36	30' 5"	TD-3601	Yellow Coach (General Motors) Pontiac, MI

Yellow Bus #306 wearing MSRy colors before the 1944 merger

Although they were not the last new buses at MSRy, this group of ten Yellow Coach "Model TD-3601" buses comprised the only diesel powered buses operated at MSRy - as all others were gasoline powered. Each Model TD-3601 bus cost MSRy $13,000. Originally built in 1940, these buses were sold off by Muni between 1948-1955. None are believed to exist in 2018.

No. 26	Years	Seats	Length	Model	Manufacturer
M401-M430	1944-1955	37	30' 5"	TG-4502	Yellow Coach (General Motors)
M431-M433	1944-1955	37	30' 5"	TG-4505	Pontiac, MI

Yellow Bus #405 wearing MSRy colors before the 1944 merger

These two groups of Yellow Coach "Model TG-4502" and "Model TG-4505" buses, built in 1941 and 1942 respectively, operated in Muni service from 1944-1952. The cost when new was $12,650 and $13,354.* After the merger most were painted in the green and cream "Wings" paint colors. Their disposition is unknown, but are not on a 1955 roster, so they are assumed to have been sold. None are believed to exist in 2018.

*The cost for Yellow Coach buses M121-M122, M150-M159, M160-M166, M201-M207, M301-M311, M401-M433, and M2-M16 is based on a price listed by an audit of the equipment obtained from MSRy in the 1944 merger. It is unknown if the prices are based upon an "acquired value" of the vehicles, or their "price when new".

A Fleet History of the San Francisco Municipal Railway
Section 3: Buses

No. 27	Years	Seats	Length	Model	Manufacturer
M1-M16	1944-1951	45	34' 10"	TG-4505	Yellow Coach (General Motors) Pontiac, MI

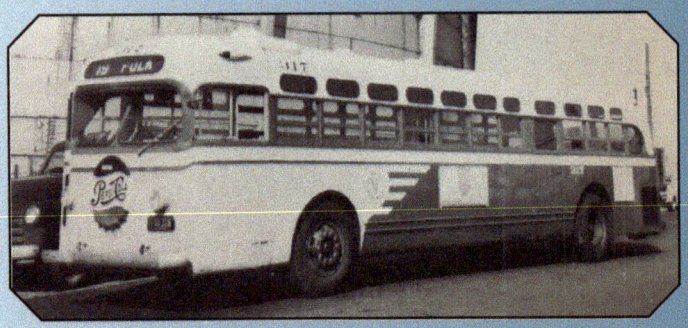

These Yellow Coach "Model TG-4505" buses were the largest buses in service at MSRy. The buses were due to go to New York, but were diverted to San Francisco as a wartime measure, and arrived in 1941. They were in Muni service from 1944-1955, where they were renumbered 312 to 327 and were repainted in the green and cream "Wings" colors. Officially the buses were leased to MSRy and then to Muni, until Muni puchased them from the War Assets Corporation for $6,606 each. In 1955 all were sold. None are believed to exist in 2018.

No. 28	Years	Seats	Length	Model	Manufacturer
075-078	1944-1955	44	35' 0"	798	White Motor Company
079-0125	1945-1955	44	35' 0"	798	Cleveland, OH
0126-0155	1946-1955	44	35' 0"	798	

This group of "Model 798" White buses was delivered in phases with the earliest buses entering service in 1944, and the last in 1946. Each bus cost between $12,350-$13,025. All were originally painted in blue and yellow, but later received the green and cream "Wings" paint colors. All were retired by 1955 when the first new buses from Mack entered service, but some were pulled from storage briefly in 1960 to supplement service during baseball season to the new stadium at Candlestick Park. The first two series of buses were delivered with standard or stick-shift transmissions, as was done on all previous Muni buses. All later buses had automatic transmissions. Disposition is unknown, and none are believed to exist in 2018.

A Fleet History of the San Francisco Municipal Railway
Section 3: Buses

No. 29 0156-0165	Years 1947-1953	Seats 44	Length 36' 1"	Model 44D	Manufacturer Fageol-Twin Coach Kent, OH

This group of 10 "Model 44D" buses by Fageol-Twin Coach were unique in post World War II San Francisco. They were built with two gasoline engines and an automatic transmission, and were designated as the replacement buses for cable car service. The buses cost $15,187 each at delivery. Although they were the first buses to use the green and cream colors, they never received the "Wings" design, probably due to the silver beltline around the entire bus. The two engines caused problems in operation, so they were modified to only use one engine, and of course they did not replace cable cars. All were retired after less than six years of service in 1953. SFMTA owns Bus #0163 in non-operable condition. Restoration of Bus #0163 was started at the Islais Creek Divison in 2018.

Muni Fageol-Twin Coach #0163 in storage at Marin Yard - 2010

In the 1952 book "Maybelle the Cable Car" a bus of this model is given the name of "Bill". Therefore, as Bus #0163 is the last Model 44D vehicle at Muni, it has earned the nickname of "Bill"

A Fleet History of the San Francisco Municipal Railway
Section 3: Buses

No. 30	Years	Seats	Length	Model	Manufacturer
0166-0195	1947-1955	39	35' 0"	798	White Motor Company
0195-0454	1948-1969	44	35' 0"	798	Cleveland, OH

A total of 288 larger White "Model 798" buses arrived in two groups in 1947-1948 as part of a large purchase following the passage of a 1947 bond measure to fund new transit equipment. These were basically the same buses that were acquired in 1944-1946, except these were delivered with automatic transmissions instead of stick-shift transmissions. They were the last gasoline powered buses at Muni. Each bus cost $16,000. The first group was retired in 1955, while the second group slowly were phased out until the last 80 buses were removed from service in 1969 following the arrival of the first GMC "New Look" buses. Buses #0392 and #0419 are owned by SFMTA and await future restoration.

Muni White Buses #0392 and #0419 in storage - 2018

A Fleet History of the San Francisco Municipal Railway
Section 3: Buses

No. 31	Years	Seats	Length	Model	Manufacturer
2100-2199	1955-1969	48	38' 6"	C49-DT	Mack Trucks Inc.
2200-2269	1956-1970	48	38' 6"	C49-DT	Allentown, PA
2300-2369	1957-1970	48	38' 6"	C49-DT	
2400-2469	1958-1970	48	38' 6"	C49-DT	
2500-2569	1959-1970	48	38' 6"	C49-DT	
2600-2669	1960-1979	48	38' 6"	C49-DT	

A total of 450 Mack "Model C-49DT" buses were acquired by Muni in six groups between 1955-1960. These were Muni's first buses that didn't contain a zero (0) in the fleet number. Following the defeat of a 1953 bond measure by voters that would have funded new buses, Muni worked out a complex lease arrangement with Mack to acquire these buses, which represent some of the last buses produced by Mack. The payment plan spread out between 1956-1966, with added minimal payments until 1969, totaled slighlty less than $11.5 million dollars. This worked out to a cost of approximately $25,000 per bus. Amazingly, Muni returned much of the completely worn out fleet to Mack in 1969-70, even though Mack was no longer producing buses. Mack scrapped most of them. Two Macks were retained for use on the 39-Coit bus route to replace the nearly 40 year old "Baby Whites". These Macks were shortened by removing the middle section, and served until the late 1970s. A few others were kept for parts or on reserve. The last Mack was removed from the Muni fleet in 1979. Several years later Muni and Market Street Railway reacquired Coach #2230, which is now owned by the SFMTA. After years of waiting, restoration began in 2016 and was completed in 2018.

Mack #2517 in gold paint for Muni 50th anniversary - 1962 (left)
Mack #2230 operating in special service - 2018

A Fleet History of the San Francisco Municipal Railway
Section 3: Buses

No. 32	Years	Seats	Length	Model	Manufacturer
3100-3179	1969-1993	48	39' 0"	T8H-5305	General Motors
3180-3189	1969-1993	48	39' 0"	T8H-5305A	Pontiac, MI
3190-3390	1969-1993	48	39' 0"	T8H-5305	

Muni was the last large transit agency in the United States to purchase GMC "New Look" buses when they were acquired in mid-1969. The official model delivered was a designated "T8H-5805". A total of 391 "New Looks" (aka "Jimmys" or "Fish Bowls") entered service in San Francisco where they replaced the last of venerable 1940s White gasoline buses, and the Mack fleet. All were delivered in the new Muni colors of maroon and gold, based on the colors of the California Street Cable Car. The new colors were adopted in 1967 to replace the green and cream colors adopted in 1946. Each "New Look" bus cost $38,500. After a dozen years of service 240 were sold in 1982, while another 151 were rebuilt and continued in service for another decade. The rebuilt buses received the "Landor" sunset glow and poppy gold colors and paint design and were renumbered as #3500-#3649. The last buses in this fleet were retired from service in 1993. SFMTA owns Coach #3287, which is restored and in operable condition, and Coach #3640, which is in non-operable condition.

GM "New Look" Muni bus in "Landor" colors - 1985

A Fleet History of the San Francisco Municipal Railway
Section 3: Buses

Muni #3287 in storage - 2017

No. 33	Years	Seats	Length	Model	Manufacturer
4000-4009	1969-1979	48	39' 0"	111-CC-C3	Flxible Corporation Loudonville, OH

Muni #4009 in storage - 2017

At the same time as the GMC fleet was acquired, a fleet of ten Flxible Model 111-CC-C3 -"New Look" buses painted in maroon and gold were purchased at a cost of about $40,000 each. The small size of this group of buses caused them to become "orphans", and within a few years they were not widely used in regular service. By 1979 they were retired and sold. SFMTA owns Coach #4009 which is non-operable, but in good shape cosmetically. In 2018 it is stored and awaiting a future restoration.

A Fleet History of the San Francisco Municipal Railway
Section 3: Buses

No. 34	Years	Seats	Length	Model	Manufacturer
4100-4200	1974-1991	41	35' 0"	9635-6	AM General Corp. South Bend, IN

The fleet of 100 AM General "Model 9635-6" buses was acquired to fill a need for smaller and quieter buses that followed public comments collected after acquisition of the GM "New Look" fleet. These buses were the first to be clad in the "Landor" sunset glow and poppy gold colors, and the first to use the Muni "worm" logo. They were also 96" wide instead of the standard 102" width. Nicknamed "Amy's", each unit cost $59,000. The last buses were retired and sold in 1991. In 2018 SFMTA owns Coach #4154, which is in operable condition and occasionally operates in special service.

No. 35	Years	Seats	Length	Model	Manufacturer
4030-4054	1980-1985	46	40' 0"	MPL-570	Grumman-Flxible Delaware, OH

After much analysis and several design and policy changes, Muni acquired a fleet of 25 advanced design "Model 870" buses produced by Grumman-Flxible. Purchased after a period of rapid inflation in the 1970s each bus cost $115,000. These buses included several "firsts" at Muni: first folding seats, first "kneeling" suspension and first wheelchair lift to accommodate persons with disabilities, oversized headsigns, and first color application using decals and not paint. Unfortunately, this fleet started out with maintenance problems and never overcame reliability concerns. In 1985 they were retired early and sold. None were retained by Muni.

A Fleet History of the San Francisco Municipal Railway
Section 3: Buses

No. 36	Years	Seats	Length	Model	Manufacturer
2700-2749	1981-1982	48	39' 0"	TDH-4801	General Motors
2800-2807	1981-1982	50	39' 0"	TDH-5105	Pontiac, MI
2900-2901	1981-1982	45	39' 0"	TDH-4512	

In fall 1981 in a desperate move driven by a high out-of-service rate on the aging GMC "New Look" fleet, Muni leased 60 GMC "old look" buses that had been retired by the Southern California Rapid Transit District (SCRTD). The lease price was $100 per month per unit. Built in 1954-1958, the buses in the best shape were placed into service with minimal Muni markings (logos and new numbers), but otherwise continued to wear their SCRTD brown, gold and and white paint colors. The buses remained in service until 1982 when they were returned to SCRTD. None are owned by Muni in 2018.

No. 37	Years	Seats	Length	Model	Manufacturer
729, 731, 742	1983	48	39' 0"	T6H	General Motors
743, 744, 745					Pontiac, MI

In 1982 plans were made to offer alternate transit service to address the Cable Car shutdown and rebuild. However, service coverage was found to be inadequate for the Union Square to Fisherman's Wharf corridor, so in 1983 an additional special shuttle was approved. For six months (late May-late November 1983) a fleet of six ex-AC Transit buses were leased and operated to provide service. The buses were leased at a cost of $8,000 each, and were outfitted with a unique cable car color inspired paint scheme. The special service was not needed in 1984 as the cable cars returned to service. None of these buses were retained by Muni.

A Fleet History of the San Francisco Municipal Railway
Section 3: Buses

No. 38	Years	Seats	Length	Model	Manufacturer
6000-6099	1984-2002	57	60' 0"	SG-310	M.A.N. Cleveland, NC

This group of 100 "Model SG-310" buses by M.A.N. (Maschinenfabrik Augsburg-Nürnberg) were the first 60-foot articulated fleet purchased by Muni. They were produced at a new plant opened as a North American subsidiary to the parent company in West Germany. Each bus cost $211,000 at delivery, and they were delivered in the "Landor" sunset glow and poppy gold colors. After proving the value of 60-foot buses in San Francisco and serving the city for over 15 years the fleet was retired and sold with the last buses ending service in 2002. SFMTA owns Coach #6099 which is in good shape, but not in operable condition in 2018.

Muni #6099 in storage - 2017

A Fleet History of the San Francisco Municipal Railway
Section 3: Buses

No. 39	Years	Seats	Length	Model	Manufacturer
4500- 4679	1984-2004	40	40' 0"	D-902	Flyer Industries Limited Winnipeg, Canada

A total of 180 40-foot Flyer "Model 902" standard transit buses were purchased to replace a large number of GMC "New Look" buses that were retired and sold in the early 1980s. The Muni buses were based on a Model 901 with some specification changes, such as wider doors, and received a "Model 902" designation. Each bus cost $144,000 when new. They were retired in the early 2000s, with the last ones being sold in 2004. Bus #4574 was reacquired by SFMTA and is in operable condition in 2018.

Muni #4574 in special service - 2017

A Fleet History of the San Francisco Municipal Railway
Section 3: Buses

No. 40	Years	Seats	Length	Model	Manufacturer
8801-8850	1988-2002	40	40' 0"	D40-80	New Flyer Industries
8901-8956	1989-2003	40	40' 0"	D40-80	Winnipeg, Canada / Union City, CA

New Flyer Industries Limited, which was a reorganzation of the older "Flyer Industries Limited", built two groups of "Model D40-80" buses for the SFMTA in the late 1980s. Each new bus cost $180,000. These were the first Muni vehicles purchased in accord with Federal Transit Administration (FTA) "Buy America" rules appoved in 1982, and revised in 1987. The new rules required 50% of vehicle content to be of U.S. origin, and that final assembly occur in the United States. The first group of 50 buses arrived as the last of the GMC "New Look" buses were being phased out and sold, and the AM General buses were being retired from service. The second group of New Flyer "Model D40-80" 40-foot buses arrived a year after the first in 1989. Each bus in this group cost $180,000 when new. Both groups would work full service careers of 14 years before being retired from the fleet in 2002 and 2003 as newer buses arrived to replace them. None of the first group of New Flyer "Model D40-80" buses is owned by Muni in 2018, but Bus #8926 of the second group is part of the historic fleet, and is in storage in non-operable service condition in 2018.

Muni #8926 in storage - 2018

A Fleet History of the San Francisco Municipal Railway
Section 3: Buses

No. 41	Years	Seats	Length	Model	Manufacturer
9000-9045	1991-2007	26	31' 7"	Orion II	Orion Missisagua, Canada / Union City, CA

Muni #CC1 in storage - 2017

A group of 45 smaller 31' Orion buses joined the Muni fleet to provide service on smaller routes on narrower streets that had been served by the 35' AM General buses. These buses were 96" wide instead of a standard 102" width. Each bus cost $165,000. All were painted in the "Landor" sunset glow and poppy orange color scheme. Coach #9030 had seats removed and was transformed into an emergency command center (CC1). The last bus was retired in 2007. CC1 and Bus #9010 are owned by SFMTA and are in operable condition.

No. 42	Years	Seats	Length	Model	Manufacturer
9101-9124	1991-2014	52	60' 0"	D60	New Flyer Winnipeg, Canada / Grand Forks, ND

Muni's second purchase of 60' articulated buses occurred in 1991 when 24 vehicles were acquired from New Flyer Industries at a cost of $285,000 per unit. These were the last buses painted in the original "Landor" design and colors of sunset glow and poppy gold. They were later repainted in the simplified sunset glow and poppy orange colors, and repainted again in the silver and red colors. These buses operated until 2004, and then several were placed into the "reserve" or "contingency" fleet where they were available for part-time use for special events. The last four of these venerable buses were finally retired in 2014. Muni owns #9120 which is in storage.

A Fleet History of the San Francisco Municipal Railway
Section 3: Buses

No. 43	Years	Seats	Length	Model	Manufacturer
Not fully sequential	1994-1998	40	40' 0"	D900-9635 D900-10235	Flyer Industries Limited Winnipeg, Canada

9635 series: 339R-341R, 343R, 345R, 352R, 355R-357R
10235 series: 601R, 603R-605R, 607R-612R, 615R-616R, 619R-629R, 633R, 645R, 647R

A group of 22 Flyer Industries "Model D900-9635" and "Model D900-10235" buses built in 1980 for SamTrans were acquired at a cost of $5,000 each in 1994 to replace GMC New Look buses in the "Reserve Fleet". The narrower "96" width buses were never painted in Muni colors, and did not see active service. The wider "102" width buses saw limited service. After rehabilitation costs are added, each bus cost about $15,000. All were sold as surplus by 1998 after the arrival of new buses. None are owned by SFMTA in 2018.

No. 44	Years	Seats	Length	Model	Manufacturer
8001-8045	1999- 2016	38	40' 0"	Model 416	North American Bus Industries Anniston, AL

In 1999 Muni bought 45 new NABI 40' buses originally ordered by AC Transit in Oakland after the East Bay transit agency decided they didn't need them. They were delivered in the simplified "Landor" color scheme with a color stripe under the windows at a cost of $315,000 per unit. Later most were repainted in the simplified stripe above the windows design, and eventually about 10 were painted gray and red. This group of buses became very popular in service due to their dependability. After a service life of 14 years, they were retired from regular service and moved to the "contingency" fleet in 2014. In 2016 the last of the fleet were sold. None were retained by the SFMTA, but two units, #8016 and #8044 were converted by the S.F. Fire Department to mass casualty transport units.

A Fleet History of the San Francisco Municipal Railway
Section 3: Buses

Bus #8016 - one of two NABI 40' buses converted to use by SFFD - 2017

No. 45 2800-2845	Years 2000-2012	Seats 38	Length 40' 0"	Model Phantom	Manufacturer Gillig Company Hayward, CA

Bus #2840 in storage in 2017

About the same time as the 40' NABI's were acquired new, Muni also purchased 45 used 1993 Gillig 40' buses from AC Transit that had been rehabilitated and repowered with an engine upgrade in 1999. Each of these buses cost $25,000. These buses also performed well with their most famous role being the uniquely colored silver, red and blue stripe NX-Judah bus service they performed near the end of the service career after they had been moved into the "reserve" or "contingency" fleet role. All were retired from service and sold in 2012. Bus #2840 is owned by SFMTA in 2018.

A Fleet History of the San Francisco Municipal Railway
Section 3: Buses

No. 46	Years	Seats	Length	Model	Manufacturer
8101-8235	2002-	38	40' 0"	AN440	Neoplan USA
8301-8371	2003-	38	40' 0"	AN440	Lamar, CO

As a replacement for the late 1980s New Flyer fleet, Muni ordered 135 40' buses from Neoplan USA, a former subsidiary of Neoplan located in Germany, and the new buses entered service in 2002. Thesse were the last buses delivered with the "Landor" colors of sunset glow and poppy gold with the simplified stripe scheme above the windows. Each bus cost $323,000. Following the initial purchase of Neoplan USA 40' buses, Muni decided to acquire 71 more buses at the same price. The second group of buses started to arrive in 2003. A few at the end of the order were delivered in red and gray which made them the first new Muni buses to wear red and gray in 70 years. These buses and their 60' counterparts are likely the last "standard" high-floor design buses to be delivered to the SFMTA as the North American market switched to low-floor buses by 2010. In 2010-2011 Muni rehabilitated 34 of these buses, and in 2012 as Muni prepared to order new buses, a decision was made to rebuild 80 more to extend their life another five years to 2020-2021. In 2018 most of the fleet has been retired.

A Fleet History of the San Francisco Municipal Railway
Section 3: Buses

No. 47	Years	Seats	Length	Model	Manufacturer
6200-6225	2002-2016	55	60' 0"	AN460	Neoplan USA
6226-6299	2003-2016	55	60' 0"	AN460	Lamar, CO
6402-6424	2003-2016	55	60' 0"	AN460	

Muni also selected Neoplan buses as a replacement for the M.A.N. 60' articulated buses. A total of 100 60' buses were ordered in 2002. Each bus cost $431,000, and like the smaller buses Neoplan produced at the same time, they were painted white with a simplified poppy orange and yellow stripe above the windows. The first group of buses entered service in 2002, and the rest entered service in 2003. Almost immediately after purchasing the first group of 100 60' articulated buses from Neoplan USA, Muni purchased 24 additional 60' articulated buses at the same price, and that group also entered service in 2003. This later group of buses arrived painted in the gray and red paint scheme. Later in their service time many of the buses from the first segment of the order were repainted to the gray and red paint colors. Like the smaller buses, they were most likely the last standard (high floor) buses to be delivered to SFMTA. All were retired by the end of 2016, and all were sold by the end of 2018. Muni owns #6255 which is non-operable in storage.

Bus #6255 - in storage - 2018

A Fleet History of the San Francisco Municipal Railway
Section 3: Buses

No. 48	Years	Seats	Length	Model	Manufacturer
8401-8456	2006 -	35	40' 0"	Model VII	Daimler Chrysler Buses (Orion)
					Mississagua, ON - Canada
					Oriskany, NY

In 2007 Muni ordered new buses that saw major changes in design. This order of 56 Orion Model VII 40' buses made by Daimler Chrysler Buses (a.k.a. Orion or Orion Industries) was Muni's first purchase of low-floor design buses, and the first order with hybrid engines (series design). The buses cost $488,000 each. Seating capacity was reduced due to the loss of seats at the wheel wells. These were also the first new buses painted in the retro Muni colors of silver (or gray) and red that were first used by Muni in 1912. These buses are scheduled for replacement in 2019.

No. 49	Years	Seats	Length	Model	Manufacturer
8501-8530	2007-	27	30' 0"	Model VIII	Daimler Chrysler Buses (Orion)
					Mississagua, ON - Canada
					Oriskany, NY

Simultaneous with the purchase of the 40' Orion buses, Muni purchased 30 Orion 30' low-floor series hybrid buses to replace an equal number of older 30' Orion buses from the early 1990s that were due for retirement. Unlike their predecessors, these small buses were a standard 102" wide. Each of the new 30' buses cost $521,000, which was more than their larger 40' siblings. They were delivered in the silver and red color scheme. These buses are due for retirement and replacement in 2019.

A Fleet History of the San Francisco Municipal Railway
Section 3: Buses

No. 50	Years	Seats	Length	Model	Manufacturer
8601-8662	2013-	37	40' 0"	XDE40-Allison	New Flyer Industries
8701-8750	2014-	37	40' 0"	XDE40-BAE	St. Cloud, MN
8751-8780	2017-	37	40' 0"	XDE40-Allison	
8800-8901	2016-	37	40' 0"	XDE40-BAE	
8902-8969	2018-	37	40'0"	XDE40-BAE	

In 2012 Muni ordered 62 New Flyer 40' low floor diesel electric hybrids with 23 being powered by BAE "series hybrid" motors and 39 being powered by Allison "parallel hybrid" motors. All were painted in retro silver and red paint colors. The BAE powered New Flyer buses cost $730,000 per unit, while the Allison powered New Flyer buses cost $789,000 per unit. The buses utilized specifications developed by the state of Minnesota to save several months of time between order and delivery, and the order included options to purchase more buses using the original contract. The options were acted upon a year later and 50 more 40' New Flyer buses powered by BAE "series hybrid" motors were delivered to Muni. The option order buses cost $761,000 per unit. A third group of buses, priced at the second option started to arrive in 2016. The contract with options allows for a purchase of up to 200 buses. The first group of these buses are scheduled to operate until 2025-2026, while the last group may be retired in 2028-2029.

A Fleet History of the San Francisco Municipal Railway
Section 3: Buses

No. 51	Years	Seats	Length	Model	Manufacturer
6500-6554	2015-	46	60' 0"	XDE60-Allison	New Flyer Industries
6560-6584	2016-	46	60' 0"	XDE60-Allison	St. Cloud, MN
6585-6628	2016-	46	60' 0"	XDE60-Allison	
6629-6697	2017-	46	60' 0"	XDE60-Allison	
6700-6705	2015-	46	60/ 0"	XDE60-BAE	
6706-6730	2016-	46	60' 0"	XDE60-BAE	

Following the 40' order for New Flyer hybrids, Muni placed an order for 60 of the 60' low floor hybrid buses with the Allison "parallel" hybrid powertrain. These are the first low floor 60-foot buses at Muni. The first ones arrived in 2015, and new buses continued to arrive into 2016. A second group of 50 60' electric hybrid low-floor buses powered by the BAE "series" hybrid also began to arrive in 2016. All buses were painted in the red and sliver colors. The Allison powered buses cost $1,042,000 per unit, and the BAE powered buses cost $1,025,000. The number of option purchases tied to this contract is 224 vehicles, although Muni may plan to acquire more if funding is available.

A Fleet History of the San Francisco Municipal Railway
Section 4: Trolley Buses

A Fleet History of the San Francisco Municipal Railway
Section 4: Trolley Buses

A Fleet History of the San Francisco Municipal Railway
Section 4: Trolley Buses

San Francisco is one of five U.S. cities that continue to operate trolley buses in 2018. The others are Seattle, WA, Philadelphia, PA, Boston, MA, and Dayton, OH. To the north this mode operates in only one Canadian city, Vancouver, BC, while to the south trolley buses continue to operate in Mexico City and Guadalajara, Mexico. These vehicles are also known as "trolleycoaches" or "trackless trolleys". The primary reasons trolley buses continue in service at Muni are: 1) geography - including hills too steep for rail service that tax the capabilities of diesel or hybrid buses, 2) zero emissions - trolley buses don't emit exhausts from internal combustion engines because they use electricity, and the power is generated via nearly emission free hydroelectric plants, 3) low and reliable energy costs - San Francisco owns the Hetch Hetchy Dam and reservoir in the Sierra Nevada that is the source of hydroelectric power used to power S.F. transit vehicles, and 4) noise pollution - trolley buses are quieter in service than diesel or hybrid buses.

For over half a century since their introduction at Muni in the 1940s, sixteen trolley bus models have operated as part of the Muni fleet, including the most recent vehicles that started to arrive in 2015. Their greatest role in Muni operations was to serve as a cheaper alternative to streetcars as many routes after World War II were converted to trolley bus service. However, the future for this mode is unclear. As battery powered vehicles of all types, including transit vehicles, continue to show dramatic improvements in performance and duration, and "rapid-charge" technology also continues to improve, the future for electric powered transit buses appears solid, but the need for miles of overhead power lines and the familiar twin poles of a trolley bus may fade into history within a generation. Only time will reveal the outcome.

No. 1	Years	Seats	Length / Width / Height / Weight	Model	Manufacturer
501-509	1941-1954	40	34' 8.5" / 8' 3.5" / ? / 20,460		St. Louis Car Company St. Louis, MO

A Fleet History of the San Francisco Municipal Railway
Section 4: Trolley Buses

Muni's first trolley buses were nine vehicles purchased from the St. Louis Car Company at a cost of $13,200 per unit that arrived painted in the short-lived blue and yellow colors. They were placed into service on a new R-Howard line that followed the route of an expired private streetcar franchise formerly owned by the Market Street Railway. The fleet was retired and scrapped in 1954, except for Trolley Bus #506 which was saved and is still owned by the SFMTA in 2018. It is cosmetically restored and is used at special events as a static display while it awaits funding for restoration to fully operable condition.

Muni Trolley Bus #506 - 2015

On September 29, 1944 the S.F. Municipal Railway (Muni) merged with the privately owned Market Street Railway (MSRy) following voter approval of Charter Measure 1 to purchase the MSRy at a cost of $7.5 million dollars. All property owned by MSRy became Muni property and the MSRy ceased to exist. Former MSRy vehicles used in revenue service by Muni are listed here with an "M" prefix to their number to designate they were ex-MSRy trolley buses that became Muni trolley buses via the merger. Most of these vehicles only briefly operated on Muni before they were retired.

A Fleet History of the San Francisco Municipal Railway
Section 4: Trolley Buses

No. 2	Years	Seats	Length / Width / Height / Weight	Model	Manufacturer
M51-M59	1944-1949	37	33' 0" / 8' 0" / ? / 19,425	T40	J.G Brill Company, Philadelphia, PA

Trolley Bus #50 - 2017

This group of nine trolley coaches represents the oldest model of this type of vehicle used in San Francisco, although they came to Muni via the merger with the Market Street Railway (MSRy). When purchased by MSRy in 1935 each unit cost $13,694. Built with two electric motors, once onsite at Muni they weren't popular and lasted only until 1949 when they were placed in storage. In storage they lasted until 1959 when they were scrapped. Muni currently owns #50 (ex-Seattle #614) which was nearly identical to the vehicles used by MSRy that Muni acquired with the merger. After acquisition it was painted in MSRy colors, renumbered as #50, and operated in special service for one day on 11/27/88. In 2018 there are no plans to restore #50.

No. 3	Years	Seats	Length / Width / Height / Weight	Model	Manufacturer
510-525	1947-1954	40	34' 10.75" / 8' 3.5" / ? / 20,580		St. Louis Car Co., St. Louis, MO

Two more groups of trolley buses from St. Louis Car Co., similar in design to the first trolley buses purchased by Muni, were acquired in 1947 at a cost of $19,000 per unit. These wore the newly adopted green and cream colors and "Wings" paint scheme. The service life of these vehicles was short lived, as all were retired after only a few years of service, and all were scrapped by 1954.

A Fleet History of the San Francisco Municipal Railway
Section 4: Trolley Buses

No. 4	Years	Seats	Length / Width / Height / Weight	Model	Manufacturer
526-549	1948-1957	40	34' 1" / 8' 6" / 10' 8.5" / 17,920	TC40	Marmon-Herrington Co. Indianapolis, IN

The next group of trolley buses acquired by Muni was the first of four groups purchased from the Marmon-Herrington Co. between 1947-1952. At the time of purchase each vehicle cost $19,000. These were delivered painted in the green and cream paint colors with the "Wings" design. Known as "Baby Marmons", because they were shorter than the other Marmons, these trolley coaches were only in regular service until 1954. Perhaps their highlight was their use in special "Seals Stadium baseball service" for a few years in the 1950s. After retirement they were stored at the Palace of Fine Arts property (before the Palace restoration in the mid-1960s), and the Potrero Division until they were scrapped in 1969. In 2018 only trolley buses #530 and #536 remain in unrestored conditiion at the Illinois Railway Museum in Union, IL after spending many years at the Orange Empire Railway Museum in Perris, CA.

No. 5	Years	Seats	Length / Width / Height / Weight	Model	Manufacturer
550-569	1949-1976	40	36' 7" / 8' 6" / 10' 8" / 18,500	TC44	Marmon-Herrington Co.
660-710	1949-1976	40	63' 7" / 8' 6" / 10' 8" / 18,500	TC44	Indianapolis, IN
711-739	1949-1976	40	36' 7" / 8' 6" / 10' 8" / 18,500	TC44	

Bus #559 "The Christmas Bus" in storage in unrestored condition - 2017

The second group of Marmon-Herrington trolley buses were the "Medium Marmons". These vehicles anchored the trolley bus fleet for over 20 years until the mid-1970s. At delivery, each vehicle cost $19,000, and like the other Marmons, these were delivered wearing the green and cream paint colors. This fleet of 100 trolley buses performed a key role in the post World War II conversion from streetcar to rubber tire transit in San Francisco. All were retired and sold off by 1977. Some went on to another life in service in Mexico City for several more years. In 2018 SFMTA owns #559, which was acquired from Dayton, OH in the 1980s as a parts source for #776. It is in unrestored and non-operable condition.

A Fleet History of the San Francisco Municipal Railway
Section 4: Trolley Buses

No. 6	Years	Seats	Length / Width / Height / Weight	Model	Manufacturer
570-659	1949-1976	44	36' 1" / 8' 8" / 10' 7.5" / 18,360	44TTW	Fageol-Twin Coach. Kent, OH

Mixed in with the large Marmon purchase was a group of 90 Fageol-Twin Coach trolley coaches that also operated for over 20 years into the mid-1970s. When delivered to Muni they cost $19,000 each. These trolley buses were distinguished by a silver belt band of aluminum below the window line that circled the entire vehicle. Perhaps due to this band, although they wore the green and cream colors of the era, they were never painted with the "Wings" design. Later near the end of service #570 was painted in the maroon and gold colors. All were retired and sold off by 1976. In 2016 only #614 remains in unrestored and non-operable condition at the Illinois Railway Museum in Union, IL after spending many years at the Orange Empire Railway Museum.

No. 7	Years	Seats	Length / Width / Height / Weight	Model	Manufacturer
740-789	1950-1976	48	39' 3" / 8' 6" / 10' 7" / 18,750	TC48	Marmon-Herrington Co.
790-849	1950-1976	48	39' 3" / 8' 6" / 10' 7" / 18,750	TC48	Indianapolis, IN

A Fleet History of the San Francisco Municipal Railway
Section 4: Trolley Buses

The third and fourth groups of Marmon-Herrington trolley buses were the "Big Marmons". A total of 110 vehicles were purchased at a cost of $17,800 per unit. All were delivered in the green and cream colors. Similar to most trolley coaches acquired by Muni in the late 1940s, these vehicles were bought to replace retired worn out streetcars on many transit lines throughout S.F. After retirement in 1976, several were scrapped and some were sold to Mexico City where they ran for several more years. SFMTA owns #786, which was renumbered #776 and painted for the U.S. Bicentennial in 1976. In the 1990s it was renovated and repainted in green and cream "Wings" paint colors.

Muni Marmon-Herrington trolley bus #776 as painted for the U.S. Bicentennial - 1976

Muni Marmon-Herrington trolley bus #776 which is restored and in full operational condition - 2017

A Fleet History of the San Francisco Municipal Railway
Section 4: Trolley Buses

No. 8	Years	Seats	Length / Width / Height / Weight	Model	Manufacturer
850-889	1952-1976	48	39' 10" / 8' 6" / 11' 1.5" / 20,520	Job 1767	St. Louis Car Co. St. Louis, MO

The last group of trolley buses acquired in the busy post World War II era of trolley bus expansion were built by St. Louis Car Co. and were delivered in 1952. The 40 vehicles cost $20,750 each, and were painted in the green and cream colors and famous "Wings" design, although later some received a simplified paint scheme. These vehicles were heavier than the Marmon trolley buses, and they also had a unique staggered seating layout. These were unpopular with operators due to their hard steering, but still completed over 20 years of service. In 1976-77 most were sold to Mexico City where they continued to operate for many more years. In 2018 none are preserved at SFMTA.

No. 9	Years	Seats	Length / Width / Height / Weight	Model	Manufacturer
5001	1971-2007	51	40' 0" / 8' 6" / 10' 5" / 20,580	E700A	Flyer Co.
5002	1973-2007	44	40' 0" / 8' 6" / 10' 5" / 20,580	E700A	Winnipeg, MT

These vehicles built by the Flyer Company of Canada were prototypes for a new series of trolley buses to replace the early 1950s fleet. The cost of each 40' vehicle was slightly over $50,000. Trolley Bus #5001 actually contained many parts from an older Marmon trolley bus placed onto a new body. These wore the short lived maroon and gold colors on a body similar in appearance to a GM "New Look" bus. Both vehicles operated a full career in San Francisco, and set the stage for a new fleet of trolley buses. Both were retired in 2007 and neither one was saved as a heritage vehicle by Muni.

A Fleet History of the San Francisco Municipal Railway
Section 4: Trolley Buses

No. 10	Years	Seats	Length / Width / Height / Weight	Model	Manufacturer
5003-5343	1975-2007	50	40' 0" / 8' 6" / 10' 5" / 20,580	E10240	Flyer Co. Winnipeg, MT

After specifications of the Flyer Co. trolley bus design were finalized in 1973, a large order for 345 new 40' trolley buses was completed, and new vehicles began to arrive in 1975, with final delivery for some vehicles occurring in 1976. Each of the new vehicles cost $74,000 and they were delivered in the "Landor" colors of sunset glow and poppy gold. These vehicles replaced all of the older trolley buses and operated up until 2002 when they started to be replaced by new trolley buses. The last units of this fleet were not retired until 2007. Trolley buses #5148 and #5300 were saved by Muni when the rest of the fleet was sold. In 2018 #5300 is operable and used by SFMTA on special occasions.

New Flyer #5300
active historic fleet 2017

A Fleet History of the San Francisco Municipal Railway
Section 4: Trolley Buses

No. 11	Years	Seats	Length / Width / Height / Weight	Model	Manufacturer
5344-5345	1978-2007	50	40' 0" / 8' 6" / 10' 5" / 20,580	E10240	Flyer Co. Winnipeg, MT

Flyer #5345 in storage - 2017

The last two 40' Flyer trolley buses arrived in 1978 to replace two vehicles (#5112 and #5113) in the first series that were damaged beyond repair during shipment. Trolley bus #5345 was saved by Muni when the last of the fleet was retired in 2007. In 2018 it is in storage, but is not operable.

No. 12	Years	Seats	Length / Width / Height / Weight	Model	Manufacturer
7000-7059	1994-2015	57	60' 0" / 8' 6" / 10' 8" / 44,000	E60	New Flyer Co. Winnipeg, MT Grand Forks, ND

This was the first group of 60' trolley buses purchased by Muni. A total of 60 were built by New Flyer Industries and delivered in 1994 at a cost of $630,000 each. These were the last vehicles delivered with the "Landor" sunset glow and poppy gold colors in the large belted paint scheme. Most were repainted with the simpler orange and yellow design, and then were repainted again in red and gray. Capable and durable, these vehicles were used on busy routes with hills where diesel 60' articulated buses struggled to operate, and in general service on other busy routes. As they neared the end of their service life they were phased out until the last group ended service in early 2015. In 2018 SFMTA has retained #7031 in its original paint scheme (which is operable) in storage as part of the heritage fleet.

A Fleet History of the San Francisco Municipal Railway
Section 4: Trolley Buses

New Flyer #7031 in storage - 2018

No. 13	Years	Seats	Length / Width / Height / Weight	Model	Manufacturer
5401-5640	2002-	38	40' 0" / 8' 6" / 11' 0" / 20,000	14TrSF	ETI, Inc. Ostrov, Czech Rep. Hunt Valley, MD

The next group of 40' trolley buses were built by Electronic Industries Incorporated (ETI) in the Czech Republic and the USA to meet "Buy America" requirements. ETI was a partnership of Skoda Corporation in the Czech Republic and AAI Corporation in the USA. Each vehicle cost $589,000 and was delivered in the simplified white with a sunset glow and poppy gold stripe above the windows paint colors between 2001 and 2004. Later some were repainted red and silver/gray, but others were never repainted. These were the first trolley buses with improved capability to reattach poles that had separated from the overhead wires, and were the first equipped with batteries to allow off-wire movement for short distances. After the SFMTA contract the production partnership was ended and ETI ceased existence. The trolley buses are being retired early due to reliability and spare parts challenges, since most parts come from Skoda facilities in the Czech Republic. At the end of 2018 only 145 remained in service.

A Fleet History of the San Francisco Municipal Railway
Section 4: Trolley Buses

No. 14	Years	Seats	Length / Width / Height / Weight	Model	Manufacturer
7101-7133	2003- 2016	52	60' 0" / 8' 6" / 11' 0" / 31,600	15TrSF	ETI, Inc. Ostrov, Czech Rep. Hunt Valley, MD

This group of 60' trolley buses were procured in 2003 to enlarge the 60' articulated trolley bus fleet that entered service in 1994. Also built by ETI, they were very similar to the smaller 40' trolley buses ordered at the same time, but all were delivered in the new red and gray/silver colors, except for the prototype, which was repainted later. They also had improved pole capabilities and batteries that allowed off-wire movement for short distances. Each new trolley bus cost $849,000. They also suffered from the same reliability and spare parts problems as the ETI 40' vehicles, and all were retired by mid-2016. None were saved by Muni.

No. 15	Years	Seats	Length / Width / Height / Weight	Model	Manufacturer
7201- 7260	2015-	46	60' 0" / 8' 6" / 11' 8" / 44,000	XT60	New Flyer Co.
7261-7293	2016-	46	60'0" / 8' 6" / 11' 8" / 44,000	XT60	Winnipeg, MT Grand Forks, ND

After receiving FTA approval to retire the 60' ETI trolley buses early, SFMTA acted to acquire new 60' articulated trolley buses from New Flyer Co. that are based on a modified design specifications set forth by King County Metro in Seattle, who ordered new vehicles simultaneous with Muni. These are the first low-floor 60' articulated trolley buses in San Francisco. These trolley buses have improved off-wire capability of operating up to at least a mile while on batteries. Each unit cost $1,374,000, and a total of 60 trolley buses painted in the red and silver colors were ordered. In 2016 33 more units were ordered.

A Fleet History of the San Francisco Municipal Railway
Section 4: Trolley Buses

No. 16	Years	Seats	Length / Width / Height / Weight	Model	Manufacturer
5701-5885	2018-	32	40' 0" / 8' 6" / 11' 8" / 33,000	XT40	New Flyer Co. Winnipeg, MT Grand Forks, ND

After receiving FTA approval to retire the 40' ETI trolley buses early, SFMTA acted to acquire 185 new 40' trolley buses from New Flyer Co. that are based on a modified design specifications set forth by King County Metro in Seattle, who ordered new vehicles simultaneous with Muni. These are the first low-floor 40' trolley buses in San Francisco. These trolley buses have improved off-wire capability of operating up to at least a mile while on batteries. Each unit cost $1,150,000, and a total of 185 trolley buses painted in the red and silver colors were ordered. Options exist to order 55 more. By the end of 2018 80 of the new trolley buses were on site and in service.

A Fleet History of the San Francisco Municipal Railway
Section 5: Cable Cars

A Fleet History of the San Francisco Municipal Railway
Section 5: Cable Cars

A Fleet History of the San Francisco Municipal Railway
Section 5: Cable Cars

The cable car is the iconic transit vehicle of San Francisco. It was invented in San Francisco by Andrew S. Halladie in 1873 with the first line running on Clay Street. At its peak in the 1890s a total of eight cable car companies operated on 52.5 miles of cable car routes in San Francisco with the last one opening for service in 1889. Although it was a huge improvement over the horsecar, and quickly spread to other American cities and around the world, the cable car era was short lived. Only fifteen years after the cable car was introduced, the electric streetcar was invented in Richmond, VA by Frank Sprague in 1888. Much cheaper, faster, and easier to expand service, the streetcar quickly drove the cable car into obsolescence.

When the S.F. Municipal Railway was established in 1912, cable cars had been in decline for over 20 years. Accordingly, Muni never built its own cable car line. Muni's first streetcar line on Geary Street followed the cable car route of the Geary Street Park & Ocean Railroad (GSP&ORR) which was purchased by the City of San Francisco in 1912. The GSP&ORR franchise expired in 1903, and city government issued short term permits for several years until the buyout. New trolley wire was installed in early 1912 as the cable car still operated. Seven months after the last cable car operated in May, Muni operated its first streetcar on December 28, 1912.

Thirty-two years later in 1944 Muni finally entered the cable car business when it merged with the Market Street Railway (MSRy), which operated two cable car lines: the Powell-Mason line and the Washington-Jackson line. Both lines originally were part of the Ferries and Cliff House Railway (F&CHRy), which started service in March, 1888. In 1893 the F&CHRy was acquired by the first MSRy, which morphed into the United Railroads in 1902, which morphed again into the second MSRy in 1921. As part of the 1944 merger Muni acquired 38 cable cars, although only 27 were used in service. In early 1947, less than three years after Muni acquired the second MSRy, Mayor Roger Lapham, sought to end cable car service on both lines. In response the San Francisco Federation of the Arts and the California Spring Blossom and Wildflower Association organized a joint meeting attended by leaders of 27 women's civic groups and the "Citizens' Committee to Save the Cable Cars" was created. Led by Friedel Klussmann, a wealthy socialite, the committee efforts led to a ballot measure to retain the cable cars. On November 4, 1947 Proposition 10 was approved by a vote of 166,989 "yes" to 51,457 "no". The two cable car lines were saved, at least temporarily.

Four years later the California Street Cable Railroad Company went bankrupt when it could no longer obtain insurance. A few months later in 1952 Muni bought the assets of the company, which had begun operations in 1878, and acquired three more lines: O'Farrell, Jones & Hyde, the Jones Street Shuttle, and the namesake California Street line. In 1954 Muni management sought once again to cut back cable car service by seeking to reduce the recently acquired lines. Friedel Klussmann again led the pro-cable car forces to oppose the plan, but was unsuccessful in this effort. The reduction in cable car service began in 1954 and by the end of 1957 over half of the old network had been removed. The portion of the O'Farrell, Jones & Hyde line located on O'Farrell and Jones Streets, which was the primary target of the anti-cable car forces, was removed, along with the majority of the Washington - Jackson line that had been acquired in 1944. The entire Jones Street Shuttle line (6 blocks) was removed. The remaining portions of the O'Farrell Jones and Hyde line on Hyde Street and Washington - Jackson line were combined and connected to the Powell Street line; with the new service operating from a unified terminal at Powell and Market Streets to twin terminals on Taylor Street and Hyde Street, both in the Fisherman's Wharf area. This change necessitated installation of a turntable at Hyde Street terminal. Finally, the California Street line lost half its length with removal of tracks between Van Ness Avenue and Presidio Avenue.

A Fleet History of the San Francisco Municipal Railway
Section 5: Cable Cars

Since 1957 the cable car lines have remained unchanged and operate 4.7 miles of service on three lines. Coincidentally, 1957 also saw the closure of the other remaining cable car system in the world in Dunedin, New Zealand. Plans to extend the Powell-Taylor line north on Taylor Street have been raised in the past 60 years, but no action has occurred. The entire cable car system was declared a National Historic Landmark in 1964.

A different challenge appeared in the early 1980s: safety and infrastructure. By 1980 the physical elements of the entire cable car system were worn out and needed to be rebuilt. At a cost of $60 million dollars the entire system was closed for 20 months and rebuilt in 1982-1984. In the thirty plus years since the system reopened for service cars have been retired, rebuilt, and new cars have come into service, but overall the system continues to service the public well as it approaches its 150th anniversary in 2023.

Unlike other SFMTA transit vehicles, cable cars are built, renovated and repaired entirely by SFMTA staff. Vehicle replacements are rare, and currently consist of retirement of an old cable car and construction of a new one that looks the same as the old one to take its place. The 2016 cost to build a cable car from scratch is approximately $1,300,000 and takes 12-18 months to complete. Renovations and rebuilds are performed by SFMTA staff at the Carpentry Shop located at the Woods Division at 22nd and Indiana Streets in San Francisco. Minor repairs are performed at a smaller shop built into the Cable Car Barn located at Washington and Mason Streets in San Francisco. A fleet history of Muni cable cars operations since 1944 that covers the four car types (Powell Street cars, California Street cars, Jones Street Shuttle cars, and Sacramento-Clay cars) in San Francisco, plus the historic fleet is presented here.

The Powell Street Cable Cars

The Powell Street Cable Cars follow two routes: Powell-Mason and Powell-Hyde, with separate northern terminals, and a joint southern terminal at Market Street. The current configuration of cable car lines and service dates to April 6, 1957 when the last route changes were made to the system. The changes consisted of removal of portions of the Washington-Jackson line, and conversion of the Hyde Street portion of the O'Farrell-Jones-Hyde line (which used larger California Street type cars) to operation using the smaller Powell Street cars. This included installation of a turntable at the foot of Hyde Street near Aquatic Park.

The service has operated with a total of 27-28 single-end Powell Street cable cars since the 1944 merger, although the lines and service were significantly changed between 1956-1957. The fleet operated by the SFMTA on the Powell Street service runs on narrow gauge track (3' 6"), are 27 feet long, and weight a little over 12,000 lbs. Single-end cars are only equipped with a cable grip at one end, and require a turntable to turn around so they can operate in a bi-directional manner. The primary builders of the Powell Street cars were the Carter Brothers Company located in Newark, CA, and the Mahoney Brothers Company located in San Francisco, CA. Carter Brothers cable cars have a simpler single level lower roofline, while Mahoney Brothers cable cars were built with a raised lower level roof (Bombay Roof). Evidence strongly suggests Mahoney Brothers contracted with two other builders: O'Brian & Sons of San Francisco, CA, and Burnham & Staudeford of Oakland, CA for production of at least some of these cars. In the Muni era (1944 - present) a toal of 37 Powell Street cable cars have been in existence: 28 are active at Muni, 2 are in storage at Muni, 2 are on display or at a museum, and 5 have been scrapped.

A Fleet History of the San Francisco Municipal Railway
Section 5: Cable Cars

All of the older existing Powell Street cable cars have been rebuilt at least once from their entry service date in the late 1800's, and many have been rebuilt twice and undergone additional partial rebuilds or renovations in their multiple decades of service. Prior to 1973 (Centennial year of service) all were numbered in a "500" series of numbers (501-528), but in 1973, they were renumbered 1-28, and that is how they are numbered in 2018.

In 2018 the Powell Street cable cars wear 11 different paint schemes that represent eras of cable car operations on Powell Street: Muni, Market Street Railway / United Railroads and the Powell Street Railway Company, which was actually a part of the aforementioned F&CHRWy that was acquired by the first MSRy in 1893, and which became part of Muni in 1944.   The paint schemes and associated cars are listed below.

Era	Car	Scheme	Painted
1888-1893	Car #1	Powell Street Railway	- painted 1973
1893-1905	Car $15	Market Street Railway	- painted 2009
1905-1907	Car #25	United Railroads	- painted 2008
1907-1927	Car #13	United Railroads / MSRy	- painted 1991
1927-1937	Car #9	Market Street Railway	- painted 1997
1893-1907	Car #11	Market Street Railway / United RRs (Sacto./Clay)	- painted 2018
1937-1944	Car #12	Market Street Railway	- painted 2016
1944-1949	Car #16	S.F. Municipal Railway (Muni)	- painted 1990
1949-1963	Car #26	S.F. Municipal Railway (Muni)	- painted 2011
1963-1982	Car #3	S.F. Municipal Railway (Muni)	- painted 1984
1984-	Car #2	S.F. Municipal Railway (Muni)	- painted 1984

The remaining 17 cars are painted like Car #2, in a dark red / maroon Muni paint scheme that was adopted in 1984. In 2015 the Powell Street cars are listed as having the same dimensions across all cars. However, since they have been extensively rebuilt on multiple occasions, actual dimensions vary slightly from car to car.

Fleet & Car No.	Length / Width / Height / Weight	Seats	Total Capacity
Cars 1-28	27'6" / 8'0" / 10'.4.75" / 15,500	30	54

Car #1
History and Disposition
1973 - Built by Muni at Elkton Shops in San Francisco, CA using new body with roof and seats from Car #506.
1973 - Painted to represent the Powell Street Railway era: 1888-1893.   1997 - Partial rebuild. 2015 - Complete rebuild.   2018- On Muni active fleet roster.

Car #1 - 2016

A Fleet History of the San Francisco Municipal Railway
Section 5: Cable Cars

Car #2 / Car #502
History and Disposition
1894 - Built by Carter Brothers of Newark, CA   1971 - Extensive repair and rebuild.   1973 - Renumbered as Car #2.   1982-1984 - Partiallly rebuilt by Muni and painted to represent the S.F. Municipal Railway era: 1984-current   2018 - On Muni active fleet roster.

Car #2
2017

Car #3 / Car #503
History and Disposition
1894 - Built by Carter Brothers of Newark, CA. Assigned #503.   1955 - Extensive repair and rebuild.
1973 - Renumbered as Car #3.   1982-1984 - Partially rebuilt by Muni and newly painted to represent the S.F. Municipal Railway era: 1963-1982.   2018 - On Muni active fleet roster.

Car #3 - 1974 (right) and
Car #3 - 2017 (below)

A Fleet History of the San Francisco Municipal Railway
Section 5: Cable Cars

Car #4 (first) / Car #504
History and Disposition
1887 - Built by Mahoney Brothers in San Francisco, CA as Car #543.   1915 - Rebuilt as a closed car and renumbered Car #504.   1973 - Renumbered as Car #4.   1998 - Removed from service in early 1990s and rebuilt for static placement display at AT&T Park. Renumbered as Car #44 to honor Willie McCovey, former S.F. Giants baseball player.   2018 - On display in the center field bleachers at AT&T Park.

Car #4 (formerly Car #504) now Car #44 at AT&T Park - 2017

Car #4 (second)
History and Disposition
1994 - Built by Muni at the Woods Carpentry Shop in San Francisco, CA as a second Car #4 and placed into service.   2018 - On Muni active fleet roster.

Car #4 - 2017

Car #5 / Car #505
History and Disposition
1894 - Built by Carter Brothers in Newark, CA.   1956 - Extensive repair and rebuild.   1973 - Renumbered as Car #5.   2018 - On Muni active fleet roster.

Car #506 (first)
History and Disposition
1894 - Built by Carter Brothers in Newark, CA as Car #506.   1965 - Removed from service and placed into storage.   1972- The roof and seats are used in the new Car #1.   1970's - The rest of the car is scrapped.

A Fleet History of the San Francisco Municipal Railway
Section 5: Cable Cars

Car #6 / Car #506 (second)
History and Disposition
1894 - Built by Carter Brothers in Newark, CA as Car #518.   1965 - Rebuilt and renumbered as Car #506 when original Car #506 was removed from service.   1971 - Appeared on 8 cent U.S. postage stamp.   1973 - Renumbered as Car #6.   2000 - Rehabilitated and partially rebuilt.   2018 - Undergoing renovation at Woods Carpentry shop.

Car #506 (now Car #6) on U.S. postage stamp - 1971   Car #6 - 1990

Car #7 / Car #507
History and Disposition
1894 - Built by Carter Brothers in Newark, CA.   1957 - Extensive repair and rebuild, and first car to operate on newly configured Powell-Hyde line.   1973 - Renumbered as Car #7.   2018 - On Muni active fleet roster.

Car #8 / Car #508
History and Disposition
1894 - Built by Carter Brothers in Newark, CA.   1958 - Extensive repair and rebuild.   1968 - Appeared in a Chevrolet Caprice TV commercial.   1973 - Renumbered as Car #8.   2016 - No longer in service. Placed into storage.   2018 - A new Car #8, which includes parts of the frame of Car #8, is under construction.

Car #9 (first) / Car #509
History and Disposition
1887 - Built as Car #110 (open sided car) by Mahoney Brothers in San Francisco, CA for the Ferries & Cliff House Railway.   1900s - Renumbered from Car #110 to Car #542.   1923 - Rebuilt as a closed car, and renumbered from Car #542 to Car #509.   1952 - Extensive repair and rebuild.   1973 - Renumbered as Car #9.   1995 - Retired from service and placed into storage.   2018 - Owned by Muni and in storage.

Car #9 (second)
History and Disposition
1997 - Built by Muni at Woods Carpentry Shop in San Francisco, CA as second Car #9 and painted to represent the Market Street Railway era: 1927-1937.   2000 - Entered into regular service.   2018 - On Muni active fleet roster.

A Fleet History of the San Francisco Municipal Railway
Section 5: Cable Cars

Car #9
2017

Car #10 / Car #510
History and Disposition
1894 - Built by Carter Brothers in Newark, CA.   1960 - Extensive repair and rebuild.   1973 - Renumbered as Car #10.   2018 - On Muni active fleet roster.

Car #11 / Car #511
History and Disposition
1894 - Built by Carter Brothers in Newark, CA.   1973 - Renumbered as Car #11.   1979-80 - Extensive repair.   2018 - Rebuilt and painted to represent Sacramento-Clay line: 1893-1907. On Muni active fleet roster.

Car #11
2018

Car #12 / Car #512
History and Disposition
1894 - Built by Carter Brothers in Newark, CA.   1959 - Extensive repair and rebuild.   1973 - Renumbered as Car #12.   2016 - Rebuilt and painted to represent Market Street Railway era: 1937-1944.   2018 - On Muni active fleet roster.

Car #12
2017

A Fleet History of the San Francisco Municipal Railway
Section 5: Cable Cars

Car #13 (first) / Car #513
History and Disposition
1894 - Built by Carter Brothers in Newark, CA.   1958 - Extensive rebuild.   1973 - Renumbered as Car #13.
1988 - Removed from service after an accident.   1990s - Given to Ardenwood Museum in Newark, CA.
Unable to restore due to poor condition, some parts are saved, but the rest of the car is scrapped.

Car #13 (second)
History and Disposition
1991 - Built by Muni at Woods Carpentry Shop in San Francisco, CA as second Car #13.   1991 - Painted to represent the United Railroads / Market St. Railway era: 1907-1927.   1992 - Entered into regular passenger service.   2018 - On Muni active fleet roster.

Car #513
2017

Car # 514 (first)
History and Disposition
1887 - Built by Mahoney Brothers in San Francisco, CA.   1893 - Renumbered as Car #528.
1929 - Renumbered as Car #514.   1963 - Scrapped.

Car #514
1949

Car #14 / Car #514 (second)
History and Disposition
1964 - Built by Muni at Elkton Shops in San Francisco, CA as second Car #514.   1973 - Renumbered as Car #14.
2018 - On Muni active fleet roster.

Car #15 (first) / Car #515
History and Disposition
1894 - Built by Carter Brothers in Newark, CA.   1954 - Extensive repair and rebuild.   1973 - Renumbered as Car #15.   1982: Removed from service and placed into storage.   2018: Owned by Muni and in storage.

A Fleet History of the San Francisco Municipal Railway
Section 5: Cable Cars

Car #15 (second)
History and Disposition
1985: Built by Muni at Woods Carpenty Shop in San Francisco, CA as second Car #15.   2009 - Extensive repair and newly painted to represent the Market Street Railway era : 1893-1905.   2018 - On Muni active fleet roster.

Car #15
2017

Car #16 / Car #516
History and Disposition
1894 - Built by Carter Brothers in Newark, CA.   1953 - Extensive repair and rebuild.   1973 - Renumbered as Car #16.   1990 - Rebuilt almost from scratch by Muni and repainted to represent the S.F. Municipal Railway era: 1944-1947.   2018 - On Muni active fleet roster.

Car #516
1952
(now Car #16)

Car #17 / Car #517
History and Disposition
1887 - Built by Mahoney Brothers in San Francisco, CA.   1929 - Renumbered from Car #532 to Car #517.
1956 - Extensive repair and rebuild.   1973 - Renumbered as Car #17.   2018 - On Muni active fleet roster.

Car #18 / Car #518
History and Disposition
1962 - Built by Muni at Elkton Shops in San Francisco as second Car #518. Original Car #518 was rebuilt and renumbered as Car #506, and is in active service as Car #6.   1973 - Renumbered as Car #18.
1982-1984 - Rebuilt by Muni.   2018 - On Muni active fleet roster.

A Fleet History of the San Francisco Municipal Railway
Section 5: Cable Cars

Car #19 (first) / Car #519 / Car #500
History and Disposition
1894 - Built by Carter Brothers in Newark, CA.   1968 - Renumbered as Car #500 following a deadly accident in 1967.   1973 - Renumbered as Car #19.   1986 - Scrapped after judged as not worthy of a rebuild due to being in very poor condition following damage that occurred while testing of a slot blade (emergency brake).

Car #19 (second)
History and Disposition
1986 - Built by Muni at Woods Carpentry Shop in San Francisco, CA as second Car #19.   2018 - On Muni active fleet roster.

Car #20 / Car #520
History and Disposition
1894 - Built by Carter Brothers in Newark, CA.   1947 - Appears in the movie Dark Passage with Humphrey Bogart as a passenger.   1968 - Extensive rebuild.   1973 - Renumbered as Car #20.   1982-1984 - Partially rebuilt by Muni.   2018 - On Muni active fleet roster.

Car #520
1966 (left)
(now Car #20)
2017 (right)

Car #21 (first) / Car #521
History and Disposition
1887 - Built by Mahoney Brothers in San Francisco, CA.   1929 - Renumbered from Car #533 to Car #521.   1956 - Extensive rebuild.   1965 - Women are allowed to "ride the running boards" after Mona Hutchins, a student at UC-Berkeley, refuses to vacate the space on Car #521.   1973 - Renumbered as Car #21.
1987 - Scrapped after being judged to be not worthy of a rebuild due to being in very poor condition.

Car #521 on Jackson Street - 1947

A Fleet History of the San Francisco Municipal Railway
Section 5: Cable Cars

Car #21 (second)
History and Disposition
1992 - Built by Muni at Woods Carpentry Shop in San Francisco, CA as second Car # 21.   2018 - On Muni active fleet roster.

Car #22 / Car #522
History and Disposition
1894 - Built by Carter Brothers in Newark CA.   1956 - Extensive rebuild.   1973 - Renumbered as Car #22.
2018 - On Muni active roster following a complete rebuild.

Car #522
1950 (left)
(now Car #22)
2018 (right)

Car#23 / Car #523
History and Disposition
1890 -Built by Ferries & Cliff House Railway in San Francisco, CA.   1969-70- Extensive rebuild.
1973 - Renumbered as Car #23.   2018 - On Muni active fleet roster following a complete rebuild.

Car #23
1974 (left)
undergoing rebuild
2017 (center),
and newly completed
2018 (right)

A Fleet History of the San Francisco Municipal Railway
Section 5: Cable Cars

Car #24 / Car #524
History and Disposition
1887 - Built by Mahoney Brothers in San Francisco, CA.   1929 - Renumbered from Car #534 to Car #524.   1949 - Car operates in temporary setup at Chicago Rail Fair.   1956 - Last car to operate on full Washington-Jackson cable car line: September 2, 1956.   1958 - Extensive rebuild.   1968 - Appeared in opening credits of the Banana Splits childrens TV show.   1973 - Renumbered as Car #24.   2018 - On Muni active fleet roster.

Car #524
1949 (above left & right)
(now Car #24)
2017 (right)

Car #25 / Car #525
History and Disposition
1890 - Built by Ferries & Cliff House Railway in San Francisco, CA.   1956 - Extensive rebuild.   1962 - Appeared in a Chevrolet commercial for the Chevy II (Nova).   1973 - Renumbered as Car #25.   1976 - Partial rebuild.   2008 - Rebuilt and newly painted to represent the United Railroads era: 1905-1907.   2018 - On Muni active fleet roster.

Car #25 - 1977

A Fleet History of the San Francisco Municipal Railway
Section 5: Cable Cars

Car #26 / Car #526
History and Disposition
1890 - Built by Ferries & Cliff House Railway in San Francisco, CA.   1973 - Renumbered as Car #26.
1975 - Extensive repairs by Muni.   2010-11 - Rebuilt and newly painted to represent the S.F Municipal Railway era 1949-1963. Nicknamed "Maybelle" after the cable car in the 1952 children's book, Maybelle the Cable Car, because it is the only cable car wearing the paint scheme in use at the time the book was written.
2018 - On Muni active fleet roster.

Car #26 - 2017 (left), Maybelle The Cable Car book (copyright 1952) (right)

Car #27 / Car #527
History and Disposition
1887- Built by Mahoney Brothers in San Francisco, CA.   1958 - Extensive rebuild.   1973 - Renumbered as Car #27.   1982-1984 - Partially rebuilt by Muni.   2018 - On Muni active fleet roster.

Car #28 (first) / Car #501
History and Disposition
1887 - Built by Mahoney Brothers in San Francisco, CA as an open car.   1912 - Rebuilt as a closed car and renumbered from Car #544 to Car # 501.   1951 - Extensive rebuild.   1973 - Renumbered as Car #28 when new Car #1 built, or else new numbering system would have made this Car #1.   2002 - Removed from service after being replaced by a new Car #28.   2018 - Sent to Shore Line Trolley Museum in East Haven, CT as part of a trade to obtain former Red Arrow SEPTA PCC cars #18 and #21, that are planned to be rebuilt to become Muni historic streetcars #1012 and #1013.

Car #501 in 1950 (left) (now Car #28) in storage 2017 (right), but sent to Shore Line Trolley Museum in 2018

Car #28 (second)
History and Disposition
2002 - Built by Muni at Woods Carpentry Shop in San Francisco, CA as second Car # 28.   2004 - Entered active service.   2018 - On Muni active fleet roster.

A Fleet History of the San Francisco Municipal Railway
Section 5: Cable Cars

The California Street Cable Cars

In 1952 Muni acquired the California Cable Railroad for $132,758 following its declaration of bankruptcy. The company consisted of three lines: California Street, O'Farrell, Jones & Hyde Street, and the Jones Street Shuttle. Two years later in 1954 Muni began implementation of major changes as it sought to reduce unprofitable cable car operations. Muni's plan was for a revised cable car service of two north-south lines using Powell Street cars, and one east-west line using California Street cars. Service ended on the Jones Street Shuttle which operated on Jones Street between O'Farrell and Market Streets on February 6, 1954. Three months later cable car service was removed from the California Street line segment between Van Ness and Presidio Avenues, and service ended on the O'Farrell, Jones and Hyde Street line which operated on O'Farrell Street between Market and Jones Streets, on Jones Street between O'Farrell and Pine Streets, on Pine Street between Jones and Hyde Streets and on Hyde Street between Pine and Beach Streets on May 16, 1954. Service on Hyde Street between Washington Street and a terminal at Beach Street was converted to operate using Powell Street cars, which required construction of a new turntable at Beach Street in Aquatic Park. The revised Powell-Hyde line opened on April 7, 1957, and the new California Street line, the sole survivor of the three Cal Cable lines opened in December 22, 1957.

These extensive route and service changes also had significant impacts on the California Street Cable Car fleet. Prior to 1954, the fleet numbered 48 cars in total: 23 California Street cars (Nos. #1-23), 22 O'Farrell-Jones & Hyde cars (Nos. #38-59), and 3 Jones Street Shuttle cars (Nos. #60-62). No cars were numbered #24-#37. All cars were built in 1907-1914 after the 1906 earthquake destroyed the entire California Street Cable Railroad Company fleet. All original cars, including the 22.5' Jones Street Shuttle cars, were double-end cars, but used only one grip - as the second set of gripman controls were connected via long rods to the hardware with the actual cable grip at the primary end of the car. The larger 30' California and O'Farrell Street cars had a capacity of 34 seated passengers and a total capacity of 60 passengers. Since the cars had controls on either end, California Street cars didn't need a turntable to operate in a bi-directional manner. All of the original California Street cable cars were painted in a maroon color scheme with gold writing, and were adorned with a "ribbon" design on the ends of the cars that listed the essential streets of the route where they operated. Car #38 and Car #39 are double counted, because they were also numbered as Car #24 and Car #15 respectively prior to 1911.

After the changes between 1954-1957, the California Street Cable Car fleet was reduced in size to 12 vehicles. The rest of the fleet was declared surplus and most were sold at auction starting in 1953 before the actual service changes were implemented. Muni records show the sale of ten cars in May 1955 netted $11,000, and six more were sold in Fall 1956 (sale amount not recorded). The individual journeys the surplus cars have taken during the past 60+ years have been remarkably varied, and because these vehicles are unlike the other modes of transit vehicle in service at Muni, including the fact they were handmade in San Francisco, a significant effort was made to follow-up on their post-Muni history. Some were reacquired by Muni, only to be sold again at a later date, others are in museums, and the whereabouts of others are currently unknown.

Several became motorized cable cars after Muni converted Jones Street Shuttle Car #62 in 1954. The process meant placing a car body on a rubber tired truck chassis with a gasoline engine, transmission and brakes. The five cars motorized at Knott's Berry Farm were different, as they kept their original steel wheels which ran on a narrow gauge rail line with a battery powered electric motor for operation and a small air-brake set up.

A Fleet History of the San Francisco Municipal Railway
Section 5: Cable Cars

The most famous motorized cable cars were created by Arnold Gridley, a real estate agent, and colorful San Franciscan, who founded Classic Cable Car Charters in 1958. Gridley was concerned all cable cars would be eliminated and disappear forever, so he bought four cars at auction from the City of San Francisco between 1956-1961 and motorized them. Later he bought several surplus cars from parties that had originally acquired them from city auction, and he also had several replica cars built by a company he helped create named Cable Car Classics in Healdsburg, CA. While Gridley helped to expand cable car lore by operating the motorized cars across Northern California - and in other places (a car was shipped to Hawaii for an event), he also took actions that challenge creation of a fleet history, including renumbering individual cars on several occasions, and by not maintaining accurate records of the cars in his ownership. After Gridley's death in 2004, the company was sold in 2008 to Ride The Ducks Inc., and the fleet, which also included several replica cable cars, was reduced from over 60 cars to around 25 cars. A handful of original former cable cars were retained by the Gridley Family, but several original cars were lost as Ride the Ducks Inc., scrapped them. In 2015 Classic Cable Cars was acquired by Hornblower Cruises and Events, a California company owned by Terry MacRae. A few original cable cars remain in service as motorized cable cars in 2018.

In 60+ years since 1957, all 12 cable cars in the Muni California Street fleet have been partially or completely rebuilt, and some have been replaced with new cars. Muni converted them to true double end cars with grip hardware on each end. A modified version of the paint colors and logo in use when Muni acquired the California Street Cable Railroad in 1952 continues to be used in 2018. Rebuilds on the fleet are performed by Muni staff at the Woods Div. Carpentry Shop at 22nd and Indiana Streets in San Francisco. Minor repairs occur at a smaller shop at the Cable Car Barn at Washington and Mason Streets in San Francisco. In the Muni era; 1952 to present, a total of 52 California Street / O'Farrell Street cable cars have been in existence: 13 are active and 1 is in storage at Muni, plus Muni has 1 motorized car, 7 are on owned by museums, 8 are privately owned in storage (5 motorized), 1 is owned by a transit agency, 4 are in private motorized service (2 currently active), 11 have been scrapped, or are likely scrapped, and 6 are status unknown.

Fleet & Car No.	Length / Width / Height / Weight	Seats	Total Capacity
Cars 1-23, 38-60	30'3" / 8'0" / 10'.2" / 16,600	34	60

Car #1
History and Disposition
1907 - Built by John Hammond Company in San Francisco, CA.   1956 - Sold to Arnold Gridley and becomes a motorized cable car for Classic Cable Car Charters.   2008 - Classic Cable Car Charters is acquired by Ride the Ducks and the fleet is reduced retaining only cars assessed to be in better shape. Car #1 is scrapped.

Car #1
1951

Car #1
motorized
1969

A Fleet History of the San Francisco Municipal Railway
Section 5: Cable Cars

Car #2
History and Disposition
1907 - Built by John Hammond Companry in San Francisco, CA.   1956 - Sold to Harrah's Casino - Reno, NV. 1980s - Sold by Harrah's to Classic Cable Car Charters. At an unknown date the car was renumbered from #2 to #3.   2008 - Classic Cable Car Charters is acquired by Ride the Ducks and the fleet is reduced retaining only cars assessed to be in better shape.   Car #2 is scrapped.

Car #2 - 1919.

Car #3
History and Disposition
1907 - Built by John Hammond Company in San Francisco, CA.   1957 - Renumbered from Car #3 to Car #18 while in storage at Muni. 1961 - Sold to Arnold Gridley and transformed into a motorized cable car for Classic Cable Car Charters. At at unknown date the car was renumbered from #3 to #2.   2008 - Classic Cable Car Charters is acquired by Ride the Ducks and the fleet is reduced retaining only cars assessed to be in better shape. Car #3 is scrapped.   2018 - Parts of Car #3 are present in the Derby Store located at 1472 Haight Street, San Francisco, although it is numbered as Car #2.

Car #3 (renumbered as Car #2) as part of a store display on Haight Street - 2017

A Fleet History of the San Francisco Municipal Railway
Section 5: Cable Cars

Car #4
History and Disposition
1907 - Built by John Hammond Company in San Francisco, CA.   1956 - Circumstances and exact date of departure from Muni currently unknown.   2018 - A motorized Cable Car #4 is currently in service with Hornblower Classic Cable Cars (successor to Classic Cable Car Charters), but it is not former California Street Cable Railroad Company Cable Car #4. It is possible this could be former Cable Car #20, or #22, or, the first Car #55, or possibly a "status unknown" car. The car retains most of its original appearance.

Car #4 - motorized - 2017

Car #4 and Car #62
stage in preparation for a parade - 2017

Car #5
History and Disposition
1907 - Built by John Hammond Company in San Francisco, CA.   1956 - Sold to an unrecorded buyer in Forest Grove, OR. Seats were removed and used in Streetcar #578, which was restored by Muni in the same year.
2018 - Status is unknown.

Car #6
History and Disposition
1907 - Built by John Hammond Company in San Francisco, CA.   1956 - Sold to Knotts Berry Farm in Buena Park, CA, converted to a motorized cable car, but on tracks.   1981 - Returned to Muni and put into storage.
1980s - Sold to Matt Etchel in Healdsburg, CA. Used as a design template to manufacture over a dozen replica cablecars - all motorized, ordered by Arnold Gridley for Classic Cable Cars.   2017 - Found derelict in a field near Healdsburg, CA - in a state beyond salvage and restoration potential, apparently after being found not worthy of restoration by Cable Car Classics, who is believed to be the last known owner of the car.

A Fleet History of the San Francisco Municipal Railway
Section 5: Cable Cars

Car #7
History and Disposition
1907 - Built by John Hammond Company in San Francisco, CA.   1956 - Sold to Arnold Gridley and made into a motorized cable car for Classic Cable Car Charters.   2008 - Classic Cable Car Charters is acquired by Ride the Ducks, but Car #7 is retained by the Gridley Family.   2018 - Owned by Phillip Wright (Gridley Family) in storage in Healdsburg, CA.

Car #7 - 1920

Car #7 as a motorized cable car - 1961

Car #8
History and Disposition
See Car #55 (first) information.

Car #9
History and Disposition
1907- Built by John Hammond Company in San Francisco, CA.   1955 - Sold to Frank Martinelli Sr. owner of Adobe Creek Lodge in Los Altos, CA.   Unknown date - acquired by Arnold Gridley and Classic Cable Cars.   2008 - Classic Cable Car Charters is acquired by Ride the Ducks, but Car #9 is retained by the Gridley Family.   2018 - Owned by Phillip Wright (Gridley Family) in storage in Healdsburg, CA. Currently numbered as Car #17.

Car #10
History and Disposition
1907- Built by John Hammond Company in San Francisco, CA.   1956 - Sold to S.F Zoo and on site 1956-1985 in the Children's Zoo.   Unknown date - acquired by Arnold Gridley and Classic Cable Cars and partially rebuilt.   2018 - Owned by Hornblower Classic Cable Cars (successor to Classic Cable Car Charters) awaiting restoration.

Car #10 - motorized, awaiting restoration - 2017

A Fleet History of the San Francisco Municipal Railway
Section 5: Cable Cars

Car #11
History and Disposition
1907- Built by John Hammond Company in San Francisco, CA.   1953 - Sold to Odd Fellows Recreational Center in San Francisco for $300.   1950s - Sent to New Jersey RR Museum.   Unknown date - Acquired by Dr. Ralph W.E. Cox of Cape May, NJ.   2014 - Sold at estate sale to an unnamed buyer for $87,500 per Bonham's Auctions.   2018 - Owner wishes anonymity, but lives in California.

Car #11 in storage - 2014

Car #12
History and Disposition
1907 - Built by John Hammond Company in San Francisco, CA.   1956 - Sold to Arnold Gridley and transformed into a motorized cable car for Classic Cable Car Charters.   2018 - A motorized Cable Car #5 is currently in service with Hornblower Classic Cable Car Charters (successor to Classic Cable Car Charters), but a closer inspection showed it is very likely Cable Car #12. It was rebuilt in 2014 and lost much of its original features.

Car #13
History and Disposition
1907 - Built by John Hammond Company in San Francisco, CA.   1953 - Sold to Man Haden Industries for $193.   1950s - Acquired by the Shriners Public Service organization.   2001- Sold at auction by D.F. Barnhardt & Associates in Georgia after making its way to South Carolina (circumstances unknown) where it was part of a restaurant. Prior to sale it was also owned by the Generation Gap Antique Auto Emporium in Georgia. It was supposed to go to Dallas, TX where it would again be part of a restaurant.   2018 - Status unknown.

Car #14
History and Disposition
1907 - Built by John Hammond Company in San Francisco, CA.   1956 - Sold or loaned to S.F. Department of Parks and Recreation for display at the Children's Playground in Golden Gate Park.   1980s - Removed from the park and scrapped.

Car #15
History and Disposition
See Car #59 (second) information.

115

A Fleet History of the San Francisco Municipal Railway
Section 5: Cable Cars

Car #16
History and Disposition
See Car #60 (second) information.

Car #17
History and Disposition
1907 - Built by John Hammond Company in San Francisco, CA.   1955 - Sold to Knott's Berry Farm in Buena Park, CA, converted to a motorized cable car, but on tracks.   1979 - Ended service at Knott's Berry Farm. 1981 - Sold to Gaslamp Trolley project in San Diego. Not used in San Diego, and later donated to the City of Poway, CA. Restored at Poway-Midland RR.   2018 - Car #17 was converted to be a battery electric car, and is still at the Poway-Midland RR where it operates in regular service.

Car #17 at Knott' Berry Farm - ca. 1965

Car #17 at Poway-Midland RR Museum - 2016

Car #18
History and Disposition
See Car #52 (first) information.

Car #19
History and Disposition
See Car #54 (second) information.

Car #20
History and Disposition
1907 - Built by John Hammond Company in San Francisco, CA.   1956 - Sold to Knotts Berry Farm in Buena Park, CA, converted to a motorized cable car, but on tracks.   1981 - Returned to Muni and placed into storage.   2018 - No longer at Muni. Status is unknown, but may have been sold in the 1980s. This could be current motorized Cable Car #4 or Car #22 that are in service with Hornblower Classic Cable Cars.

116

A Fleet History of the San Francisco Municipal Railway
Section 5: Cable Cars

Car #21
History and Disposition
1907 - Built by John Hammond Company in San Francisco, CA.   1956 - Sold or loaned to Travel Town in Griffith Park in Los Angeles.   2018 - Car #21 is in poor condition at Travel Town in Griffith Park in Los Angeles. Currently the car is painted a tan color and is wears #28 following its use in a movie several years ago.

Car #21 at Griffith Park in Los Angleles - 2017

Car #22
History and Disposition
1907 - Built by John Hammond Company in San Francisco, CA.   1956 - Sold to A. Williamson of Sacramento, CA where it was used as part of a swimming pool display.   2018 - A motorized Cable Car #22 is currently in service with Hornblower Classic Cable Cars (successor to Classic Cable Car Charters). It is an authentic original California Street Cable Railroad Company cable car. The car retains most of its original appearance. It isn't clear how this car was acquired by Classic Cable Car Charters (now Hornblower Classic Cable Cars), or if this is the original Car #22, or another original cable car that had its fleet number changed to Car#22.

Car #22
motorized - 2017

Car #23
History and Disposition
1907 - Built by John Hammond Company in San Francisco, CA.   1956 - Sold to Santa Clara County and placed on display at the Santa Clara County Fairgrounds in San Jose, CA shortly thereafter. At an unknown date it was donated to the California Trolley Corporation (historic railroad) and placed into storage.   2005 - The car was sold to an unrecorded party.   2018 - Status unknown.

A Fleet History of the San Francisco Municipal Railway
Section 5: Cable Cars

Car #24 / Car #38
History and Disposition
See Car #38 information.

Car #25 / Car #39
History and Disposition
See Car #39 information.

Car #38 / Car #24
History and Disposition
1907 - Built by John Hammond Company in San Francisco, CA.   1911 - Rebuilt by the California Street Cable Railroad Company and moved from California Street route to O'Farrell & Jones route, and renumbered from Car #24 to Car #38.   1956 - Sold to an unrecorded buyer in Lakeport, CA. The car was a display at the Lake County Fairgrounds for over 50 years.   2007 - Placed into storage for restoration.   2013 - After a partial restoration Car #38 was moved to the Ely Stage Stop and Country Museum (Lake County Historical Society).   2018 - On public display at the Ely Stage Stop and Country Museum in Kelseyville, CA.

Car #38 at Ely Stage Stop and County Museum Kelseyville, CA 2017

Car #39 / Car #25
History and Disposition
1907 - Built by John Hammond Company in San Francisco, CA.   1911 - Rebuilt by California Street Cable Railroad Company, and moved from California Street route to O'Farrell & Jones route, and renumbered from Car #25 to Car #39.   1956 - Sold or loaned to the San Francisco Youth Guidance Center.   2018 - No longer on site, believed to have been scrapped, but officially, status is unknown.

Car #39 at S.F. Youth Guidance Center - 1960's

A Fleet History of the San Francisco Municipal Railway
Section 5: Cable Cars

Car #40 / Car #49
History and Disposition
See Car #49 (second) information.

Car #41
History and Disposition
1907 - Built by W.L. Holman Company in San Francisco, CA.   1953 - Sold to Al Williams, owner of the Papagayo Room in the Fairmont Hotel in San Francisco for $225.   Unknown date -Scrapped.

Car #41 in service - 1909

Car #42
History and Disposition
1907 - Built by W.L. Holman Company in San Francisco, CA.   1955 - Sold to H. Stanley Brown of Betteravia, CA. It was motorized and used as a work car on a private narrow gauge railroad operated on the Stinton and Brown cattle feedlot.   1979 - The feedlot is closed and Car #42 is placed into storage.   1993 - Donated by the Brown family to the non-profit Market Street Railway. Restoration is started.   2012 - Operated in service for the first time to celebrate the Muni Centennial.   2016 - Operated for the first time since 1954 on the Hyde Street segment of the former O'Farrell, Jones and Hyde line where it ran when in regular service over 50 years earlier.   2018 - On Muni fleet roster and used in service for special occasions.

Car #42 with Fageol bus that was supposed to replace cable cars. - 1947

Car #42 -On private railroad in cattle ranch Betteravia, CA - 1960

A Fleet History of the San Francisco Municipal Railway
Section 5: Cable Cars

Car #42 in 2014

Car #43 (first)
History and Disposition
1907 - Built by W.L. Holman Company in San Francisco, CA.   Pre-1952 - never owned by Muni as it was scrapped at an unknown date by California Street Cable Railroad Company.

Car #43 (second) / Car #4
History and Disposition
1907 - Built by W. L. Holman Company in San Francisco, CA.   Unknown date - Renumbered as Car #4 after original Car #4 is scrapped.   1954 - Last cable car to operate on California line west of Van Ness to Presidio Ave.   1955 - Renumbered from Car #4 to Car #43.   1955 - Sold to Knotts Berry Farm in Buena Park, CA, converted to a motorized cable car, but on tracks.   1981 - Acquired by the Orange Empire Railway Museum.   2018 - On display at the Orange Empire Railway Museum in Perris, CA.

Car #4 - 1912 - renumbered as Car #43 in 1955

Car #43 at Orange Empire Museum 2012

A Fleet History of the San Francisco Municipal Railway
Section 5: Cable Cars

Car #44
History and Disposition
1907 - Built by W.L. Holman Company in San Francisco, CA.   1953 - Sold to Jorgensen Steel in Oakland, CA for $150 and motorized.   1958 - Acquired by Western Airlines of Los Angeles, CA and used it as a promotional vehicle to advertise air service to San Francisco.   1987 - Western Airlines is acquired by Delta Airlines, and Car #44 winds up (circumstances unknown) as a static display at Trolley Square in Salt Lake City, UT. Subsequentially it was moved again to the Lagoon Amusement Park in Farmington, UT.   2003 - Acquired by S & S Shortline Railroad of Farmington, UT with plans for a restoration, but found to be beyond repair. Scrapped.

Car #44 - Western Airlines 1958

Car #45
History and Disposition
1907 - Built by W.L. Holman Company in San Francisco, CA.   1953 - Sold to Victor Meats in San Francisco for $225.   1956 - Purchased by Damon Trout at Marelco Ranch located west of Portland in North Plains, OR.   1989 - Following an unknown journey Car #45 was acquired by Snowmass Village Ski Area in Colorado and was used as a fast food stand.   2003 - Sold to an unrecorded buyer via EBay.   2018 - Status unknown.

Car #46
History and Disposition
1907 - Built by W.L. Holman Company in San Francisco, CA.   1955 - Sold to Steve's Gay 90s Cafe in Tacoma, WA where it was on site until it closed in 1977.   1977 - Purchased by Arnold Gridley of Classic Cable Cars. 2008 - Classic Cable Car Charters is acquired by Ride the Ducks, but Car #46 is retained by the Gridley Family. 2018 - Owned by Phillip Wright (Gridley Family) in storage in Healdsburg, CA.

Car #46 following sale in 1955

Car #46 in storage 2018

A Fleet History of the San Francisco Municipal Railway
Section 5: Cable Cars

Car #47
History and Disposition
1907 - Built by W.L. Holman Company in San Francisco, CA.   1955 - Sold to Harold Warp and displayed at the Pioneer Village Museum in Minden, NE.   2018 - On display at the Pioneer Village Museum in Minden, NE.

Car #47 at Pioneer Village Museum in Minden, NE 2017

Car #48
History and Disposition
1907 - Built by W.L. Holman Company in San Francisco, CA.   1955 - Sold to Josef Gest of Montreal, QU. At an unknown date Car #48 passed into ownershp of Herbert J. O' Connell, and then to M. Paul Bienvenu.   1983 - Acquired by the Seashore Trolley Museum in Kennebunkport, ME.   2018 - On display at the Seashore Trolley Museum in Kennebunkport, ME.

Car #48 at Seashore Trolley Museum in Kennebunkport, ME 2017

Car #49 (first)
History and Disposition
1912 - Built by California Street Cable Railroad Company in San Francisco, CA.   1956 - Sold to Knott's Berry Farm in Buena Park, CA, converted to a motorized cable car, but on tracks.   1981 - Returned to Muni placed in storage, but later sold at unknown date.   2018 - Owned by Brett Folena, Auburn, CA - for sale on Facebook.

Car #49 (second) / Car #40
History and Disposition
1912 - Built by California Street Cable Railroad Company in San Francisco, CA.
1957 - Renumbered from Car #40 to Car # 6, and then quickly renumbered again as Car #49, on Muni fleet roster.   1990 - Damaged in an accident and judged not repairable. Scrapped.

A Fleet History of the San Francisco Municipal Railway
Section 5: Cable Cars

Car #49 (third)
History and Disposition
1992 - Built by Muni at Woods Carpentry Shop in San Francisco, CA.   2018 - On Muni active fleet roster.

Car #50
History and Disposition
1910 - Built by the California Street Cable Railroad Company in San Francisco, CA.   1982-1984 - Rebuilt by Muni.   2018 - On Muni active fleet roster.

Car #50 - 1960

Car #50 - 2017

A Fleet History of the San Francisco Municipal Railway
Section 5: Cable Cars

Car #51
History and Disposition
1907 - Built by W.L. Holman Company in San Francisco, CA.   1954 - Last car to operate on the full O'Farrell, Jones & Hyde cable car line: May 16, 1954.   1982-1984 - Partially rebuilt by Muni.   2014 - Rebuilt by Muni.   2018 - On Muni active fleet roster.

Car #51 with protestors opposing reduction of cable car service - 1954

Car #51 - 2017

Car #52 (first)
History and Disposition
1907 - Built by John Hammond Company in San Francisco, CA.   1953 - Sold to Odd Fellows San Leandro for $300, and used as a static display playground piece at Guerneville, CA in the Russian River area. Within a decade the car had succumbed to natural elements and vandals, and was removed from display.   Unknown date: Acquired by Arnold Gridley and Classic Cable Cars.   2008 - Classic Cable Car Charters is acquired by Ride the Ducks, but Car #52 is retained by the Gridley Family.   2018 - Owned by Phillip Wright (Gridley Family) in storage in Healdsburg, CA. Currently renumbered as Car #11.

Car #52 - 1955

Car #52 - 2018

Car #52 (second) / Car #18
History and Disposition
1907 - Built by John Hammond Company in San Francisco, CA.   1957 - Renumbered from Car #18 to Car #3, and then quickly renumbered again as Car #52. Placed into storage for 27 years.   1981 - Scrapped, but some hardware used in construction of new Car #52 (third), and seats were used in restoration of Car #56 in 1984.

A Fleet History of the San Francisco Municipal Railway
Section 5: Cable Cars

Car #52 (third)
History and Disposition
1995 - Built by Muni at Woods Carpentry Shop in San Francisco, CA as third Car #52. 2017 - On Muni active fleet roster.

Car #53
History and Disposition
1907 - Built by W.L. Holman Company in San Francisco, CA.   2018 - Out of service undergoing renovation and repair.

Car #53 - 1960

Car #54 (first)
History and Disposition
1907 - Built by W.L. Holman Company in San Francisco, CA.   1955 - Sold to Hal Wilmunder of Roseville, CA, who owned the Camino, Cable & Northern RR near Camino, CA. Unknown if regauged for use on the line which stopped operation before 1970.   2018 - Status is unknown.

A Fleet History of the San Francisco Municipal Railway
Section 5: Cable Cars

Car #54 (second) / Car #19
History and Disposition
1907 - Built by John Hammond Company in San Francisco, CA.   1957 - Renumbered from Car #19 to Car #4, and renumbered again as Car #54.   1982-1984 - Partial rebuild by Muni.   2018 - On Muni active fleet roster.

Car #55 (first)
History and Disposition
1907 - Built by John Hammond Company in San Francisco, CA.   1956 - Sold to Valley Fair Shopping Center in San Jose, CA where it remained until 1984 as part of a restaurant.   1985- Acquired by Arnold Gridley and Classic Cable Cars.   2008 - Classic Cable Car Charters is acquired by Ride the Ducks and the fleet is reduced. Car #55 is believed to be scrapped., but there is a chance it could be Hornblower Car # 4 or Car #22.

Car #55 (second) / Car #8
History and Disposition
1907 - Built by John Hammond Company in San Francisco, CA.   1952 - Briefly painted green and cream after Muni acquires California Cable RR. Repainted maroon and gold.   1957 - Renumbered from Car #8 to Car #55. 1982-1984 - Rebuilt by Muni.   2006 - In an accident where the cable car ran a "split switch", which damaged the cable car and removed it from service.   2018 - Undergoing restoration at Muni in San Francisco.

Car #8 in 1952

Car #8 - renumbered as Car #55 in 1957

Car #55 in storage in preparation for restoration - 2018

Car #56
History and Disposition
1913 - Built by California Cable Railroad Company in San Francisco, CA.   1982-1984 - Rebuilt by Muni including use of seats from first Car #52.   2016- Rebuilt by Muni.   2018 - On Muni active fleet roster.

A Fleet History of the San Francisco Municipal Railway
Section 5: Cable Cars

Car #57
History and Disposition
1914 - Built by California Street Cable Railroad Company in San Francisco, CA.   1957 - Renumbered from Car #57 to Car #11, and then quickly renumbered back to Car #57.   2018 - Rebuilt by Muni and on Muni active fleet roster.

Car #58
History and Disposition
1914 - Built by California Street Cable Railroad Company in San Francisco, CA.   1954 - Last car to operate on Jones Street Shuttle cable car line: February 6, 1954.   2018 - On Muni active fleet roster.

Car #58 in 2017

Car #59 (first)
History and Disposition
1915 - Built by the California Street Cable Railroad Company in San Francisco, CA.   1955 - Sold to Knott's Berry Farm in Buena Park, CA, converted to a motorized cable car, but on tracks.   1981 - Returned to Muni placed into storage, and sold at unknown date.   2018 - On display at Oakwood Village Senior Retirement Facility in Auburn, CA.

Car #59 - in Auburn, CA in 2017

A Fleet History of the San Francisco Municipal Railway
Section 5: Cable Cars

Car #59 (second) / Car #15
History and Disposition
1907 - Built by John Hammond Company in San Francisco, CA.   1957 - Renumbered from Car #15 to Car #59.   1996 - Traded to New Orleans as part of a lease agreement that sent New Orleans streetcar #952 to S.F. Placed on static display at Popp's Fountain Park.   2010 - Removed from the park and placed into storage in poor condition in New Orleans.   2018 - In storage in New Orleans.

Car #59 (second) at Carrolton Shops
New Orleans, LA - 2017

Car #59 (third)
History and Disposition
1998 - Built by Muni at Woods Carpentry Shop in San Francisco, CA as the third Car #59.   2017 - On Muni active fleet roster.

Car #60 (first)
History and Disposition
See Jones Street Shuttle sub-section.

Car #60 (second) / Car #16
History and Disposition
1907 - Built by John Hammond Company in San Francisco, CA.   1957 - Renumbered from Car #16 to Car #60. 1969 - Extensive rebuild using original roof and seats.   2002 - Removed from service and placed into storage by Muni.   2018 - In storage owned by Muni in San Francisco.

Car #60 (second) - 1976

Car #60 (third)
History and Disposition
2002 - Built by Muni at Woods Carpentry Shop in San Francisco, CA as the third Car #60.
2003 - Entered revenue service.   2018 - On Muni active fleet roster.

A Fleet History of the San Francisco Municipal Railway
Section 5: Cable Cars

The Jones Street Shuttle Car Fleet

As stated in the California Street section, the Jones Street Shuttle was the third California Street Cable Car Company line, and it operated on a six-block segment of Jones Street between O'Farrell Street and Market Street starting in 1891. The last day of service was February 6, 1954 and after closure it was completely removed. Although regular sized O'Farrell, Jones & Hyde cable cars were used on the shuttle, three smaller double end cable cars that were only 22.5' in length were specifically designed for the line and were used for over 40 years until the service ended. The Jones Street Shuttle cars were the highest numbered cars (Nos. 60-62) in the California Street Cable Car Company / Muni fleet. The Jones Street Shuttle cars had a capacity of 28 seated passengers and a total capacity of 48 passengers. The Jones Street Shuttle cable cars were painted in the Cal Cable maroon color scheme with yellow / gold writing, and were adorned with a "ribbon" design on the ends of the cars that listed the essential streets of the route where they operated. Basic specifications for the cars are shown below. Surprisingly, all three Jones Street Shuttle cars are still in existence in 2018; 1 has been motorized and is owned by Muni, 1 is motorized and in storage in Healdsburg, CA, and 1 is in a museum in Japan.

Fleet & Car No.	Length / Width / Height / Weight	Seats	Total Capacity
Cars 60-62	22'5" / 8'0" / 10'3" / 10,500	28	48

Car #60 (first)
History and Disposition
1908 - Built as a Jones Street Shuttle Car by the California Street Cable Railroad Company in San Francisco, CA. 1956 - Sold to Rothschild, Raffin & Werric Construction Co.   Unknown date - Acquired by Arnold Gridley and transformed into a motorized cable car for Classic Cable Car Charters.   2008 - Classic Cable Car Charters is acquired by Ride the Ducks, but Car #60 is retained by the Gridley Family.   2014 - After being stored in Hayward for several years while owned by Christine Bennett of the Gridley family, it was acquired by Phillip Wright, another member of the Gridley Family.   2018 - Currently in storage in Healdsburg, CA.

Car #60 (first) - 1950

Car #60 (first) - 2018

A Fleet History of the San Francisco Municipal Railway
Section 5: Cable Cars

Car #61 / Car #62
History and Disposition
1908 - Built as a Jones Street Shuttle car by California Street Cable Railroad Company in San Francisco, CA.
1947 - Renumbered from Cable Car #62 to Cable Car #61 following the return of sibling Car #61 from being used in a movie in Los Angeles, during which it had been renumbered as Cable Car #62. In short the two cars switched numbers.   1954 - Placed on rubber tires but not motorized by Muni following the closure of the Jones Street Shuttle cable car line.   1959 - Shipped to Japan for display at the Osaka Transportation Museum.   2014 - Osaka Museum is closed. Car is placed into storage in Osaka and is not on display.   2017 - A plan arises to build a display space for Cable Car #61 at the Osaka Institute of Technology.

Car #61 in 1953, and Car #61 as it was prepared to be sent to Japan in 1959

Car #61 in the Osaka Transport Museum in Osaka, Japan - 2014

Car #61 at annoucement for new home at the Osaka Institute of Technology and artist rendering of new display area - 2017

A Fleet History of the San Francisco Municipal Railway
Section 5: Cable Cars

Car #62 / Car #61
History and Disposition
1908 - Built as a Jones Street Shuttle car by the California Street Cable Railroad Company in San Francisco, CA. 1947 - Renumbered from Cable Car #61 to Cable Car #62 during painting in Los Angeles in preparation for use on the movie "I Remember Mama".   1954 - Motorized and placed on rubber tires and the chassis of a retired bus (ACF Brill Model 31S) by Muni following the closure of the Jones Street Shuttle cable car line. In the late 1950s, the banner logo on the car was changed from "O'Farrell, Jones & Hyde Streets" to "San Francisco Municipal Railway", and at some point after the early 1960s, it was changed again to read "Van Ness, California & Market Streets". This was a route that was never operated by this cable car when it was in active service, but the banner does match the current name of the California Street line.   2018 - Owned by Muni as a motorized cable car and used for special events, such as the annual Cable Car Bell Ringing Contest.

Car #61 - (renumbered as current #62) - ca. 1945

Car #62 - the only motorized cable car owned and operated by Muni - 1954

Car #62 - 2018

A Fleet History of the San Francisco Municipal Railway
Section 5: Cable Cars

The Sacramento-Clay Cable Car Fleet

The fourth cable car fleet owned by Muni was acquired along with the first cable car fleet as part of the 1944 merger with MSRy. Twelve cable cars from the Sacramento-Clay cable car line were placed in storage when MSRy closed the line down on February 15, 1942 and replaced the cars with buses. MSRy was ordered by the U.S. Office of Defense Transportation to hold onto the cars in case they were needed to be used again, so they were placed into storage. All were built by the Southern Pacific RR Shops in Sacramento, CA in the 1880s and were used in service on Market Street prior to the 1906 Earthquake. In 1907 they were remodeled for use on the Sacramento-Clay line (including conversion to narrow gauge of 3'6") where they ran 1907-1942. The cars were numbered #15-#26. This line was originally a part of the Ferries and Cliff House Railway, along with the Powell Street and Washington-Jackson lines. The cars were four feet longer than California Street cars, and with a seated capacity of 40, and a total capacity of 72 passengers, these cars were the largest of the four car types acquired by Muni. The fleet did not operate in passenger service while owned by Muni. In 1948 eleven cars were sold for scrap for $50 each. The last car was sold for scrap in 1953.

The outcomes of several of these cars following their departure from Muni are known. The first motorized cable car to be created was Sacramento-Clay Car #21, which was built in 1952. It was shortened to resemble a Powell St. car and was used in parades or as a rolling billboard. It was last used as a billboard for the Johnson-Humphrey Presidential campaign in 1964 before it burned in a warehouse fire in December 1964. Car #16 was moved to the roof of the Emporium Department Store on Market Street in September 1948 and became part of a Christmas holiday season roof-top carnival until the 1990s. In 1996 it was removed in poor condition and was scrapped. Car #17 was bought third-hand in 1962 by the Erie County Fair in Hamburg, NY, was motorized in S.F., and was driven to upstate N.Y. by its new owners. In 2018 it is in good condition and continues to be a part of the annual fair, although it is no longer operational. Car #18 was found in Fall 2018 in poor condition being used as a sales kiosk and storage building for a river raft rental agency in Healdsburg, CA. Car #20 was purchased by the non-profit Friends of the Cable Car Museum in 1996 with plans for a rebuild, but after years of weather exposure it was scrapped in 2015. Car #22 was stored for many years at the Western Railway Museum in Suisun City, CA, but weather exposure has damaged the car and only pieces remain. Car #24 was supposedly sold to a movie studio in Hollywood around 1950, but its location isn't known today. One car remains in nearly complete restored condition today: Car #19, which is owned by Muni, is in storage at the Cable Car Barn. More information on Car #19 is on the next page.

Market St. Railway (MSRy.) Car #16 in service - ca. 1920 at Sacramento and Fillmore Streets (left) and ca. 1960 as a display on the roof of the Emporium Department Store on Market Street (right)

A Fleet History of the San Francisco Municipal Railway
Section 5: Cable Cars

Market St. Railway (MSRy.) Car #17 at Erie County (NY) fair ca. 1960s (left) and ca. 1980s (right)

The Historic Cable Car Fleet

Although the entire San Francisco Municipal Railway cable car fleet is classified as a historic fleet (one of only a few moving National Historic Landmarks), Muni owns three unique cable cars that are not used in regular service. Two of these vehicles, Car #42 and Car #62, have been profiled because both were part of the California Street Cable Car roster. Information on the third historic cable car is listed below.

Fleet & Car No.	Length / Width / Height / Weight	Seats	Total Capacity
Cars 19	34'0" / 8'2" / 10'2" / N/A	40	72

History and Disposition
1883 - Built by Southern Pacific RR shops in Sacramento, CA for the Market Street Cable Railway Company. 1907 - Rebuilt by United RR for use on the Sacramento - Clay Street line. 1942 - Service ends on the Sacramento - Clay line and Car #19 is placed into storage. 1944 - Muni acquires 12 ex-Sacramento-Clay cable cars via the merger with Market Street Railway 1948 - Eleven cars are sold at auction, most for $50 each. Car #19 is acquired by the Pacific Coast Chapter: Railway & Historical Locomotive Society and stored in S.F. 1953 - Car #26 is sold. 1966 - Car #19 is moved to Cable Car Barn to be part of the new museum, but is not used in museum displays. Enters storage. 2000 - Car is moved to storage at Pier 80. 2002 - After restoration offsite, Cable Car #19 returns to the Cable Car Barn, but a test trip ends when its size and a wheel truck issue cause a clearance and a safety problem. 2018 - Owned by Muni in storage at the Cable Car Barn.

Market St. Railway (MSRy.) Car #19 in service on Sacramento-Clay line - ca. 1940 (above) and being moved into storage - 1966 (right)

Former Market St. Railway (MSRy.) Car #19 at Muni Car Barn - 2017

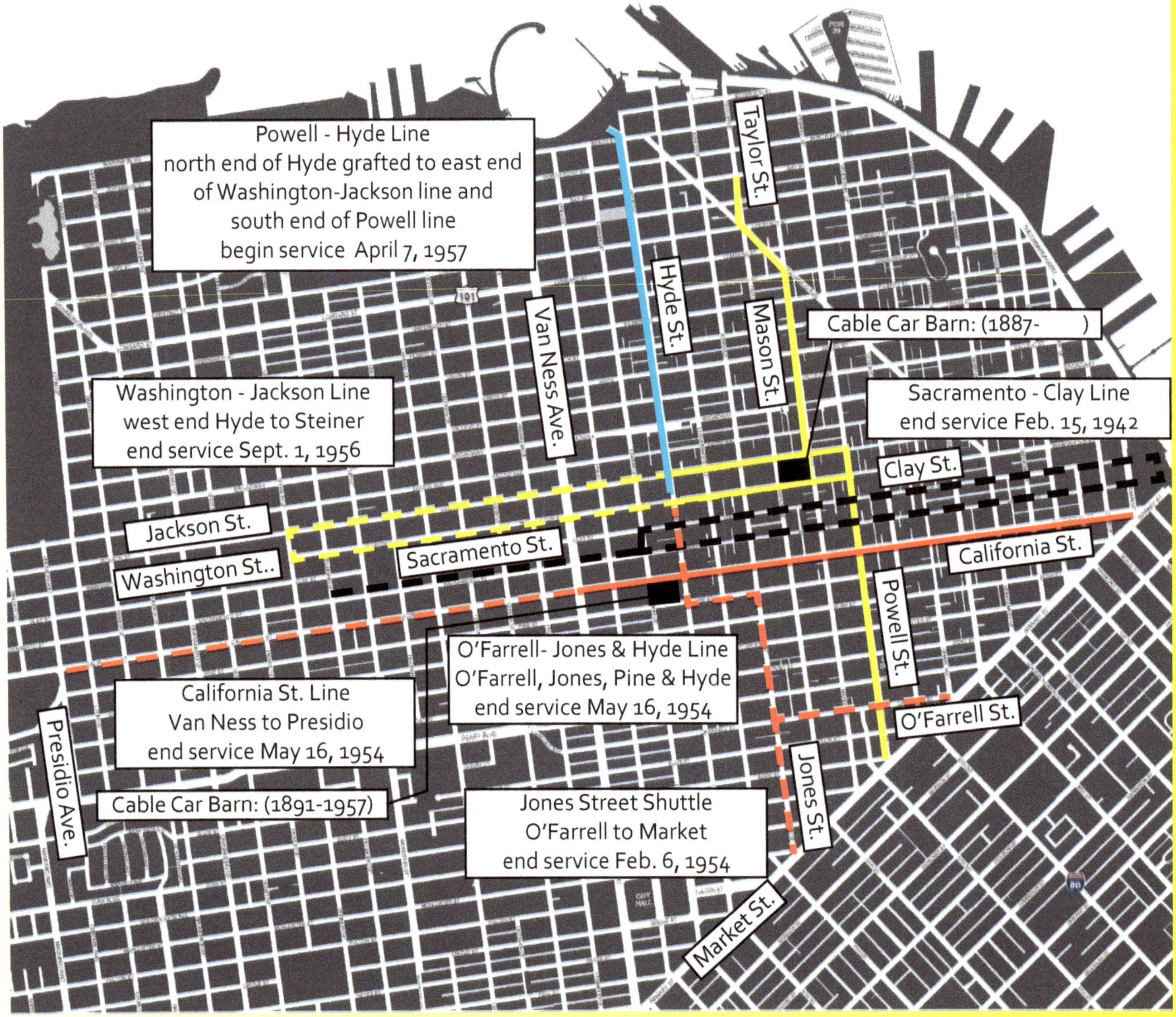

A Fleet History of the San Francisco Municipal Railway
Section 5: Cable Cars

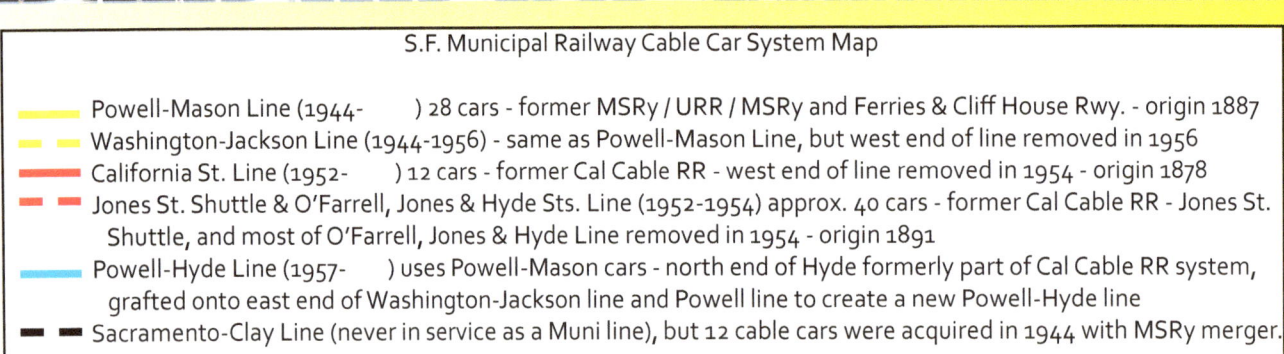

S.F. Municipal Railway Cable Car System Map

- ▬ Powell-Mason Line (1944-) 28 cars - former MSRy / URR / MSRy and Ferries & Cliff House Rwy. - origin 1887
- ▬ ▬ Washington-Jackson Line (1944-1956) - same as Powell-Mason Line, but west end of line removed in 1956
- ▬ California St. Line (1952-) 12 cars - former Cal Cable RR - west end of line removed in 1954 - origin 1878
- ▬ ▬ Jones St. Shuttle & O'Farrell, Jones & Hyde Sts. Line (1952-1954) approx. 40 cars - former Cal Cable RR - Jones St. Shuttle, and most of O'Farrell, Jones & Hyde Line removed in 1954 - origin 1891
- ▬ Powell-Hyde Line (1957-) uses Powell-Mason cars - north end of Hyde formerly part of Cal Cable RR system, grafted onto east end of Washington-Jackson line and Powell line to create a new Powell-Hyde line
- ▬ ▬ Sacramento-Clay Line (never in service as a Muni line), but 12 cable cars were acquired in 1944 with MSRy merger.

134

A Fleet History of the San Francisco Municipal Railway
Section 6: Divisions, Yards, Barns and Work Cars

A Fleet History of the San Francisco Municipal Railway
Section 6: Divisions, Yards, Barns and Work Cars

A Fleet History of the San Francisco Municipal Railway
Section 6: Divisions, Yards, Barns and Work Cars

A vehicle fleet requires a location for storage and maintenance of the vehicles, and Muni has utilized several locations in San Francisco to perform this task. There have been no clear distinctions within Muni between the terms, division, yard or barn, aside from the fact that barns are enclosed spaces. In slightly longer than a century of operations, Muni has utilized 22 divisions, yards and barns to service its transit fleet, although one site has transformed so completely at different times it has had three different names at the same location. Nine sites were acquired via the merger with the Market Street Railway in 1944, and three of these remain in service as part of 10 divisions, yards and barns that are active in 2018. Muni's oldest division: Presidio (aka Geary Car House) remains one of the active sites. Information on all locations is in this section.

Division Name	Location	Mode(s)	Active Years	Approx. Capacity
Presidio Division (aka Geary Division / Geary Car House)	Geary Blvd. & Presidio Ave.	Streetcar	1912-1956	136 (pre-1949) streetcars
		Bus	1918-1944*	20 25'-30' buses
		Trolley Bus	1950-	115 (40') T-buses

* Buses have been temporarily stored at the division at various times after 1944.

History and Disposition

1912 - The Geary Division opened shortly before Muni began streetcar service on December 28, 1912. It was originally built with 16 tracks on an upper level at grade on Geary Street, and four tracks on the lower level facing Presidio Avenue.   1915 - A second level of offices was added over the sixteen streetcar tracks facing Geary Street.   1918 - Muni starts to store a small number of buses from its initial bus fleet at Geary.   1944 - Muni ends bus storage at Geary following the merger with MSRy, but in times with a shortage of vehicle storage space (1950s-80s), Muni stored limited numbers of buses at Presidio.   1949 - Muni expands the facility by remodeling the lower level shop areas and by building a new open surface storage yard for the growing trolley bus fleet on the former Laurel Hill Cemetery site.   1956 - Streetcar service ends on Geary Street and Balboa Streets on December 29, 1956, and the facility transforms into the Presidio Trolley Bus Division.   2004- Most Muni administrative offices are moved out of Presidio to offices located in the downtown area near Civic Center. Transit Schedules was the last main group to leave. Reproduction services (print shop) remains at Presidio in 2018.   2016 - A planning process to rebuild / replace the 104 year-old division building is initiated. A tentative timeline calls for a new facility to open before 2030.

Geary Division under construction - 1912

Geary Division - 1923

A Fleet History of the San Francisco Municipal Railway
Section 6: Divisions, Yards, Barns and Work Cars

Geary Car House (Presidio Division after 1956) - 1948

Trolley Bus Yard at Presidio Division - 1958

Presidio Division - 2015

Division Name	Location	Mode(s)	Active Years	Approx. Capacity
Presidio & Ferries RR Car Barn	Filbert Street / Gough Street	Streetcar	1913-1922	25-30 streetcars

History and Disposition
1908- Car Barn is built for the Presidio & Ferries RR (P&FRR).   1913 - Muni buys the P&FRR, but doesn't buy the car barn, which is leased. Muni operates Type G streetcars on Union Street from this facility until 1922 when the cars are replaced by new Type J cars and the lease ends.   2018 - A bowling alley existed on this site for several years, but in 1980 an apartment building was built that continues to occupy this location.

Presidio & Ferries RR Car Barn - 1908

Apartment building on site - 2018

A Fleet History of the San Francisco Municipal Railway
Section 6: Divisions, Yards, Barns and Work Cars

Division Name	Location	Mode(s)	Active Years	Approx. Capacity
Potrero Division (aka 17th Street Car House)	17th Street / Bryant Street	Streetcar Trolley Bus	1914-1949 1944-	110 streetcars 20 (pre-1949) T-buses 250 40' (pre-1994) T-buses 140 40' / 95 60' T-buses

History and Disposition

1914 - The Potrero Car House / Potrero Division opened in 1914 with 14 tracks facing Mariposa Street. 1923 - A second level of offices was added over the streetcar tracks facing Mariposa Street. 1941 - Muni builds a temporary deck on the building roof to accommodate the first trolley buses obtained for the R-Howard line. Trolley buses access the deck from 17th Street. 1946 - Muni builds a new trolley bus yard west of the existing car barn which closes York Street between Mariposa and 17th Streets. 1949 - Muni starts a major renovation and reconstruction program to transform the facility to an all trolley bus division. The new construction includes permanent trolley bus storage and maintenance on the roof of the heavily rebuilt 1914 building. 1994 - Muni initiates 60' trolley bus vehicles, and the new longer trolley buses are maintained and stored at the Potrero Division. 2016 - A planning process to rebuild / replace the 102 year-old division building is initiated. A very tentative timeline calls for a new facility to open before 2030.

Potrero Car House - 1921

Potrero Car House with second level - 1926

Initial trolley bus upper level - 1941

Conversion to an all trolley bus division - 1949

A Fleet History of the San Francisco Municipal Railway
Section 6: Divisions, Yards, Barns and Work Cars

Potrero Division - 2018

Division Name	Location	Mode(s)	Active Years	Approx. Capacity
Geary Street Park & Ocean RR Car Barn	Geary Street / Arguello Blvd.	Bus	1935-1944	40 25'-30' buses

History and Disposition
1892 - Car Barn is built for the cable cars of the Geary Street Park & Ocean RR (GSP&ORR).   1912 - Muni buys the GSP&ORR to build the first streetcar line, but doesn't buy the car barn.   1935 - Muni leases space in the upper level of the significantly remodeled building for bus storage.   1944 - After the merger with the MSRy all bus operations are moved to the 24th & Utah Division.   2018 - The car barn building is still standing, and was an Office Depot office supplies store (closed in 2018), with customer parking inside on the upper level.

Geary Street, Park & Ocean RR Barn - 1912

Geary Street, Park & Ocean RR Barn - 2017

On September 29, 1944 the S.F. Municipal Railway (Muni) merged with the privately owned Market Street Railway (MSRy) following voter approval of Charter Measure 1 to purchase the MSRy at a cost of $7.5 million dollars. All property owned by MSRy became Muni property and the MSRy ceased to exist. Former MSRy vehicles used in revenue service by Muni are listed here with an "M" prefix to their number to designate they were ex-MSRy cars that became Muni cars via the merger.   Most of these cars only briefly operated on Muni before they were retired.

A Fleet History of the San Francisco Municipal Railway
Section 6: Divisions, Yards, Barns and Work Cars

Division Name	Location	Mode(s)	Active Years	Approx. Capacity
Cameron Beach Yard (aka Geneva Division)	Geneva / San Jose Avenue	Streetcar	1944-	88 (1940s era) streetcars 30 (2017) streetcars

History and Disposition

1901 - The facility (20 track barn and administration building) is constructed for the S.F. & San Mateo Electric Railway (first electric system in S.F). 1903 - The facility becomes part of United RR's (URR). 1906 - The facility buildings are damaged in the 1906 Earthquake. Support bracing is added to the offices that will remain for over 100 years. 1944 - Merger between Muni and MSRy officially brings this facility into Muni ownership and control. 1956 - Geneva becomes the only Muni streetcar railway facility shop following closure of rail service on Geary and Balboa Streets and conversion of Geary Car House to Presidio Division. 1958 - The last of the "old" non-PCC streetcars are retired - leaving Geneva as home to five rail lines with all PCC vehicles. 1977 - Green Division opens across the street as new yard for new Boeing LRV fleet. Geneva transforms into a support facility for Green Division. 1984 - Decrepit streetcar storage barns on site are torn down. 1986 A new smaller streetcar maintenance building opens on site. 1989 - Following additional damage from the Loma Prieta Earthquake, Muni closes the administration building. 1998 - The building is saved from demolition by Mayor Willie Brown. 2004 - SFMTA sells the administration building to the Parks and Recreation Department for $1. 2012 - A new shelter over six tracks (reminiscent of the old barn) opens, and the facility is renamed the Cameron Beach Yard after SFMTA Board Member and transit professional who rose to be the Operations Manager of the Sacramento Regional Transit District. 2018 - The facility continues in service, and Parks and Rec plans for the Administration building move forward.

Geneva Division - 1904

Geneva Divison - 1945

Geneva Car Barn - 1965

Car shed and 1986 maintenance building - 2017

A Fleet History of the San Francisco Municipal Railway
Section 6: Divisions, Yards, Barns and Work Cars

Division Name	Location	Mode(s)	Active Years	Approx. Capacity
Haight Street Division	Haight / Stanyan Streets	Streetcar	1944-1946	40 streetcars
		Trolley Bus	1944-1946	10 T-buses

History and Disposition
1883 - The facility was built for the Market Street Cable Railway and housed cable cars.   1902 - The company was reorganized as United RRs.   1907 - The cable cars are replaced by streetcars after the 1906 Earthquake.   1935 - The facility was partially converted to a trolley bus garage.   1944 - Merger between Muni and MSRy officially brings this facility into Muni ownership and control.   1946 - Operations cease after a trolley bus damaged the building structure. Shortly afterward the wooden building is torn down.   1980s - The site was occupied by a bowling alley (Park Bowl / Rock ' Bowl), which later became Amoeba Records.   2018 - The site continues to be the location of Amoeba Records.

Haight Street Car Barn - 1942

Ameoba Records - 2018

Division Name	Location	Mode(s)	Active Years	Approx. Capacity
Turk & Fillmore Car House & Compound	Turk / Fillmore Streets	Streetcar	1944-1948	70 streetcars

History and Disposition
1895 - The car house located on the south side of Turk Street, and west side of Fillmore Street, is built by Market St. Railway on the site of an earlier car house from 1877.   1902 United RRs (URR) is created and unifies most private transit in S.F. Property owned by Central RR on the east side of Fillmore Street is also acquired, and a powerhouse is built a year later.   1921 - URR transforms into the second MSRy.   1944 - Merger between Muni and MSRy officially brought this facility into Muni ownership and control.   1949 - The site, which had been primarily used for storage of retired streetcars prior to their disposition is closed, and the car barn site is sold. The powerhouse remains in service.   1950s - A Safeway grocery store is built on the car barn site.   1978 - The powerhouse is closed and the site turned over to the City of S.F.   1970s - Safeway closed the building becomes a California state employment office.   2018 - The site is the Northern Police Station.

142

A Fleet History of the San Francisco Municipal Railway
Section 6: Divisions, Yards, Barns and Work Cars

Turk & Fillmore Car Barn - 1928

Northern Police Station - 2018

Division Name	Location	Mode(s)	Active Years	Approx. Capacity
McAllister Division	McAllister / Fulton Street	Streetcar	1944-1948	75 streetcars
		Bus	1948-1950	130 35' buses

History and Disposition

1883 - The car barn is built for Market Street Cable Railway to house cable cars.   1902 - As part of a larger merger, the facility becomes part of the newly created United RRs.   1907 - The cable cars are replaced by streetcars following conversion after the 1906 Earthquake.   1921 - Following bankruptcy of URR, the company is reorganized as the second Market Street Railway (MSRy).   1944 - Merger between Muni and MSRy officially brings this facility into Muni ownership and control.   1948 - Streetcar operations end at site.   1949 - The streetcar barn is torn down.   1950 - Bus operations end, and the land is sold.   2018 - The site is occupied by housing over retail, which includes a Lucky supermarket and an underground parking garage.

McAllister Street Car Barn - 1921

McAllister Street Car Barn - 1948

Multi-unit housing, with ground floor retail, including Lucky grocery store and underground parking - 2018

143

A Fleet History of the San Francisco Municipal Railway
Section 6: Divisions, Yards, Barns and Work Cars

Division Name	Location	Mode(s)	Active Years	Approx. Capacity
Lincoln Way Yard (aka Lincoln Way Boneyard or Funston Boneyard))	Lincoln Way / Funston Ave.	Streetcar	1944-1950	120 streetcars

History and Disposition

1905 - MSRy purchases the property and opens a storage yard.   1906 - Plans to build a car barn at the site are postponed by the 1906 Earthquake. The car house was not built, but for the next 38 years the site was used for streetcar storage and occasional dispatching of streetcars for special events.   1944 - Merger between Muni and MSRy officially brought this facility into Muni ownership and control.   1950 - After six years of additional use as a storage yard by Muni, the site is sold.   2018 - The site is occupied by a large apartment building and an Andronico's grocery store, with an accompanying parking lot.

Lincoln Way Yard - 1942

Park West Apartments and Andronico's grocery store - 2017

Division Name	Location	Mode(s)	Active Years	Approx. Capacity
Sutro Division	32nd Ave. / Clement St.	Streetcar	1944-1951	107 streetcars

History and Disposition

1895 - The car house is built for Sutro RR.   1902 - The facility becomes part of the United RRs.   1944 - Merger between Muni and MSRy officially brought this facility into Muni ownership and control.   1948 - All MSRy lines from this division are replaced with streetcars that serve Muni lines.   1951 - After using the facility briefly for storage, the site is sold.   2018 - The site is occupied by a CVS Pharmacy and a Fresh and Easy grocery store (now closed), which replaced an earlier structure that was a Safeway grocery store.

Sutro Divsion - 1942 (2 years before it is acquired by Muni)

CVS Pharmacy and former Fresh & Easy Grocery Store - 2018

A Fleet History of the San Francisco Municipal Railway
Section 6: Divisions, Yards, Barns and Work Cars

Division Name	Location	Mode(s)	Active Years	Approx. Capacity
Elkton Shops	Ocean / San Jose Avenues	Streetcar	1944-1977	Not a regular operations division

History and Disposition

1907 - Elkton Shops is built and opened by United RR's in a lightly populated location named for an old train station very near to the Geneva Division. Elkton Shops was built with a focus on heavy duty maintenance activities.   1933 - The last of over 200 wooden streetcars is built at this site by MSRy employees. Muni #798 (former MSRy car) is the sole known survivor of this extraordinary accomplishment.   1944 - Merger between Muni and MSRy officially brought this facility into Muni ownership.   1948 - The east side of the property along San Jose Avenue is cleared and Ocean Division (buses) is built and opens for service.   1954 -Geneva Avenue is extended west using a slice of property that bi-sected the site. This separated the paint shop from the other buildings.   1969 - The paint shop is removed.   1973 - A new Powell-Hyde Cable Car - numbered Cable Car #1, to celebrate the Cable Car Centennial, is built at Elkton Shops.   1973 - The Balboa Park BART station opens for revenue service.   1977 - The new Metro Rail Center (renamed Green Division), built on eastern portion of Elkton Shops property and the former Ocean Bus Division (which closed in 1975), opens for service. 1977 - Elkton Shops is closed and the remaining buildings are removed.   1986 - The Green Annex building is opened.   2018 - The Green Division Rail Yard, Green Division Maintenance Buildings, part of I-280, part of Geneva Avenue and the Balboa Park BART station comprise the former Elkton Shops site.

Elkton Shops under construction - 1906

Elkton Shops - 1928

Elkton Shops - 1942
looking south on San Jose Avenue - The Geneva Car House Administration Building is in the far back left area of photo. Elkton Shops was the future site of Ocean Division (bus) 1948-1975, and Green Division (rail) 1977-present

A Fleet History of the San Francisco Municipal Railway
Section 6: Divisions, Yards, Barns and Work Cars

Elkton Shops - paint shop - 1942 - pre-Geneva Avenue addition (above) - and 1967 - after Geneva Avenue addition was built in 1954 (right)

Elkton Shops site - 1973 I-280 (foreground), Balboa Park BART (left), Elkton Shops (center), Ocean Division (right), Geneva Ave. cuts through the middle, parked cars in foreground are the former paint shop site, Ocean Division buses (foreground right)

Elkton Shops undergoing demolition - 1977

A Fleet History of the San Francisco Municipal Railway
Section 6: Divisions, Yards, Barns and Work Cars

Division Name	Location	Mode(s)	Active Years	Approx. Capacity
24th & Utah Division (aka 24th & Utah Barn)	24th / Utah Streets	Streetcar	1944-1952	75 (assumes 0 buses)
		Bus	1944-1994	130 40' (assumes 0 streetcars)

History and Disposition

1904 - The facility is built by United RRs (URR) as a streetcar barn with sixteen tracks and facilities for heavy duty repair work. 1921 - URR becomes the second Market Street Railway (MSRy). 1932 - Buses obtained for more lighly patronized routes begin to be stored and maintained at this location. 1944 - Merger between Muni and MSRy officially brings this facility into Muni ownership. 1952 - A large portion of the facility is destroyed in a fire that also destroyed 20 buses. The damaged area is rebuilt, and 24th & Utah is converted to be a bus only facility with a focus on heavy duty maintenance and special shop activities. 1978 - The new Woods Division and Central Shops facilities replace 24th & Utah as the primary heavy duty maintenance facility, but Muni continues to use the property for bus storage and some maintenance activites. 1994 - The facility is closed and the property is transferred to S. F. Dept. of Parking and Traffic (SFDPT) to become a parking garage for S.F. General Hospital. Special shop activity is mostly transferred to a Muni facility at 700 Pennsylvania Avenue, which does not operate as a transit division. 1999 - The SFDPT and Muni are merged to create a new agency, the San Francisco Municipal Transportation Agency (SFMTA). 2018 - The main parking garage for S.F. General Hospital is at this site.

24th & Utah Car House - 1904

24th & Utah Car House after merger - 1946.

24th & Utah Car House fire - 1952

Rebuilt division and shops - 1955

S.F. General Hospital Garage - 2018

A Fleet History of the San Francisco Municipal Railway
Section 6: Divisions, Yards, Barns and Work Cars

Division Name	Location	Mode(s)	Active Years	Approx. Capacity
Cable Car Barn	Washington / Mason Streets	Cable Car	1944-1982	42 cable cars
(aka Washington & Mason Barn)		Cable Car	1984-	42 cable cars

History and Disposition

1887 - The first barn is built for cable cars of the Ferries and Cliff House RR.   1902 - The railroad and barn are acquired by the newly formed United RRs, which transformed into the second MSRy in 1921.   1906 - The car barn is destroyed in the 1906 Earthquake, and is rebuilt.   1944 - Merger between Muni and MSRy officially brings this facility into Muni ownership, and results in the first operation of cable cars by Muni.   1957 - The cable for the California Cable Car Line is routed to the Washington & Mason location as part of the 1954-57 cable car consolidation and reconfiguration of service by Muni.   1960s - The building is painted white by Muni. 1967 - The museum opens inside the car barn.   1982 - The entire cable car system is shut down for a rebuild when widespread infrastructure and safety issues are found. Exterior walls are preserved, but the remainder of the building is entirely replaced. The rebuild lasted 18 months. 1984 - The cable car system and new car barn reopen.   2018 - The Cable Car Barn continues in service, complete with a museum and a small carpentry shop to perform woodwork often needed to keep the cars in operation.

Cable Car Barn (first) - 1904

Ruins after the 1906 Earthquake and fire.

Cable Car Barn (second) - 1921

Cable Car Barn (second) in white paint - 1965

A Fleet History of the San Francisco Municipal Railway
Section 6: Divisions, Yards, Barns and Work Cars

Cable Car Barn (third) during rebuild - 1983

Cable Car Barn (third) - 2017

Division Name	Location	Mode(s)	Active Years	Approx. Capacity
Ocean Division	Geneva / San Jose Avenues	Bus	1948-1975	150 40' buses

History and Disposition
1948 - The Ocean Division, built new by Muni, opens on a portion of the Elkton Shops facility. It was built as a division capable of only light maintenance (running repair) - similar to the other division opened a short time later - Kirkland.   1975 - The facility is closed and buildings are torn down to make space for the new Metro Rail Center.   2018 - The site is part of the Green Division (rail).

Ocean Division - 1949

Ocean Division demolition - 1975

A Fleet History of the San Francisco Municipal Railway
Section 6: Divisions, Yards, Barns and Work Cars

Division Name	Location	Mode(s)	Active Years	Approx. Capacity
Kirkland Division	Beach / Stockton Streets	Bus	1950-	125 40' buses

History and Disposition
1950 - The Kirkland Division opens near Fisherman's Wharf. The division is named for William B. Kirkland, who died in 1942. Kirkland was a former Southern Pacific RR official employed by the U.S. Army during WWII at this site when it was a rail yard serving nearby Fort Mason. Kirkland was built as a division capable of only light maintenance (running repair) - similar to the Ocean division opened in 1948.   1967 - A concept plan is drafted to replace the facility, but no action is taken.   2016 - A planning process to rebuild the 70 year-old division is initiated. A very tentative timeline calls for a new facility to open before 2030.

Kirkland Division - 1950

Kirkland Division - 2015

Division Name	Location	Mode(s)	Active Years	Approx. Capacity
California Cable RR Car Barn & Powerhouse	California / Hyde Streets	Cable Car	1952-1957	48 cable cars

History and Disposition
1890 - The facility is built with cable car storage on two levels, a powerhouse and winding machinery to pull the cables.   1906 - The car barn is damaged in the 1906 Earthquake, but is repaired.   1951 - The California St. Cable Car RR ceased operations when it could not obtain insurance. Essentially, the business was bankrupt. 1952 - Muni purchases the holdings of the company and begins service with the cars and staff operating from this location.   1957 - Muni centralizes cable car operations at the Washington and Mason Car Barn, and closes this location.   1960 - The property is sold and the facility is demolished.   A supermarket is built at the site. 2018 - A Trader Joes and CVS Pharmacy s are located at this site.

California St. Cable RR Barn - 1948

Trader Joe's Market & CVS Pharmacy - 2017

A Fleet History of the San Francisco Municipal Railway
Section 6: Divisions, Yards, Barns and Work Cars

Division Name	Location	Mode(s)	Active Years	Approx. Capacity
Woods Division (aka Central Shops)	22nd / Indiana Streets	Bus	1975-	225 40' buses

History and Disposition

1975- Muni's first new operations division in over 20 years, the Woods Division, named for former Muni General Manager John M. Woods, opens on the west side of Indiana Street at 22nd Street. While being developed, it was named the Tubbs Division after a short street at the southern end of the property, but the Woods name was adopted after the retirement of John M. Woods. 1977 - The large heavy maintenance area, sometimes known as Central Shops, but also often referred to as Woods Division, opens on the east side of Indiana Street at 22nd Street. The Central Shops complex replaced the 24th & Utah site as the heavy maintenance facility at Muni. A separate smaller building onsite (the Carpentry Shop) is built to specialize in woodworking and has become the main location for repair or replacement of cable cars. 2018 - Woods Division / Central Shops / Carpentry Shop continues to perform the role it was built for over 40 years ago. Renovations of some areas of the facility are planned for the near future.

Woods Division - Vacant parcels - except for dark colored warehouse (removed before new construction began) - 1974

Woods Division - Operations active - Carpentry Shop and Central Shops across Indiana Street are under construction - 1975

A Fleet History of the San Francisco Municipal Railway
Section 6: Divisions, Yards, Barns and Work Cars

Woods Division - Carpentry Shop (front) and Central Shops (rear) - 2018

Woods Division Bus Operations. - 2018

Woods Division - Central Shops (front) Carpentry Shop (rear) and Indiana Street - 2018

Division Name	Location	Mode(s)	Active Years	Approx. Capacity
Green Division (aka Metro Rail Division)	Geneva / San Jose Avenues	LRV Streetcar	1977- 2008-	100 75' LRVs (capacity included in number above)

History and Disposition
1977 - The Metro Rail Divison opens on the site of the former Elkton Shops facility. The Geneva Division (located across Geneva Avenue - which was renamed Cameron Beach Yard in 2012) becomes a support facility to the new Metro Rail Division. 1980 - The facility is renamed for Curtis E. Green; a former Muni General Manager. 1985 - A new building, known as Green Annex, is built adjacent to the the existing Green facility buildings. 2018 - The Green Division continues in service.

Model of Green Division - 1975

A Fleet History of the San Francisco Municipal Railway
Section 6: Divisions, Yards, Barns and Work Cars

Green Division under construction - 1976

Green Division and LRV Yard - 1985

Green Annex Bldg. - 2018

Green Division Shops - 2018

A Fleet History of the San Francisco Municipal Railway
Section 6: Divisions, Yards, Barns and Work Cars

Division Name	Location	Mode(s)	Active Years	Approx. Capacity
Army Street Yard	Army / 3rd Streets	Bus	1984-1995	100 60' buses

History and Disposition
1984 - This parcel located at Army St. (now Cesar Chavez St.) & 3rd Streets was leased at a time when Muni was desperately short on division space to park buses. The site is used to store about 100 new 60' articulated buses. The buses are serviced at the Woods Division.   1989 - The opening of Flynn Division eases the space issue significantly, but the location continues to be used to store "The Reserve Fleet".   1995 - The Army Street Yard is closed.

Army Street Yard 1985

Office Building 2018

Division Name	Location	Mode(s)	Active Years	Approx. Capacity
Flynn Division (aka Harrison St. Division)	15th / Harrison Streets	Bus	1989-	102 60' buses

History and Disposition
1989 - Muni rehabilitates a large covered warehouse built for U.S. Steel in 1941 and opens the Harrison Street Division, its first 60' articulated bus division. It was and continues to be Muni's only covered bus division.
1989 - The facility is renamed after H. Welton Flynn, a longtime member of S.F. Public Utilities Commission, and later a member of the SFMTA Board of Directors.   2018 - Flynn Division continues in service.

U.S. Steel Bldg - 1985

Flynn Division - 2018

A Fleet History of the San Francisco Municipal Railway
Section 6: Divisions, Yards, Barns and Work Cars

Division Name	Location	Mode(s)	Active Years	Approx. Capacity
Metro East Division (aka MME)	25th St. / Illinois St.	LRV Streetcar	2008- 2008-	125 75' LRVs (capacity included in number above)

History and Disposition
2008 - Adjacent to the newly opened T-LRV line, the Metro East Division (aka MME or Muni Metro East)) opens as the second LRV and streetcar facility with space to accommodate a planned expansion of the Muni rail fleet.
2018 - This division continues in service without major changes since it was opened.

Metro East Division - 2018

A Fleet History of the San Francisco Municipal Railway
Section 6: Divisions, Yards, Barns and Work Cars

Division Name	Location	Mode(s)	Active Years	Approx. Capacity
Islais Creek Division	22nd St. / Ceser Chavez St.	Bus	2014-	85 40' buses 80 60' buses

History and Disposition
2014 - Phase 1 of the Islais Creek Division (fuel, wash and parking) opens. The opening coincided with a large fleet replacement program, and this yard in coordination with leased property (adjacent Marin site) became the hub of the replacement program. The program is due to be completed in 2020 as old buses and trolley buses are removed from service and new ones are delivered and enter into service.   2018 - Phase 2 (heavy duty maintenance and administration) is completed, and the fully functional division enters service.

Islais Creek Division - Phase 1 - 2014

Islais Creek Division - Phase 2 model - 2015

Islais Creek Division Phase 1 (left) and Phase 2 (right) under construction 2018

Islais Creek Division Phase 2 under construction 2018

A Fleet History of the San Francisco Municipal Railway
Section 6: Divisions, Yards, Barns and Work Cars

A transit vehicle fleet not only consists of vehicles used in revenue service, but support and non-revenue vehicles that are required to perform different tasks. Work cars is a term used to designate non-revenue vehicles that assist revenue vehicles by performing special tasks. Tow trucks, electric overhead line maintenance vehicles, and pusher vehicles are examples of this type of vehicle. Other common non-revenue vehicles include cars and pickup trucks used by supervisors and repair staff.

In over a century of transit operations hundreds of non-revenue / work car vehicles have been in service at Muni. In more recent times, many have been leased from larger pools of vehicles that are procured by the City of San Francisco for all city agencies. A comprehensive list is not a part of this document, but the role these vehicles perform in the successful operation of Muni requires acknowledgement. Some of the more unique vehicles are truly one of a kind and pre-date World War II. They continue in service, because while very old, they still are able to perform the task they were designed to do. Others are newer, but just as unique, and will likely remain on site for several decades.

Perhaps the most famous work car is Streetcar #578, Muni's oldest operating streetcar, which came to Muni in the 1944 merger with the Market Street Railway. For over a decade Car #578, numbered as Car #0601, operated as a sand car, but in 1956 the car was restored to original appearance as an operational streetcar for the 50th anniversary of the 1906 Earthquake and Fire. Over 60 years later, Car #578 remains in service.

Below are a few of the many Work Cars and Non-Revenue vehicles that have been in service at Muni during the past 100+ years.

Car #0601 - operating as a sand car, was put to use as a campaign billboard to promote approval of Propositions 1-7 in the 1947 election

Truck #002 - at Potrero Division - 1927

157

A Fleet History of the San Francisco Municipal Railway
Section 6: Divisions, Yards, Barns and Work Cars

Work Car #C-1, which has been in service for over a century. It is parked near the Geary Carhouse in photo at left (1916), and is part of the N-Judah rail project photo at right (2012)

Overhead electric line maintenance vehicles in 1948 (left) and in 2014 (right)

Ford F1 pickup #00101 in Muni green and cream with "Wings paint scheme - 1954

Ford Escape pool car #7350001 - 2018

A Fleet History of the San Francisco Municipal Railway
Section 7: Figures and Graphics

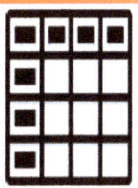

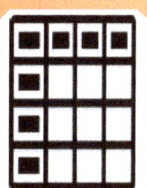

A Fleet History of the San Francisco Municipal Railway
Section 7: Figures and Graphics

A Fleet History of the San Francisco Municipal Railway
Section 7: Figures and Graphics

Figures and Graphics Information

This section contains tables and charts that summarize fleet and vehicle information. The assembled data shows the growth, contraction and most recently, growth again of the entire transit fleet. Information graphically displays the fleet size of all transit vehicle types, the lengths of service of all transit vehicle types, and the costs of each vehicle type when acquired by Muni.

A sub-section is present for each vehicle type comprised of an information table, which includes a number assigned to each vehicle type in the earlier sections. The number (e.g. #10) in the first column corresponds to the same number in the accompanying charts, that follow the table.

As the information shows, the cost of new transit vehicles has dramatically increased in the past 40 years, although the complexities of the vehicles have substantially increased too. The conversion from a streetcar based transit agency - with a few buses and trolley buses before World War II, to a bus and trolley bus based transit agency, with a few streetcars by the 1950s is very evident. The thriftiness of Muni and its acquisition of PCC streetcars in the late 1950s and early 1960 stands out, as does the cost of rehabilitation of old streetcars when compared to the purchase price of new LRVs. The same tables and analysis are present for buses and trolley buses and similar trends of increased cost and vehicle complexity are present.

The table on cable cars summarizes the known histories of each car, prior to Muni operations (if applicable), and after Muni operations (if applicable). Similar to the cable car table, a table summarizes information of all divisions, yards and barns, the approximate size of each site, its period of operation, and the current land use if the site is no longer owned or operated by the SFMTA. A map of S.F. shows the location of all Muni divisions, yards and barns past and present.

A short sub-section addresses the different logos and color schemes worn by Muni vehicles while in service during agency history.

A table shows a log of Muni annual ridership, revenue collection, and farebox recovery 1913-2016. An accompanying graph shows annual ridership for Muni over the same time period, plus MSRy data prior to the 1944 merger, along with census data for San Francisco 1910-2017. A second graph shows a record of the U.S. inflation rate 1913-2017, the Muni adult fare history, the average Muni fare collected, and Muni farebox recovery 1913-2016.

Finally the last table in this section lists the leadership of Muni as it evolved from a unit within the Public Works Department, to a unit of the San Francisco Public Utilities Commission, to a stand alone agency that in 2018 is a part of the San Francisco Municipal Transportation Agency (SFMTA).

A Fleet History of the San Francisco Municipal Railway
Section 7: Figures and Graphics

A summary information table of Muni streetcars / LRVs is below.

No.	Model	Service Numbers	Number in Service	Year Built	First Year in Muni Service	Last Year in Muni Service	Seats	Length
1	A	1-20*	20	1912	1912	1951	48	47'1"
2	A	21-43	22	1913	1913	1951	48	47'1"
3	G	301-329	29	1895-1898	1913	1922	26	26'10"
4	B	44-168*	124	1913-1914	1913	1958	50	47'1"
5	J	352-371	20	1922	1922	1948	32	29'10"
6	K	169-188	20	1923	1923	1958	50	47'1"
7	L	189-213	25	1926-1928	1926	1958	50	47'1"
8	C	1001-1005	5	1939	1939	1959	60	50'5"
9	N/A	M101-M180**	79	1911	1944	1949	46	47'0"
10	N/A	M200-M265	65	1913	1944	1950	50	47'0"
11	N/A	M266-M285 M286-M305	20 20	1920-1921 1924-1925	1944 1944	1949 1949	44 44	47'0" 47'0"
12	N/A	M778-M808 M809-M994	31 185	1923-1924 1926-1933	1944 1944	1948 1950	50 50	47'0" 47'0"
13	N/A	M735-M736	2	1916	1944	1946	40	43'9"
14	G	Mo601(578)	1	1896 1956	1944 1956	in service	26	26'10"
15	N/A	M740-M749	10	1918	1944	1946	40	42'0"
16	N/A	M1225-M1244	18	1903	1944	1949	46	48'1"
17	N/A	San Francisco	1	1901	1944	1948	26	37'0"
18	N/A	M1553-M1722	9	1906-1907	1944	1949	44	46'4"
19	N/A	M788(II)	1	1948	1944	1948	44	47'0"
20	N/A "Torpedoes"	1006-1015	25	1948	1948	1982	59	50'5"
21	N/A "Baby Tens"	1016-1040***	25	1951-1952	1952	1982	58	46'5.5"
22	N/A	1101-1166	66	1946	1957	1982	53	46"0"
23	N/A	1167-1170	4	1946	1962	1982	53	46'0"

A Fleet History of the San Francisco Municipal Railway
Section 7: Figures and Graphics

Manufacturer / Seller	Manufacturer Location	Cost	2017 Fleet	Muni Historic Fleet	Saved in Museum
W.L. Holman Brookville Equip Company (Car #1) (2012)	San Francisco, CA Brookville, PA	$7,700 $1.3 M		X	X
Union Iron Works	San Francisco, CA	$7,700			
Hammond Car Company purchased as part of Presidio & Ferries RR	San Francisco, CA	N/A		X	
Jewett Car Company S.F. Municipal Railway - Woods Div. (Car #130 & Car #162) (1983, 2008) Carlos Guzman, Inc. (Car #162) (2017)	Newark, OH San Francisco, CA Long Beach, CA	$7,100		X X	
American Car Company	Philadelphia, PA	$11,500			
Bethlehem Steel	San Francisco, CA	$16,500			
St. Louis Car Company	St. Louis, MO	$19,200			
St. Louis Car Company	St. Louis, MO	$22,400			X
Jewett Car Company	Newark, OH	N/A**			
American Car Company	Philadelphia, PA	N/A			
Market Street Railway -Elkton Shops	San Francisco, CA	N/A			
Market Street Railway -Elkton Shops Brookville Equip. Co. (Car #798) (2018)	San Francisco, CA Brookville, PA	N/A $2.0M		X	
J.G Brill Company	Philadelphia, PA	N/A			
Hammond Car Company S.F Municipal Railway - Elkton Shops	San Francisco, CA San Francisco, CA	N/A unknown		X	
St. Louis Car Company	St. Louis, MO	N/A			
Laclede Car Company	St. Louis, MO	N/A			
St. Louis Car Company	St. Louis, MO	N/A			X
St. Louis Car Comapny	St. Louis, MO	N/A			
Market Street Railway -Elkton Shops	San Francisco, CA	N/A			
St . Louis Car Company	St. Louis, MO	$27,500		X	X
St. Louis Car Company	St. Louis, MO	$37,750		X	X
St. Louis Car Company (purchased from St. Louis Public Transport)	St. Louis, MO	$7,400		X	X
St. Louis Car Company (purchased from Toronto Transit Commission)	St. Louis, MO	$6,800			X

A Fleet History of the San Francisco Municipal Railway
Section 7: Figures and Graphics

No.	Model	Service Numbers	Number in Service	Year Built	First Year in Muni Service	Last Year in Muni Service	Seats	Length
24	N/A	1180-1190	11	1946	1974	1979	50	46'5"
25	USSLRV	1200-1299	100	1977	1979	2003	68	71'0"
26	USSLRV	1300-1329	30	1981	1982	2003	68	71'0"
27	LRV2	1400-1473	75	1996-1999	1997	in service	60	75'0"
28	LRV3	1474-1500	76	2000-2013	2000	in service	60	75'0"
29	LRV4****	2000 series	10 (175)	2017	2017	in service	60	75'0"
30	Big Tens or Torpedoes	1000 series	3	(1948) 1995	1995	in service	60	50'6"
31	Philadelphia PCCs	1000 series	14	(1948) 1995	1995	in service	47	46'8.2"
32	Milans	1800 series	11	(1928) 1998	1998	in service	30	45'7"
32	Minneapolis-Newark PCCs	1000 series	11	(1946) 2007	2007	in service	50	46'5"
33	Torpedoes II***	1000 series	5	(1948-1952) 2012	2012	in service	60/50	50'5"/ 46'5"
34	Shoreline Museum Topedoes	1012-1013	2	2018	2018-19	in storage - pending restoration	60	50'5"
35	Non Op. PCCs Baby Tens II	N/A	11	1951-1952	N/A	N/A	50	46'5"
36	Non Op. PCCs St. Louis Cars II	N/A	6	1946-1947	N/A	N/A	50	46'0"-46'5"
37	Non Op. PCCs Disposition Fleet	N/A	12	1946-1952	N/A	N/A	50-59	46'0"-46'8.2"
38	Wheels of the World *****	N/A	18	1923-1954	1995	some in service	N/A	N/A

Notes

* Streetcars #1, #130, #162 and #798 are not shown separately in this table, although they also have undergone extensive rebuild / rehabilitation to allow them to be in service vehicles in 2018.

** Streetcars acquired via MSRy merger are designated with an 'M' prefix to differentiate from Muni cars.

*** Streetcar #1040 (last U.S. built PCC) is active in service following rehabilitation as part of Vehicle Group #33 - Torpedoes II and a Baby Ten.

A Fleet History of the San Francisco Municipal Railway
Section 7: Figures and Graphics

Manufacturer / Seller	Manufacturer Location	Cost	2018 Fleet	Muni Historic Fleet	Saved in Museum
St. Louis Car Company (purchased from Toronto Transit Commission)	St. Louis, MO	$1,800			X
Boeing-Vertol Company	Norton, PA	$310,000			X
Boeing-Vertol Company	Norton, PA	$715,000			
Breda Construzioni Ferrovarie	Pistoia, Italy/ South S.F., CA	$1,800,000	X		
Breda Construzioni Ferrovarie	Pistoia, Italy/ South S.F., CA	$1,800,000	X		
Siemens Corporation	Sacramento, CA	$3,700,000	X		
St. Louis Car Company (original) Morrison-Knudsen (refurbishment)	St. Louis, MO Hornell, NY	See #14 $1,500,000	X		
St. Louis Car Company (orignial) Morrison-Knudsen (1st refurbishment) Brookville Equip. Co. (2nd refurbishment)	St. Louis, MO Hornell, NY Brookville, PA	$12,000 $1,500,000 $1,000,000	X	X	
Carminati & Toselli San Francisco Municipal Railway	Milan, Italy San Francisco, CA	$30,000 SF rehab	X	X	
St. Louis Car Co. (original) Brookville Equipment Co.	St. Louis, MO Brookville, PA	$15,000 $700,000	X	X	
St. Louis Car Co. (original) Brookville, Equpment Co.	St. Louis, MO Brookville, PA	See #14,15 $2.0-$2.5M		X	
St. Louis Car Co. (original) Brookville Equipment Co.	St. Louis, MO Brookville, PA	$84,500 TBD		X	
St. Louis Car Co.	St. Louis, MO	N/A			
St. Louis Car Co.	St. Louis, MO	N/A			
St. Louis Car Co.	St. Louis, MO	N/A			
Various manufacturers around the U.S. and the world	Various cities around the U.S. and the world	Wide range of purchase / restoration cost		X	

Notes
**** A total of 175 LRV4s have been purchased, and 40 more are authorized and funded for future delivery.
***** The Wheels of the World Fleet has been loosely defined to focus on the old and unique streetcars from around the world, which in this book has included the five pre-PCC Muni historic streetcars: #1, #130, #162, #578, and #798.

165

A Fleet History of the San Francisco Municipal Railway
Section 7: Figures and Graphics

A summary information table of Muni streetcars / LRVs is shown on these pages

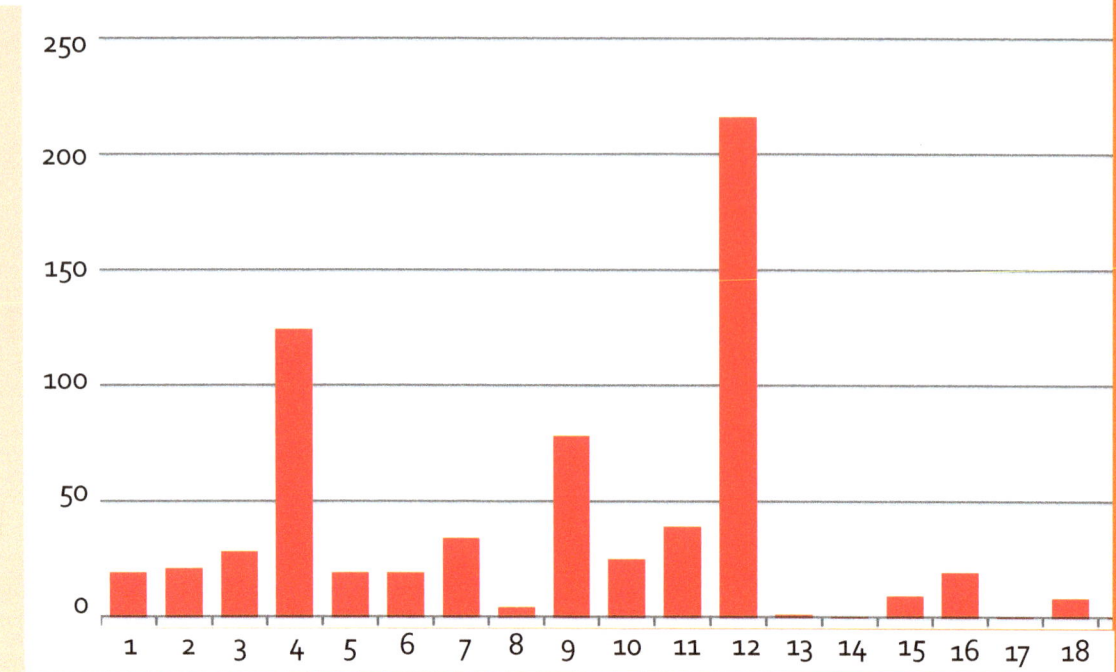

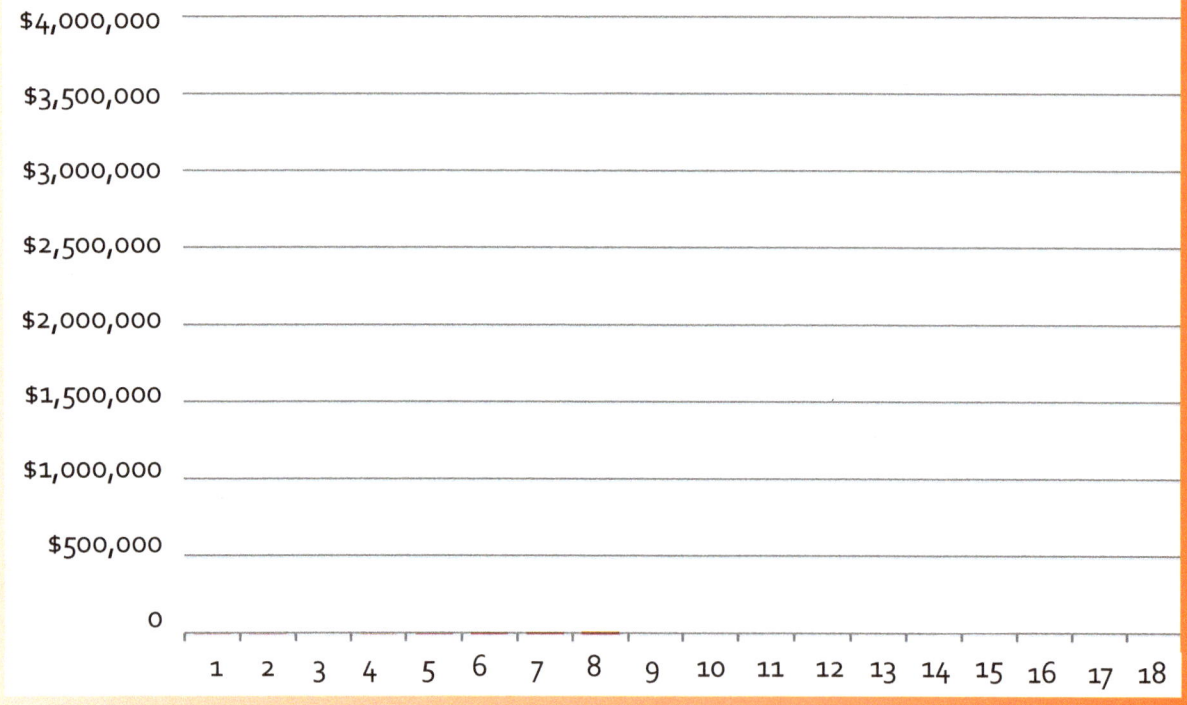

A Fleet History of the San Francisco Municipal Railway
Section 7: Figures and Graphics

Table with information used in graph - See pages 162-165

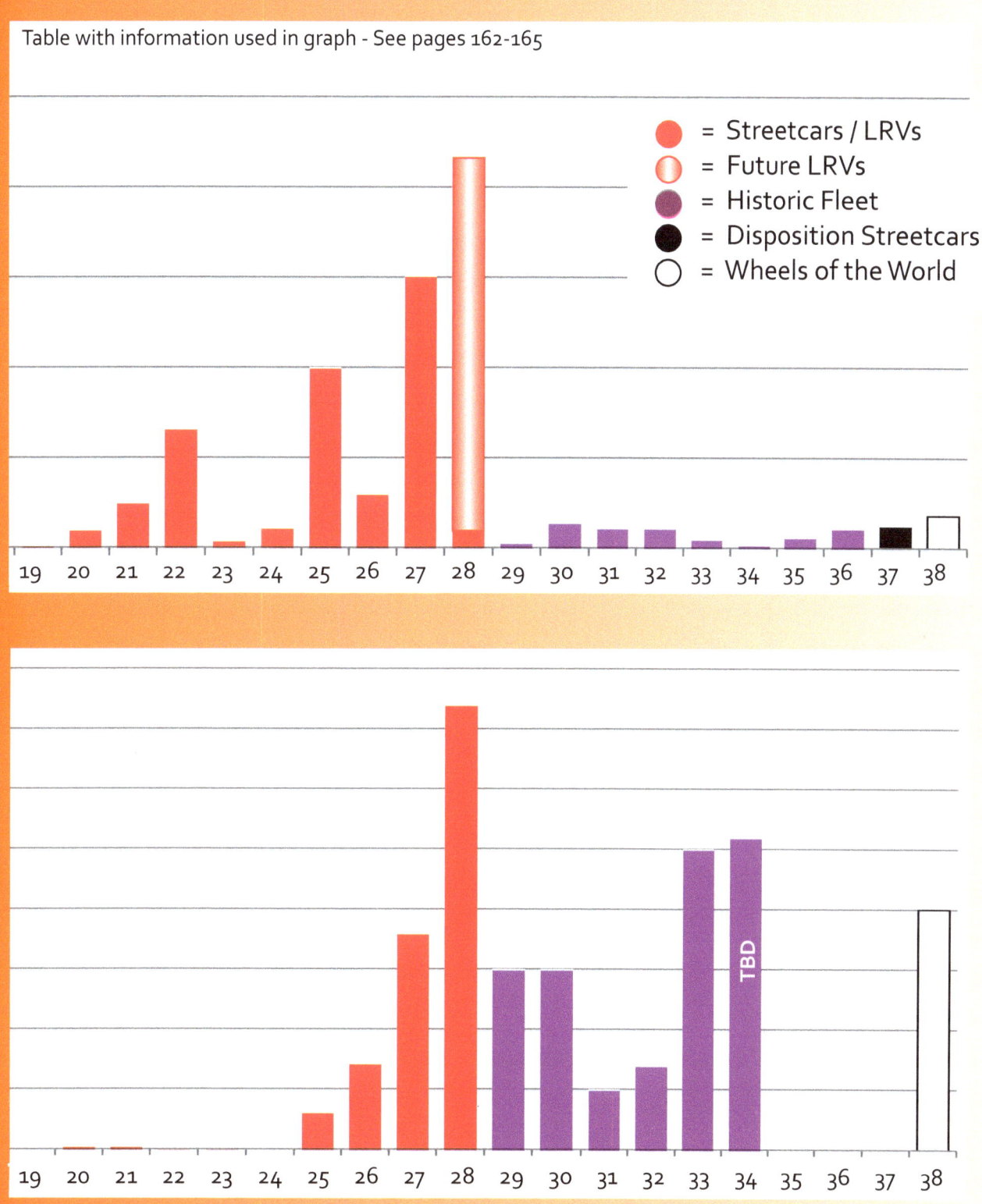

A Fleet History of the San Francisco Municipal Railway
Section 7: Figures and Graphics

A summary information table of Muni buses is below.

No.	Model	Service Numbers	Number in Service	Year Built	First Year in Service	Last Year in Service	Seats	Length
1	TDB	01-06	6	1918	1918	1927	19	20'6"
2	20-45	07-09	3	1920	1920	1930	18	??
3	50A	010-012	3	1924	1924	1931	25	??
4	Z	013-015	3	1925	1925	1933	29	25'
5	AB	016-017	2	1927	1927	1934	29	??
6	Streetcar	018-019	2	1927	1927	1937	29	??
7	50A	020-021	2	1927	1927	1934	29	??
8	AB	022-024	3	1927	1927	1938	29	??
9	105	025	1	1927	1927	1938	29	??
10	BK	026	1	1929	1929	1938	29	??
11	160	027-029	3	1930	1930	1938	28	??
12	155-6	030-031	2	1931	1931	1938	27	??
13	54	032-033	2	1933	1933	1941	29	??
14	684	034-036	3	1934	1934	1955	32	??
		037-038	2	1936	1936	1955	32	??
		039-040	2	1937	1937	1955	32	??
15	784	041-062	22	1938	1938	1975	32	30'0"
16	26-S	063-072	10	1941	1941	1954	26	30'0"
17	31-S	074-075	2	1941	1941	1954	31	32'0"
18	1932	M8	1	1932	1944	1946	30	
19	T-26-C	M21	1	193	1944	1946	17	14'1"
20	23-R	M25-M28*	4	1937	1944-	1946	23	22'9"
21	739	M30-M41	12	1939	1944	1948	25	24'2"
		M60-M76	17	1939	1944	1948	27	24'2"
22	731	M101-M120	20	1939-1940	1944	1948	36	30'10"
23	TG-3601	M121-M122	2	1940	1944	1955	36	30'5"
		M150-M159	9	1941	1944	1955	36	30'5"
		M160-M166	7	1942	1944	1954	36	30'5"
24	TG-3201	M201-M207	7	1939	1944	1953	32	28'0"
25	TG-3601	M301-M311	11	1940	1944	1955	36	30'5"
26	TG-4502	M401-M430	30	1941	1944	1955	37	30'5"
		M431-M433	3	1942	1944	1955	37	30'5"
27	TG-4505	M1-M16	16	1941	1944	1955	45	34'10"

A Fleet History of the San Francisco Municipal Railway
Section 7: Figures and Graphics

Manufacturer / Seller	Manufacturer Location	Cost	2017 Fleet	Muni Historic Fleet	Saved in museum
Meister & Sons	Sacramento, CA	$4,500 est.			
White Motor Motor Company.	Cleveland, OH	$4,500 est.			
White Motor Motor Company	Cleveland, OH	$5,000 est.			
Pierce-Arrow Motor Company	Buffalo, NY	$5,850			
Mack Truck	Allentown, PA	$5,500 est.			
Fageol Motors	Oakland, CA	$7,000 est.			
White Motor Company	Cleveland, OH	$7,500 est.			
Mack Truck	Allentown, PA	$7,500 est.			
Fageol Motors	Oakland, CA	$8,000 est.			
Mack Truck	Allentown, PA	$7,500 est.			
Fageol Motors	Oakland, CA	$8,000 est.			
Fageol Motors	Oakland, CA	$8,000 est.			
White Motor Company	Cleveland, OH	$9,724			
White Motor Company White Motor Company White Motor Company	Cleveland, OH	$9,855 $10,278 $10,117			
White Motor Company	Cleveland, OH	$10,328		X	X
ACF Brill Motor Company	Philadelphia, PA	$7,933			
ACF Brill Motor Company	Philadelphia, PA	$9,969			
Fageol Motors	Oakland, CA	N/A			
Yellow Coach (General Motors)	Pontiac, MI	N/A			
Twin Coach	Kent, OH	N/A*			
Yellow Coach (General Motors) Yellow Coach (General Motors)	Pontiac, MI	N/A* $7,365*			
Yellow Coach (General Motors)	Pontiac, MI	$9,822*			
Yellow Coach (General Motors) Yellow Coach (General Motors) Yellow Coach (General Motors)	Pontiac, MI	10,916* 12,105* 13,328*			
Yellow Coach (General Motors)	Pontiac, MI	9,513*			
Yellow Coach (General Motors)	Pontiac, MI	$13,000			
Yellow Coach (General Motors) Yellow Coach (General Motors)	Pontiac, MI	12,650* 13,354*			
Yellow Coach (General Motors)	Pontiac, MI	$6,606*			

A Fleet History of the San Francisco Municipal Railway
Section 7: Figures and Graphics

No.	Model	Service Numbers	Number in Service	Year Built	First Year in Service	Last Year in Service	Seats	Length
28	798	075-078	4	1944	1944	1955	44	35'0"
		079-0125	47	1944	1944	1955	44	35'0"
		0126-0155	30	1946	1946	1955	44	35'0"
29	44D	0156-0165	10	1947	1947	1953	46	36'1"
30	798	0166-0195	30	1947	1947	1955	39	35'0"
		0196-0454	258	1948	1948	1969	44	35'0"
31	C49-DT	2100-2199	100	1955	1955	1969	48	38'6"
		2200-2269	70	1956	1956	1970	48	38'6"
		2300-2369	70	1957	1957	1970	48	38'6"
		2400-2469	70	1958	1958	1970	48	38'6"
		2500-2569	70	1959	1959	1979	48	38'6"
		2600-2669	70	1960	1960	1979	48	38'6"
32	T8H-5305	3000-3179	180	1969	1969	1993	48	39'0"
	TBH-5305A	3180-3189	10	1969	1969	1993	48	39'0"
	T8H-5305	3190-3390	201	1969	1969	1993	48	39'0"
33	111-CC-C3	4001-4009	10	1969	1969	1979	48	39'0"
34	9635-6	4101-4200	100	1974	1974	1991	41	35'0"
35	MPL-570	4030-4054	25	1980	1980	1985	46	40'0"
36	TDH-4801	2700-2749	50	1954	1981	1982	48	39'0"
	TDH-5105	2800-2807	8	1958	1981	1982	50	39'0"
	TDH-4812	2900-2901	2	1958	1981	1982	45	39'0"
37	517	700 series	6	1962	1983	1983	45	40'0"
38	SG-310	6000-6099	100	1984	1984	2002	57	60'0"
39	D-902	4500-4679	180	1984	1984	2004	40	40'0"
40	D40-80	8801-8850	50	1988	1988	2002	40	40'0"
	D40-80	8901-8956	56	1989	1989	2003	40	40'0"
41	Orion II	9000-9045	46	1991	1991	2007	26	31'7"
42	D60	9101-9124	24	1991	1991	2007	52	60'0"
43	D900-9635	300 series	9	1980	1994	1998	40	40'0"
	D900-10235	600 series	13	1980	1994	1998	40	40'0"
44	Model 416	8001-8045	45	1999	1999	2016	38	40'0"
45	Phantom	2800-2845	45	1993	2000	2012	38	40'0"
46	AN440	8101-8235	135	2002	2000		38	40'0"
		8301-8371	71	2003	2003		38	40'0"
47	AN460	6200-6225	26	2002	2002	2016	55	60'0"
		6226-6299	74	2002	2002	2016	55	60'0"
		6401-6424	24	2003	2003	2016	55	60'0"

A Fleet History of the San Francisco Municipal Railway
Section 7: Figures and Graphics

Manufacturer / Seller	Manufacturer Location	Cost	2017 Fleet	Muni Historic Fleet	Saved in museum
White Motor Company	Cleveland, OH	$12,362			
White Motor Company		$12,429			
White Motor Company		$13,024			
Fageol-Twin Coach	Kent, OH	$15,187		X	
White Motor Company	Cleveland, OH	$15,811		X	
White Motor Company		$16,286			
Mack Truck	Allentown, PA	$25,000		X	X
Mack Truck		$25,000			
Mack Truck		$25,000			
Mack Truck		$25,000			
Mack Truck		$25,000			
Mack Truck		$25,000			
General Motors	Pontiac, MI	$38,500		X	X
General Motors		$38,500			
General Motors		$38,500			
Flxible Corporation	Loudonville, OH	$40,000 est.		X	
AM General Corporation	South Bend, IN	$59,000		X	
Grumman-Flxible Corporation	Delaware, OH	$115,000		X	
General Motors	Pontiac, MI	$100 per month lease			X
General Motors					
General Motors					
General Motors (leased from AC Transit)	Pontiac, MI	$8,000 lease			
M.A.N.	Cleveland, NC	$211,000		X	
Flyer Industries, Ltd.	Winnipeg, MT	$144,000		X	
Flyer Industries, Ltd.	Winnipeg, MT	$180,000		X	
Flyer Industries, Ltd.		$180,000			
Orion Corporation	Winnipeg, MT	$165,000		X	
		$165,000			
New Flyer Industries, Ltd.	Mississagua, ON / Grand Forks, ND	$285,000		X	
Flyer Industries, Ltd. (bought from SamTrans)	Winnipeg, MT	$15,000			
		$15,000			
North American Bus Industris (NABI)	Anniston, AL	$315,000			
Gillig Corporation (bought from AC Transit)	Hayward, CA	$25,000		X	
Neoplan USA	Lamar, CO	$323,000	X		
Neoplan USA		$323,000			
Neoplan USA	Lamar, CO	$431,000		X	
Neoplan USA		$431,000			
Neoplan USA		$431,000			

A Fleet History of the San Francisco Municipal Railway
Section 7: Figures and Graphics

No.	Model	Service Numbers	Number in Service	Year Built	First Year in Service	Last Year in Service	Seats	Length
48	Model VII	8401-8456	56	2006	2006		35	40'0"
49	Model VIII	8501-8530	30	2007	2007		27	30'0"
50	XDE40	8601-8622	22	2013	2013		37	40'0"
		8701-8750	50	2014	2014		37	40'0"
		8751-8780	30	2017	2017		37	40'0"
		8800-8901	102	2016	2016		37	40'0"
		8902-8969	68	2018	2018		37	40'0"
51	XDE60	6500-6554	55	2015	2015		46	60'0"
		6560-6584	25	2016	2015		46	60'0"
		6585-6628	44	2016	2016		46	60'0"
		6629-6697	69	2017	2017		46	60'0"
		6700-6705	6	2015	2015		46	60'0"
		6706-6730	25	2016	2016		46	60'0"

Notes

* The cost for Yellow Coach buses M121-M122, M150-M159, M160-M166, M201-M207, M301-M311, M401-M433, and M2-M16 is based on a price listed by an audit of the equipment obtained from MSRy in the 1944 merger. It is unknown if the prices are based upon an "acquired value" of the vehicles, or their "price when new".

A Fleet History of the San Francisco Municipal Railway
Section 7: Figures and Graphics

Manufacturer / Seller	Manufacturer Location	Cost	2017 Fleet	Muni Historic Fleet	Saved in museum
Daimler-Chrysler (Orion) Bus	Mississagua, ON / Oriskany, NY	$488,000 / $488,000	X		
Daimler-Chrysler (Orion) Bus	Mississagua, ON / Oriskany, NY	$521,000 / $521,000	X		
New Flyer Industries - Allison New Flyer Industries - BAE New Flyer Industries - Allison New Flyer Industries - BAE New Flyer Industries - BAE	St. Cloud, MN	$789,000 $730,000 $789,000 $730,000 $730,000	X		
New Flyer Industries - Allison New Flyer Industries - Allison New Flyer Industries - Allison New Flyer Industries - Allison New Flyer Industries - BAE New Flyer Industries - BAE	St. Cloud, MN	$1,042,000 $1,042,000 $1,042,000 $1,042,000 $1,025,000 $1,025,000	X		

A Fleet History of the San Francisco Municipal Railway
Section 7: Figures and Graphics

A summary information graphic of Muni buses is shown on these pages

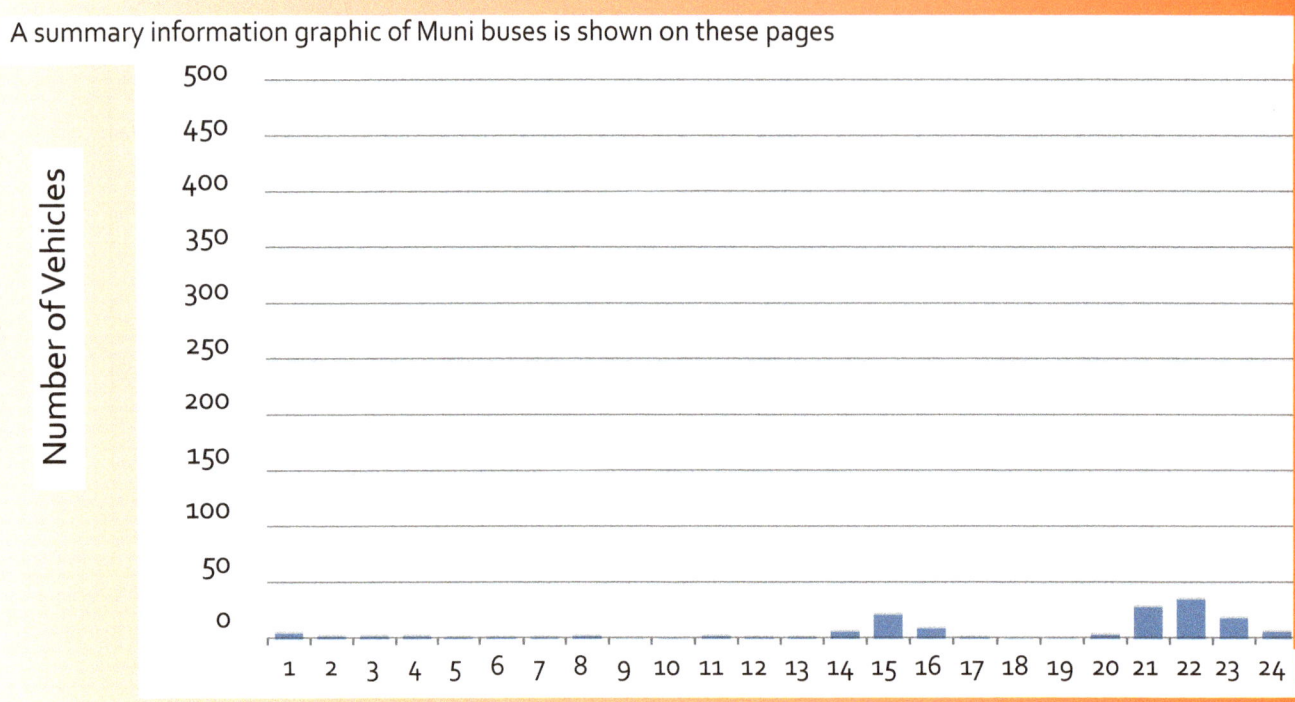

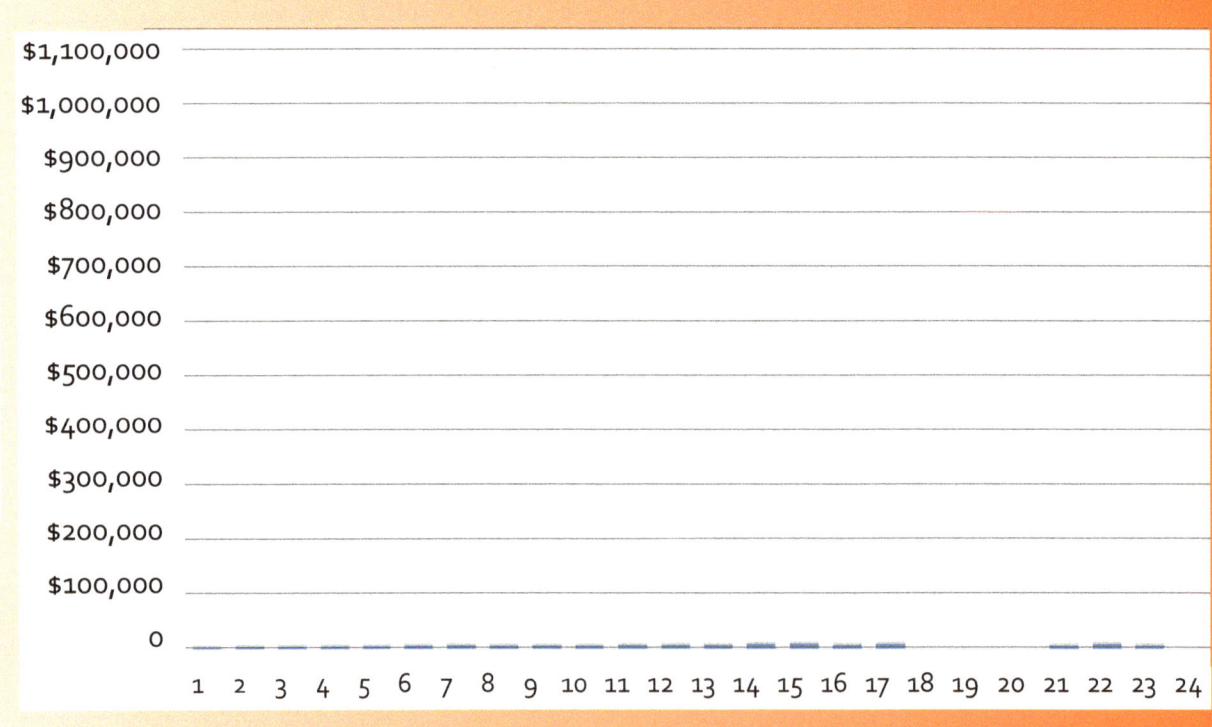

A Fleet History of the San Francisco Municipal Railway
Section 7: Figures and Graphics

Table with information used in graph - See pages 168-173

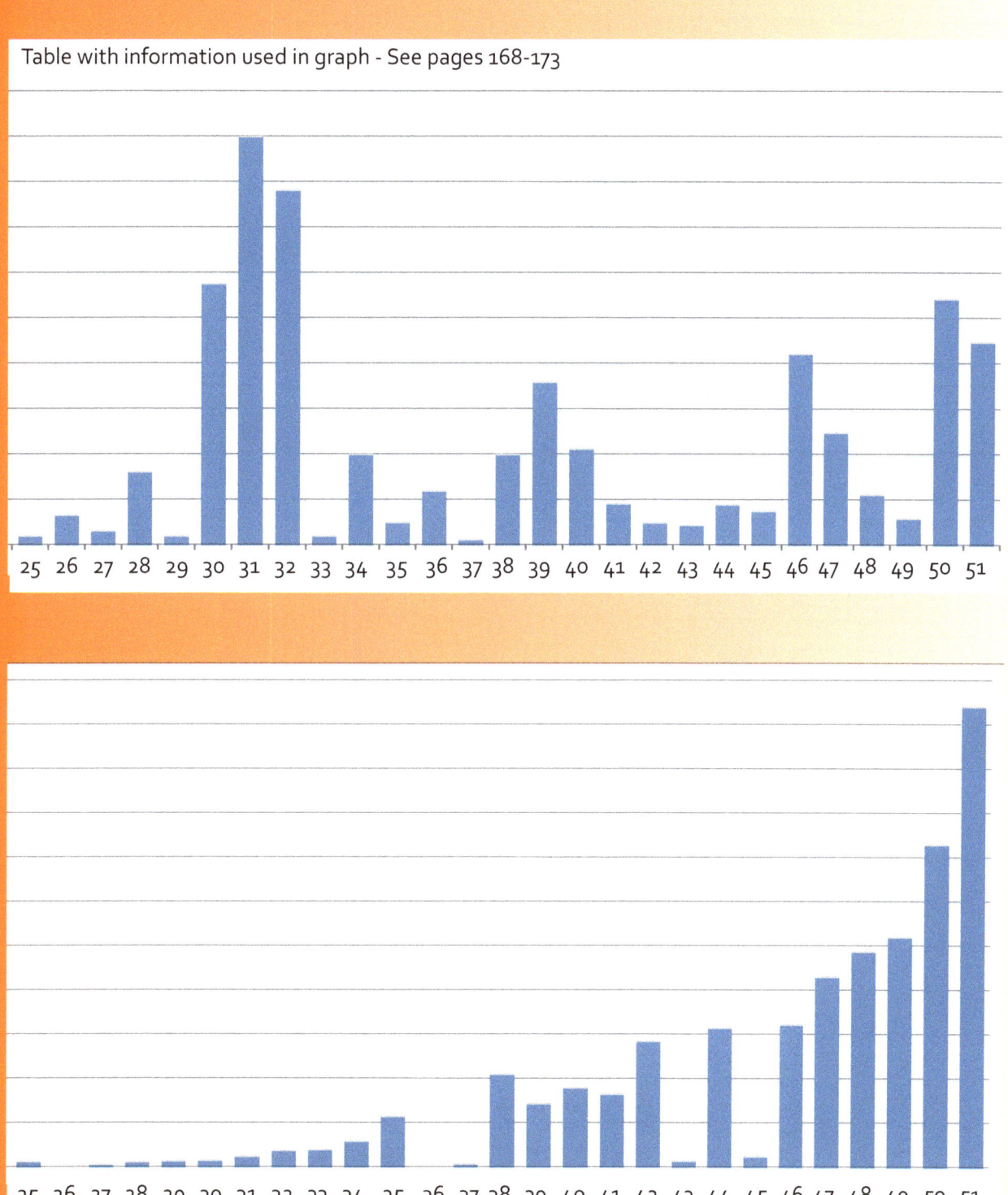

A Fleet History of the San Francisco Municipal Railway
Section 7: Figures and Graphics

A summary information table of Muni trolley buses is below.

No.	Model	Service Numbers	Number in Service	Year Built	First Year in Service	Last Year in Service	Seats	Length
1		501-509	9	1941	1941	1954	40	34'9"
2		M51-M59	9	1935	1944	1954	37	33'0"
3		511-525	15	1947	1947	1954	40	34'11"
4	TC40	526-549	25	1948	1948	1957	40	34'1"
5	TC44	550-569 660-710 711-739	20 51 29	1949 1949 1949	1949 1949 1949	1976 1976 1976	44 44 44	36'7" 36'7" 36'7"
6	44TTW	570-659	90	1949	1949	1976	44	36'1"
7	TC48	740-789 790-849	50 60	1950 1950	1950 1950	1976 1976	48 48	39'3" 39'3"
8	Job 1767	850-889	40	1952	1952	1976	48	39'0"
9	E700A	5001	1	1970	1970	2007	51	40'0"
10	E700A	5002	1	1973	1973	2007	44	40'0"
11	E20240	5003-5343	340	1973	1973	2007	50	40'0"
12	E20240	5344-5345	2	1978	1978	2007	50	40'0"
13	E60	7000-7059	60	1994	1994	2005	57	60'0"
14	14TrSF	5401-5640	230	2002	2002		38	40'0"
15	15TrSF	7101-7233	133	2003	2003	2016	52	60'0"
16	XT60	7201-7260 7261-7293	60 33	2015 2016	2015 2016		46	60'0"
17	XT40	5701-5885	185	2017	2018		32	40'0"

A Fleet History of the San Francisco Municipal Railway
Section 7: Figures and Graphics

Manufacturer / Seller	Manufacturer Location	Cost	2017 Fleet	Muni Historic Fleet	Saved in museum
St. Louis Car Company	St. Louis, MO	$13,200		X	
J.G. Brill Company	Philadelphia, PA	$13,694		X	
St. Louis Car Company	St. Louis, MO	$19.000			
Marmon-Herrington Company	Indianapolis, IN	$19,000			
Marmon-Herrington Company	Indianapolis, IN	$19,000			
Fageol-Twin Coach Company	Kent, OH	$19,000			
Marmon-Herrington Company	Indianapolis, IN	$17,800		X	
St. Louis Car Company	St. Louis, MO	$20,750			
Flyer Company	Winnipeg, MB	$50,000			
Flyer Company	Winnipeg, MB	$50,000			
Flyer Company	Winnipeg, MB	$74,000		X	
Flyer Company	Winnipeg, MB	$74,000		X	
New Flyer Company	Winnipeg, MB Grand Forks, ND	$630,000		X	
ETI Incorporated	Ostrov, Czech Rep. Hunt Valley, MD	$589,000	X		
ETI Incoporated	Ostrov, Czech, Rep. Hunt Valley, MD	$849,000			
New Flyer Company	Winnipeg, MB Grand Forks, ND	$1,374,000	X		
New Flyer Company	Winnipeg, MB Grand Forks, ND	$1,185,000	X		

A Fleet History of the San Francisco Municipal Railway
Section 7: Figures and Graphics

A summary information table of Muni trolley buses is shown on these pages

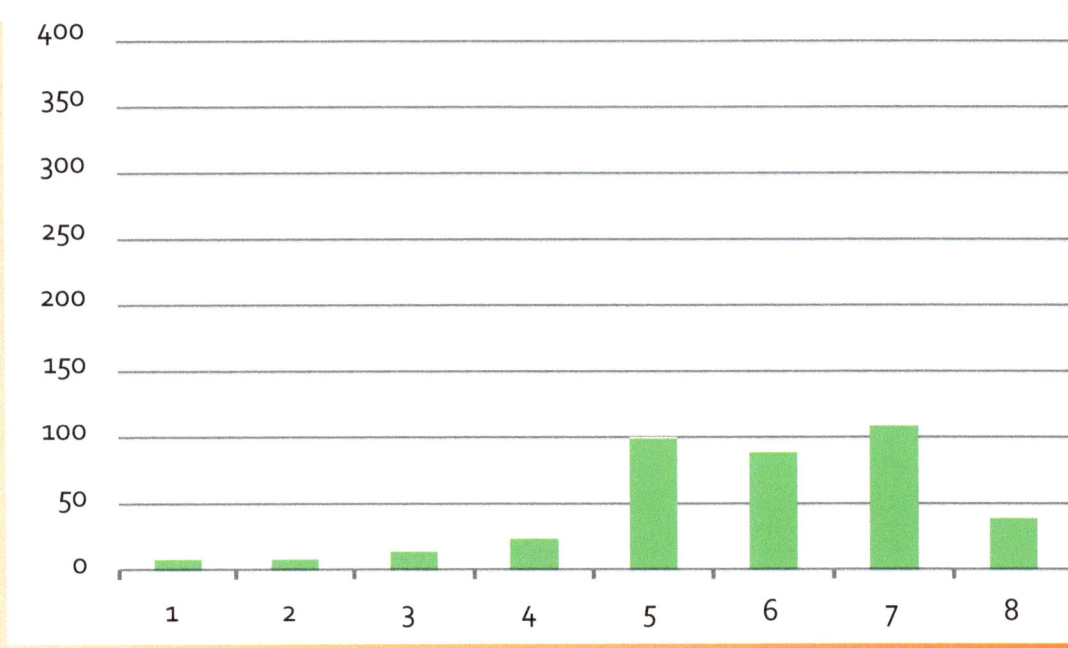

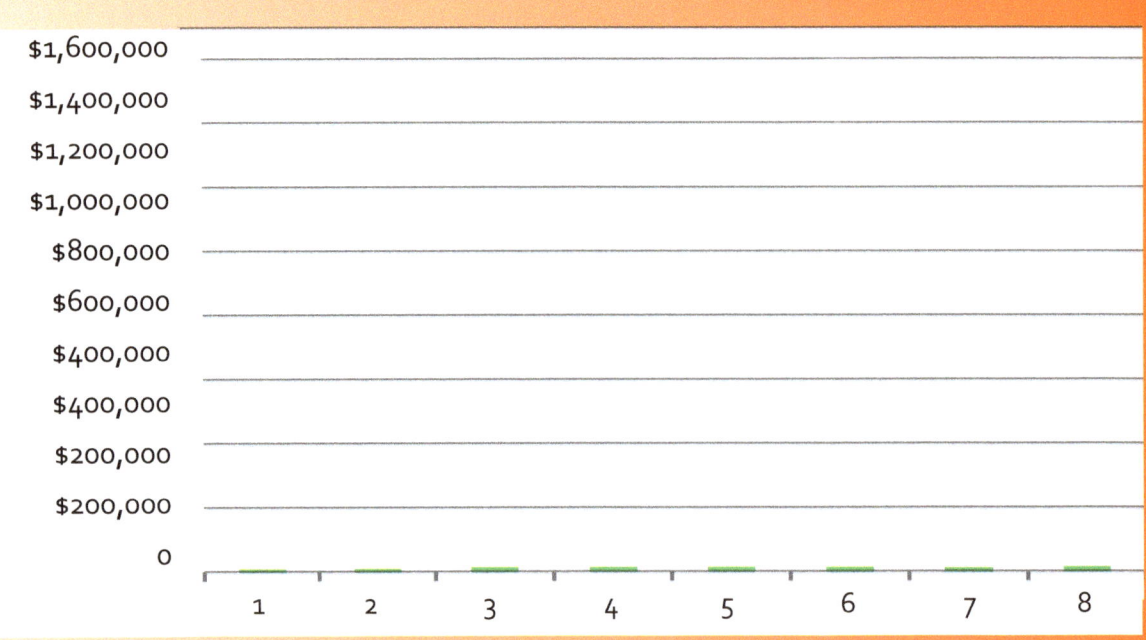

A Fleet History of the San Francisco Municipal Railway
Section 7: Figures and Graphics

Table with information used in graph - See pages 176-177

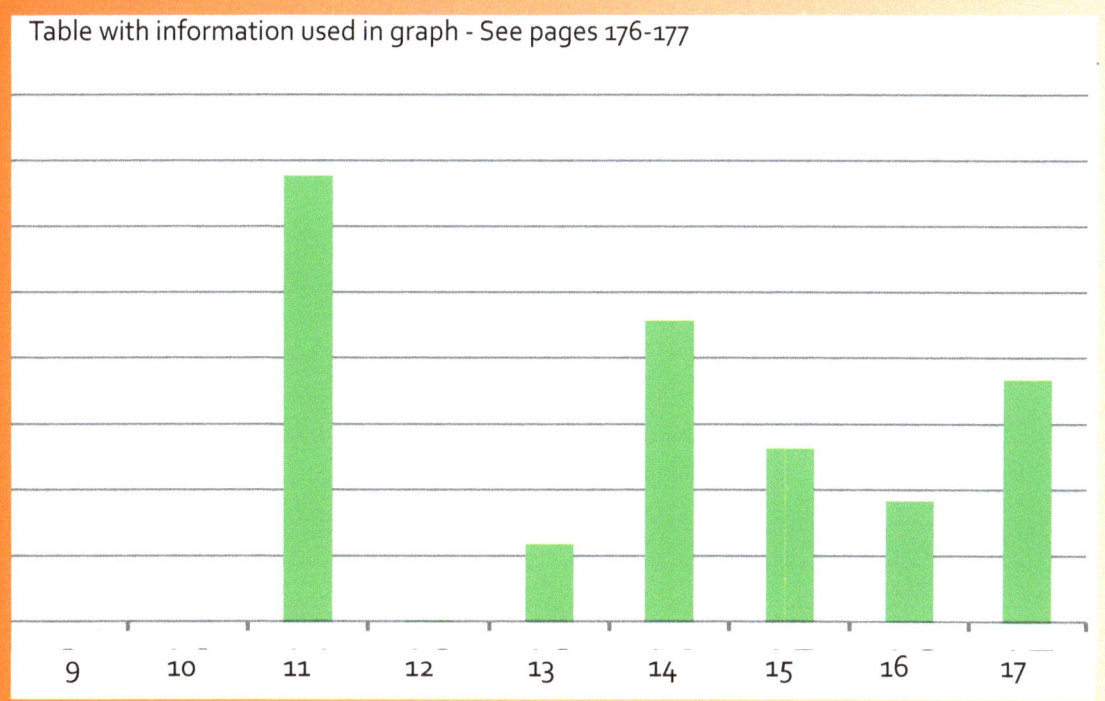

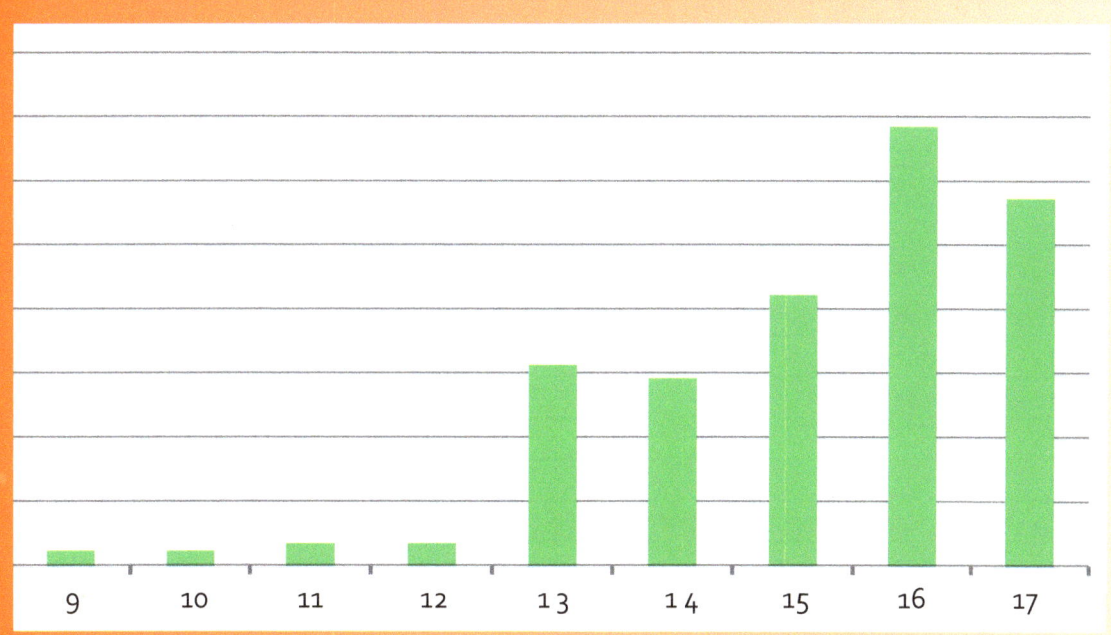

A Fleet History of the San Francisco Municipal Railway
Section 7: Figures and Graphics

Powell Cable Car Fleet List - 2018

Color Codes	= in Muni service as a cable car	= renumbered - see other Car #
	= in service as a motorized cable car	= status unknown
	= in storage	= scrapped / destroyed
	= in a museum	

No.	Disposition
1	On Muni active fleet roster
2 / 502	On Muni active fleet roster
3 / 503	On Muni active fleet roster
4 (1) / 504	On display Oracle Park, San Francisco, CA - renumbered as Car #44
4 (2)	On Muni active fleet roster
5 / 505	On Muni active fleet roster
506 (1)	Scrapped by Muni (1970s)
6 / 506 (2)	On Muni active fleet roster, but undergoing rebuild at Woods Carpentry Shop, San Francisco, CA
7 / 507	On Muni active fleet roster
8 / 508	Scrapped by Muni (2015), a new Car #8 is planned
9 (1) / 509	In storage at Muni since retirement in 1995
9 (2)	On Muni active fleet roster
10 / 510	On Muni active fleet roster
11 / 511	On Muni active fleet roster
12 / 512	On Muni active fleet roster
13 (1) / 513	Ended service in 1988, given to Ardenwood Museum, Fremont, CA, unable to restore, scrapped.
13 (2)	On Muni active fleet roster
514 (1)	Scrapped by Muni (1963)
14 (1) / 514 (2)	On Muni active fleet roster
15 (1) / 515	Ended service in 1982, placed into storage at Muni
15 (2)	On Muni active fleet roster
16 / 516	On Muni active fleet roster
17 / 517	On Muni active fleet roster
18 / 518	On Muni active fleet roster
19 (1) / 519	Scrapped by Muni (1986); also briefly Car # 500 (1968-1973)
19 (2)	On Muni active fleet roster
20 / 520	On Muni active fleet roster
21 (1) / 521	Scrapped by Muni (1987)

A Fleet History of the San Francisco Municipal Railway
Section 7: Figures and Graphics

Powell Cable Car Fleet List - 2018 continued	
No.	Disposition
21 (1) / 521	Scrapped by Muni (1987)
21 (2)	On Muni active fleet roster
22 / 522	On Muni active fleet roster, recently completed rebuild in 2017
23 / 523	On Muni active fleet roster, recently completed rebuild in 2018
24 / 524	On Muni active fleet roster
25 / 525	On Muni active fleet roster
26 / 526	On Muni active fleet roster
27 / 527	On Muni active fleet roster
28 (1) / 501	In storage at Muni since retirement in 2002. Sent to ShoreLine Trolley Museum, East Haven, CT in 2018
28 (2)	On Muni active fleet roster

California - O' Farrell Cable Car Fleet List - 2018	
No.	Disposition
1	Scrapped (2008)
2	Renumbered from Car # 2 to Car #3, scrapped (2008)
3	Renumbered from Car # 3 to Car # 2, scrapped (2008); partially saved in a Haight St. clothing store
4	An original cable car (not Car #4) is in service w/ Hornblower Cable Cars, but the original #4, is #43
5	Current status unknown.
6	Former Knott's Berry Farm Car, pieces found in a field in Healdsburg, CA (2017), essentially scrapped
7	Owned by Phillip Wright (Gridley Family) in Healdsburg, CA
8 / 55	See Car # 55 information
9	Owned by Phillip Wright (Gridley Family) in Healdsburg, CA and currently numbered Car #17
10	A motorized cable car - in storage, owned by Hornblower Classic Cable Cars, awaiting restoration
11	Sold at Bonham's Auction in New Jersey (2014) - current owner wishes anonymity - lives in California
12	Believed to be In service as motorized Cable Car #5 with Hornblower Classic Cable Cars
13	Current status is unknown
14	Scrapped (1980s)
15 / 59 (2)	See Car # 59(2) information
16 / 60 (2)	See Car # 60 (2) information
17	Former Knott's Berry Farm Car, currently at Poway-Midland Museum, Poway, CA
18 / 52 (1)	See Car # 52 (1) information

A Fleet History of the San Francisco Municipal Railway
Section 7: Figures and Graphics

California - O'Farrell Cable Car Fleet List continued: 2018	
No.	Disposition
19 / 54 (2)	See Car #54 (2) information
20	Knott's Berry Farm Car, sold 1980s, possibly Car #4 or #22 at Hornblower Cable Car, or status unknown
21	At Travel Town Museum, Griffith Park, Los Angeles, CA
22	Assuming not renumbered, in service as motorized Cable Car #22 with Hornblower Classic Cable Cars
23	Sold to an unrecorded party (2005), current status is unknown
24 / 38	See Car #38 information
25 / 39	See Car #39 information
26-37	Numbers not used by California Cable RR after 1907
38 / 24	At Ely Stage Stop & Museum, Lake County, CA
39 / 25	Status unknown, but very likely scrapped
40 / 49 (2)	See Car #49 (2) information
41	At an unknown date - scrapped.
42	On Muni active roster - restored to early 1900s appearance - used for special occasions
43 (1)	Never owned by Muni, scrapped by California Cable RR at unknown pre-1952 date
43 (2) / 4	Knott's Berry Farm Car, at Orange Empire Museum, Perris, CA, Car #4 when Muni bought Cal Cable RR
44	Scrapped at S & S Shortline Railroad Museum, Farmington, UT (2003)
45	Sold to unrecorded party on Ebay (2003), current status is unknown
46	Owned by Phillip Wright (Gridley Family), in Healdsburg, CA
47	At Pioneer Village Museum, Minden, NE
48	At Seashore Trolley Museum, Kennebunkport, ME
49 (1)	Knott's Berry Farm Car, returned to Muni, later sold, owned by Brett Folena, Meadow Vista, CA
49 (2) / 40	Scrapped by Muni (1990s)
49 (3)	On Muni active fleet roster, undergoing restoration work at Cable Car Barn, San Francisco, CA
50	On Muni active fleet roster
51	On Muni active fleet roster
52 (1)	Owned by Phillip Wright (Gridley Family) in Healdsburg, CA and currently numbered as Car #11
52 (2) / 18	Scrapped by Muni (1981)
52 (3)	On Muni active fleet roster
53	On Muni active fleet roster, but undergoing repair at Cable Car Barn, San Francisco, CA
54 (1)	Current status is unknown
54 (2) / 19	On Muni active fleet roster
55 (1)	Believed to be scrapped (2008), but there is a chance this is Hornblower Cable Car #4
55 (2) / 8	On Muni active fleet, but undergoing rebuild at Carpentry Shop, Woods Division, San Francisco, CA

A Fleet History of the San Francisco Municipal Railway
Section 7: Figures and Graphics

California - O'Farrell Cable Car List continued: 2018	
No.	Disposition
56	On Muni active fleet roster. Recently completed a rebuild in 2018
57	On Muni active fleet roster
58	On Muni active fleet roster
59 (1)	Former Knott's Berry Farm Car, currently at Oakwood Senior Retirement Facility, Auburn, CA
59 (2) / 15	In storage at New Orleans Regional Transit Authority, New Orleans, LA
59 (3)	On Muni active fleet roster
60 (2) / 16	In storage at Muni since retirement in 2002
60 (3)	On Muni active fleet roster

Jones Street Shuttle Cable Car Fleet List: 2018	
No.	Disposition
60 (1)	Converted to a motorized cable car, owned by Phillip Wright (Gridley Family), in Healdsburg, CA
61 / 62	Originally Jones Street Shuttle Car # 62, in storage in Osaka, Japan
62 / 61	Originally Jones Street Shuttle Car # 61, in service as motorized Cable Car # 62, owned by Muni

Sacramento-Clay Cable Car Fleet List 2018	
No.	Disposition
15, 23, 25-26	Sold to private parties - current status for these cable cars is unknown
16	Scrapped in 1996 after removal from Emporium roof
17	Motorized but not operating - owned by Erie County Fair in Hamburg, NY
18	Owned by Phillip Wright (Gridley Family) in Healdsburg, CA, in use as a ticket office and storage shed
19	See historic fleet below
20	Scrapped in 2015 when determined condition was too deteriorated to restore
21	Sold to Mrs. W. Ballard, converted to first motorized cable car 1952, destroyed in warehouse fire 1964
22	Stored at Western Railway Museum in Suisun City, CA, but mostly destroyed by outside exposure
24	Sold to a unnamed movie studio in Los Angeles - late 1940s, believed to be scrapped.

Historic Cable Car Fleet List: 2018	
No.	Disposition
19	Sold to Pacific Railway & Locomotive Society, acquired by Muni, currently owned by Muni in storage

A Fleet History of the San Francisco Municipal Railway
Section 7: Figures and Graphics

No.	Name	Location	Built	Years of Muni service
1	Presidio Division / Geary St. Car House	Geary Blvd. & Presidio Avenue	1912	1912-
2	Presidio & Ferries RR Car Barn	Filbert St. & Gough St.	1908	1913-1922
3	Potrero Division / 17th St. Car House	17th St. & Bryant St.	1914	1914-
4	Geary St., Park & Ocean RR Car Barn (former)	Geary Blvd. & Arguello Blvd.	1892	1930s-1944
5	Cam Beach Yard / Geneva Division	Geneva Ave. & San Jose Ave.	1901	1944-
6	Haight Division	Haight St. & Stanyan St.	1883	1944-1948
7	Turk & Fillmore Car House	Turk St. & Fillmore St.	1902	1944-1948
8	McAllister Division	McAllister St. & Masonic Ave.	1883	1944-1950
9	Lincoln Way Yard (aka Boneyard)	Lincoln Way & Funston Ave.	1905	1944-1950
10	Sutro Division	32nd Ave. & Clement St.	1895	1944-1951
11	Elkton Shops	Ocean Ave. & San Jose Ave.	1907	1944-1977
12	24th & Utah Division & Shops	24th Ave. & Utah St.	1904	1944-1994
13	Cable Car Barn	Washington St. & Mason St.	1887 / 1907 1984	1944-
14	Ocean Division	Ocean Ave. & San Jose Ave.	1949	1949-1975
15	Kirkland Division	Beach St. & Stockton St.	1950	1950-
16	California Cable RR Car Barn & Powerhouse	California St. & Hyde St.	1890	1952-1957
17	Woods Division (aka Central Shops)	22nd St. & Indiana St.	1975	1975-
18	Green Division (aka Metro Rail Green)	Geneva Ave. & San Jose Ave.	1977	1977-
19	Flynn Division	15St. & Harrison St.	1989	1989-
20	Army Street Yard	Army St. & 3rd St.	1982	1982-1990
21	Metro East Division (aka MME)	25th St. & Illinois St.	2007	2007-
22	Islais Creek Division	22nd Ave. & Cesar Chavez St.	2014	2014-

Notes

- • = a division in active service which currently stores and operates this type of vehicle
- X = a division that formerly stored and operated this type of vehicle

A Fleet History of the San Francisco Municipal Railway
Section 7: Figures and Graphics

Bus	Trolley Bus	Street Car	LRV	Cable Car	Current Status
X	•	X			Active Division
		X			Apartment building
	•	X			Active Division
X					Was recently Office Depot store, with upper level parking garage
		•	•		Active Yard, part of Green Division
	X	X			Ameoba Music (former Park Bowl)
		X			Northern Police Station
X		X			Multi-unit housing, ground level retail stores, including Lucky grocery store
		X			Andronico's grocery store, Park West apartments, large parking lot
X		X			CVS Pharmacy and former Fresh and Easy grocery store and parking lot
		X			Green Division (rail), Balboa Park BART station, I-280 freeway right of way
X					S.F. General Hospital parking garage - under control of SFMTA
				•	Active Division
X					Green Division (rail)
•					Active Division
				X	Trader Joe's / CVS Pharmacy stores, parking garage and parking lot
•					Active Division
		•	•		Active Division
•					Active Division
X					Warehouse site and parking lot
		•	•		Active Division
•					Active Division

185

A Fleet History of the San Francisco Municipal Railway
Section 7: Figures and Graphics

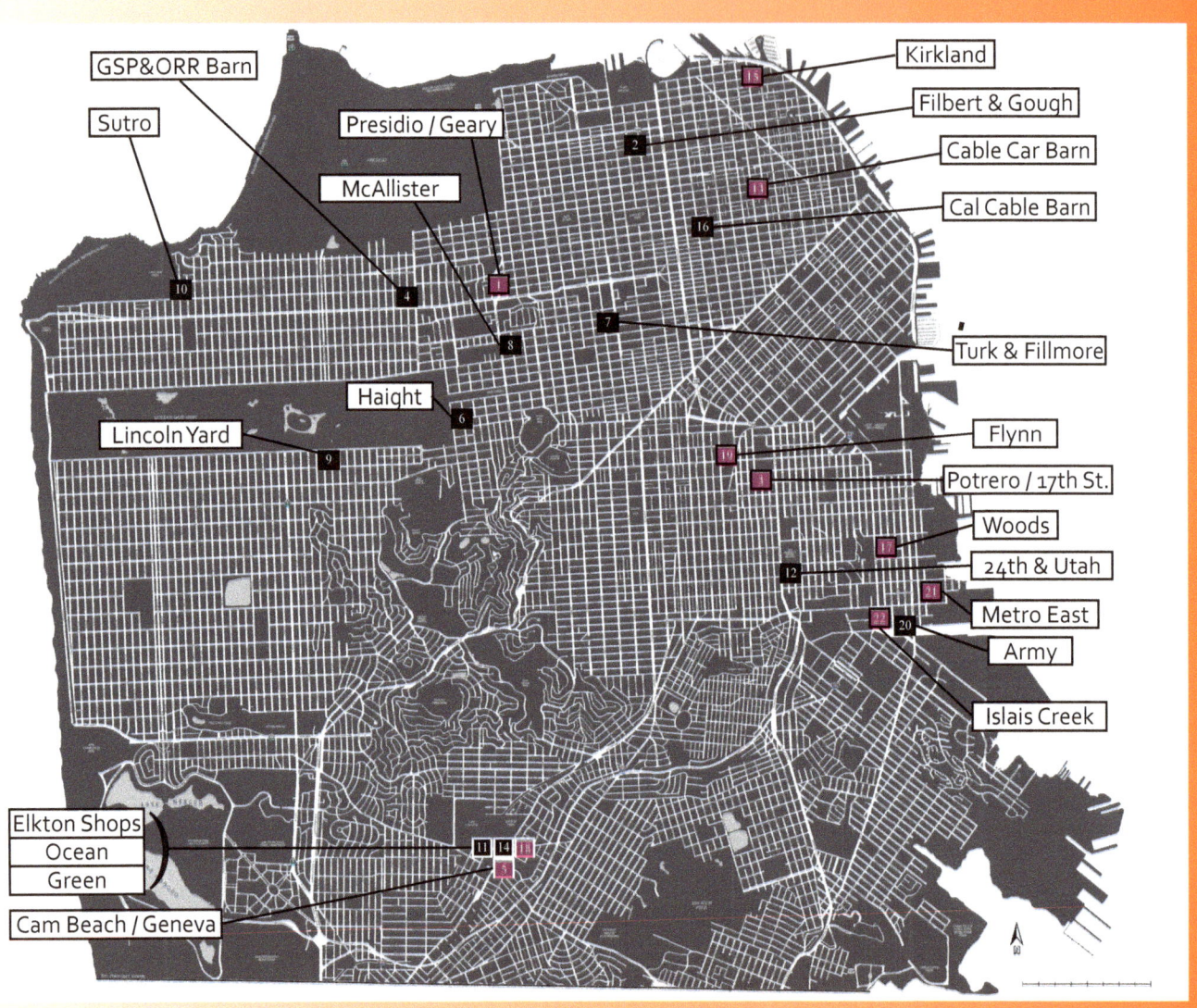

Notes

- ▪ = active division, yard or barn
- ▪ = a closed facility that formerly was the site of an active division, yard or barn

A Fleet History of the San Francisco Municipal Railway
Section 7: Figures and Graphics

LOGOS AND COLOR SCHEMES

During a century of transit operations Muni has used three logos and six color schemes, although the sixth color scheme was actually a return to the first color scheme. In 1912 as Muni prepared to initiate service, a decision was made to paint the first streetcars gray with red trim and gold lettering. No records are known to exist that detail how the colors were selected or who was responsible for the decision. In 1912, the newly formed San Francisco Municipal Railway did not have a logo. The first 194 street cars and 5 buses entered service with the printed words "Municipal Railway" on their side, but without a logo.

The circular logo with the letters "SF" in the center and the words "Municipal Railway" printed along the contours of the circle first appeared on Bus # 06 in 1918. It appeared slightly different than the logo shown, but this logo became the identification of Muni for the next 50 years. This logo has become known by the name of the "O'Shaughnessy logo", although the origin of its design is not known. It is doubtful that M.M. O'Shaughnessy personally designed it. It's not color specific as it appeared with the different Muni color scehmes during the era, sometimes with the writing being dark and the background being light, and other times with the writing being light and the background being dark. Although a new logo was adopted in 1968, this logo never was retired, and is still used on occasion in 2018.

In the late 1930's, Muni ordered buses that were delivered in orange and black, which were never official Muni colors, but shortly afterward, Muni did officially change colors to "Commodore Blue" and "Coca-Cola Yellow", or simply blue and yellow to commemorate the 1939 Golden Gate International Exposition, or "World's Fair" on Treasure Island in the middle of San Francisco Bay. No records exist to detail who authorized the change. The five new "Magic Carpet" streetcars (very similar to PCC cars) were painted this color, as were multiple orders of buses, and initially, former MSRy vehicles after the 1944 merger. This color scheme was short-lived, and was replaced in 1946.

Muni's most famous color scheme and design treatment was the green and cream with "Wings" design adopted in 1946-47. As with the earlier color schemes, no records exist that state the persons who authorized the change, and it is unknown who was responsible for the "Wings" design. Part of the rationale for the change appears to be almost of necessity, because of the huge increase in fleet size following the 1944 merger, coupled with green and white being the MSRy colors. Although the MSRy shade of green used on vehicles was different from that adopted by Muni, the two colors were marginally similar. The change to green has been seen by some to be a reflection of power of displaced MSRy staff, many of whom settled into senior level positions at Muni.

There were variations in the green and cream with "Wings" design as it was applied to vehicles. No cable cars ever wore the "Wings" design. Designs with "squared-off" and "angled ends" were both used. Type A streetars had "mini-Wings" where the design was only applied above a raised body-length edge rail in a small space below the windows. The Fageol-Twin Coach buses bought to replace cable cars in 1947 didn't use the "Wings" design at all due to a conflict with a large aluminum band that circled the vehicle.

A Fleet History of the San Francisco Municipal Railway
Section 7: Figures and Graphics

The last new vehicles to wear the colors and design were Mack buses, although the last vehicles of any type to wear the colors and design were four second-hand PCC cars from St. Louis obtained in 1962.

 In 1967 Muni updated transit operator uniforms by adopting colors based on the California Cable Car line. In 1968 a new logo, known as the "Ribbon" logo, was introduced. It resembled the ribbon design found on the Calfornia Cable Car line, and included the word "Muni" with serifs to give it a "Victorian" style, and a plain sans serif "S" and "F" on different parts of the lower ribbon. Simultaneously, Muni adopted the California Cable Car colors of maroon and yellow/gold.  The new logos and colors were on all 391 GM "New Look" buses that arrived in 1969, and the colors were used on some, but not all old vehicles when repainted. The majority of trolley buses and PCC streetcars remained painted in green and cream until replaced in the 1970s and 1980's. The "Ribbon" logo is no longer in use.

 In 1975 under Curtis Green as General Manager, Muni prepared to implement a new trolley bus fleet, LRV operations were on the horizon, and Muni paid the design firm of Walter Landor Associates a fee of $100,000 for a new logo and color scheme. The fee was an unusual action by a public agency at that time, and still would be today, but Landor delivered the only Muni complete "branding campaign" that has occurred in agency history. Almost everything, the colors, the logo, operator uniforms, stop flags, transit service maps, etc. were changed.  The iconic logo has come to be known as the "Muni Worm", due to its resemblence to a wriggling worm. The new colors were "Sunset Glow" (orange) and "California Poppy Gold" (yellow). The adopted paint scheme liberally used white with the orange and yellow colors appearing in a triple band with two broad stripes flanking a very narrow stripe of contrasting color which wrapped around vehicles. Near the front of most vehicles, the color bands reversed the colors found on the rest of the vehicle. The only transit vehicles that did not wear this paint scheme were the cable cars. Starting in the mid-1990s a much simpler and much narrower single stripe color scheme was adopted in an effort to reduce maintenance costs. Initially the stripe was applied below the windows, but later the stripe was moved to be above the windows. The final order of Neoplan "standard floor" buses were the last to wear the Landor color scheme. Older buses and trolley buses were painted in the simplified stripe design, but it was not used on Boeing LRVs.

The most recent color scheme at Muni appeared in 1996 when the new Breda LRVs arrived painted in silver (gray) and red, which were Muni's first colors in 1912. The decision to paint the LRVs in Muni's original colors was made while Johnny Stein was General Manager, although it isn't clear who authorized this action.  Once the LRVs were in service, a decision was made while Michael Burns was the General Manager to paint future buses and trolley buses in silver (gray) and red to match the LRV fleet. Some units of the 2002-03 Neoplan contract for 40' and 60' buses were the first to be painted in the retro colors. Once adopted as the new color scheme, older vehicles were repainted as the need arose when they came in for major maintenance actions. Although the colors changed, the "Muni Worm" logo continued to be the official Muni logo. The silver or gray and red color scheme has not been used on cable cars. In 2018 the "Muni Worm" logo continues to be the primary logo, although the O'Shaughnessy logo is used in certain situations, often when old / historic vehicles are involved.

A Fleet History of the San Francisco Municipal Railway
Section 7: Figures and Graphics

PASSENGER LEVELS, FARES, FAREBOX RECOVERY AND OTHER FINANCIAL INFORMATION

Tables and graphics on the next few pages detail several pieces of historic data. The first table contains the progression of the basic cash fare required for travel on Muni from 1912-2017. The issue of fares is more complex than use of a basic cash fare and cannot be addressed in detail here, but a few notes illustrate some key elements. During earlier years in its history, Muni offered reduced fares based on "volume" purchases (e.g. 3 tokens for 25c at a time when single fares were 10c each), but generally the basic fare applied to most passengers. Although Muni charged reduced fares to some groups (youths and seniors), beginning in 1974 a 50% reduced fare for seniors and disabled passengers - at least during off-peak times - became a requirement for all agencies accepting federal funding. This came as a result of a modification to the Urban Mass Transit Act of 1964, which created the Urban Mass Transit Administration (UMTA), that later became the Federal Transit Administration (FTA) in 1991. The 1964 legislation and various amendments established the framework for federal support for public transit that continues into 2018. Also starting in 1974 Muni offered its first volume pass, the Fast Pass (cost $11), which allowed unlimited rides for the duration of a month. Use of the paper passes ended in 2011 as the program adopted use of a stored value plastic card. Starting in 1984, following the passage of Proposition E, cable car fares were allowed to be set separately from base transit fares. In 2014 the reduced fare for youth was modified by a program to provide free fares to lower income youth. These examples show that fares remain a dynamic changing issue in San Francisco.

The data for the second table in this section was compiled from multiple sources. Pre-1981 data was taken from a table in the book Inside Muni, which likely used data found in annual reports. 1981-1996 data was generally taken from Muni Short Range Transit Plans and agency budget documents. The 1997-2017 data utilizes Muni data reported annually to the FTA that is recorded as part of the National Transit Database (NTD). NTD Tables 1 and 12 were utilized 1997-2012, and the agency profile summary was used 2012-2015. After the SFMTA was created in 1999, a "clear" budget that separated Muni from the other parts of the larger agency increasingly has not been available, aside from the NTD data, as certain actions (e.g. fare inspectors) have been absorbed by other divisions.

Data appears to have transitioned from calendar year to fiscal year in 1915. There is data gap between 1980-1988, because ridership data collected during this time was later realized to be inaccurate and inflated. Actions occurred almost simultaneously that are believed to have caused this problem, including changes in data collection techniques, implementation of Muni Metro Market Street subway service, and major bus and trolleybus service changes. An example of "ridership inflation" is a 1984 count which registered 313 million passengers, while revenue figures were only slightly changed from a few years earlier when a reliable figure of 184 million passengers was recorded.

An issue also concerns farebox recovery data. Older data (pre-1979) may include other revenue (advertising), while later data (post 1996) does not. Earlier data include accounting changes that impacted costs more than revenues. An example is 1953, the last year with a 100% farebox recovery, which was made possible by counting accumulated surplus from sources that hadn't been yet shown on the books. Exact certainty on the affect of these elements on farebox recovery isn't possible, but assuming a variance of 3% up or down is likely a reasonable "margin of error", with higher variances in certain years. While the data shown is believed to be "credible", there is no one definitive souce of Muni / SFMTA ridership figures and farebox recovery statistics.

A Fleet History of the San Francisco Municipal Railway
Section 7: Figures and Graphics

Muni Cash Fare History

Year	Cash Fare / % increase		Cable Car / % increase		Year	Cash Fare / % increase		Cable Car / % increase	
1912-1944	$ .05		N/A		1992-1993	$ 1.00		$ 2.00 / $3.00 RT	
1944-1946	$ .07	28%	$ .07		1993-1998	$ 1.00		$ 2.00	
1946-1952	$ .10	30%	$ .10		1998-2003	$ 1.00		$ 3.00	33%
1952-1969	$ .15	33%	$ .15		2003-2005	$ 1.25	20%	$ 5.00	40%
1969-1970	$ .20	25%	$ .20		2005-2009	$ 1.50	17%	$ 5.00	
1970-1980	$ .25	20%	$ .25		2009-2011	$ 2.00	25%	$ 5.00	
1980-1982	$ .50	50%	$ .50		2011-2014	$ 2.00		$ 6.00	17%
1982-1984	$ .60	17%	$ .60		2014-2015	$ 2.25	11%	$ 7.00	14%
1984-1986	$ .60		$ 1.00	40%	2015-2017	$ 2.50	10%	$ 7.00	
1986-1988	$ .75	20%	$ 2.00 / $ 2.50 RT	100%	2017-	$ 2.75	9%	$ 7.00	
1988-1992	$ .85	12%	$ 2.00 / $ 2.50 RT					RT = round trip fare	

Ridership and Revenue

Year	Annual Passengers*	Annual Fare Revenue	Farebox Recovery %	Year	Annual Passengers	Annual Fare Revenue	Farebox Recovery %
1913	9,723,177	444,745	123.7%	1938	90,290,519	3,444,745	108.4%
1914	27,933,049	1,150,236	123.2%	1939	106,478,465	4,107,365	110.6%
1915	40,369,865	1,630,788	116.3%	1940	111,305,527	4,135,903	108.5%
1916	47,886,784	1,970,478	114.6%	1941	108,822,011	4,057,698	104.2%
1917	36,234,723	1,470,193	102.1%	1942	113,956,341	4,290,238	107.1%
1918	62,396,036	2,363.366	104.8%	1943	142,896,226	5,571,933	117.9%
1919	59,341,253	2,391,176	95.3%	1944*+	167,348,356	6,661,889	115.6%
1920	66,169,246	2,702,289	99.2%	1945	295,306,166	15,008,834	123.8%
1921	69,960,834	2,868,616	93.8%	1946*	326,007,393	17,290,400	106.7%
1922	70,757,908	2,884,815	97.4%	1947	314,623,064	18,890,017	97.2%
1923	70,633,760	2,993,829	91.7%	1948	307,975,046	18,171,522	92.3%
1924	77,736,617	3,173,181	91.5%	1949	298,475,999	18,456,459	88.9%
1925	79,900,145	3,268,383	91.5%	1950	259,177,321	18,411,169	88.9%
1926	83,390,900	3,395,950	91.5%	1951	248,630,182	17,860,166	92.4%
1927	83,603,652	3,398,187	93.5%	1952*	241,405,841	18,083,097	87.3%
1928	85,281,171	3,461,859	92.2%	1953	221,981,258	21,976,748	102.3%
1929	85,683,684	3,482,133	89.1%	1954	211,477,453	21,456,987	95.8%
1930	87,673,608	3,553,592	88.5%	1955	203,887,807	20,898,346	94.7%
1931	85,250,742	3,409,103	86.4%	1956	198,049,970	20,252,610	92.3%
1932	80,123,258	3,163,189	85.3%	1957	197,397,641	20,027,769	92.6%
1933	71,815,286	2,795,456	82.1%	1958	195,471,709	19,842,118	86.8%
1934	73,063,608	2,819,549	106.3%	1959	198,040,839	19,818,277	84.4%
1935	78,849,085	3,008,011	104.2%	1960	200,054,717	19,717,769	81.0%
1936	79,116,866	3,049,141	104.2%	1961	198,639,884	19,928,935	78.5%
1937	80,754,084	3,137,584	106.1%	1962	199,388,421	19,683,629	77.4%

A Fleet History of the San Francisco Municipal Railway
Section 7: Figures and Graphics

Ridership and Revenue

Year	Annual Passengers	Annual Fare Revenue	Farebox Recovery %	Year	Annual Passengers	Annual Revenue	Farebox Recovery %
1963	196,313,284	19,614,395	82.7%	1991	238,933,414	79,844,000	30.0%
1964	198,102,066	19,765,491	79.7%	1992*	238,294,492	82,494,000	30.6%
1965	196,794,746	19,626,207	73.6%	1993*	229,918,154	90,337,000	33.3%
1966	200,215,911	20,100,665	69.3%	1994	219,916,249	97,266,000	34.9%
1967	204,727,040	20,618,719	68.0%	1995	215,998,232	93,497,000	33.8%
1968	203,394,030	20,812,485	63.5%	1996	214,048,267	94,603,000	33.2%
1969*	198,810,265	20,531,789	54.1%	1997	217,209,022	98,007,252	33.8%
1970*	187,564,375	24,945,349	54.3%	1998	219,089,550	97,587,835	31.4%
1971	178,988,593	26,400,550	53.7%	1999	216,411,575	97,650,766	28.3%
1972	164,780,943	25,689,123	56.2%	2000	225,671,849	102,074,623	26.4%
1973	158,531,072	24,799,796	47.7%	2001	234,912,828	104,176,336	24.2%
1974	162,169,654	24,682,002	42.3%	2002	233,015,741	97,287,281	21.9%
1975	164,811,156	24,936,207	36.4%	2003	215,594,488	97,886,438	21.8%
1976	148,127,619	21,975,611	31.4%	2004	215,743,701	115,526,988	25.7%
1977	159,356,666	23,412,191	30.4%	2005*	216,948,400	121,588,335	25.7%
1978	170,118,499	24,788,486	29.9%	2006	210,848,300	135,966,057	28.7%
1979	184,303,380	26,936,009	29.8%	2007	206,458,615	142,993,754	28.1%
1980*	Ridership Data gap 1980-1987 due to incorrect data	32,666,281	31.4%	2008	227,135,348	151,530,920	25.9%
1981		45,585,449	36.7%	2009*	217,021,058	152,114,110	25.9%
1982*		46,876,066	31.0%	2010	214,653,212	187,629,138	24.9%
1983		51,077,743	30.8%	2011	222,936,618	191,619,436	30.3%
1984*		51,847,132	30.3%	2012	222,922,607	202,266,644	31.3%
1985		55,262,000	26.5%	2013	223,851,332	220,093,193	32.9%
1986		62,129,000	28.7%	2014*	228,748,481	212,823,751	29.8%
1987		68,315,000	31.1%	2015	229,442,770	214,676,015	28.8%
1988*	244,733,183	69,551,000	29.7%	2016	232,348,165	206,735,189	25.7%
1989	235,793,859	76,766,000	32.6%	2017			
1990	233,468,239	78,168,000	31.2%				

+ Muni and Market Street Railway merger: September 29, 1944
* Fare increase year

A Fleet History of the San Francisco Municipal Railway
Section 7: Figures and Graphics

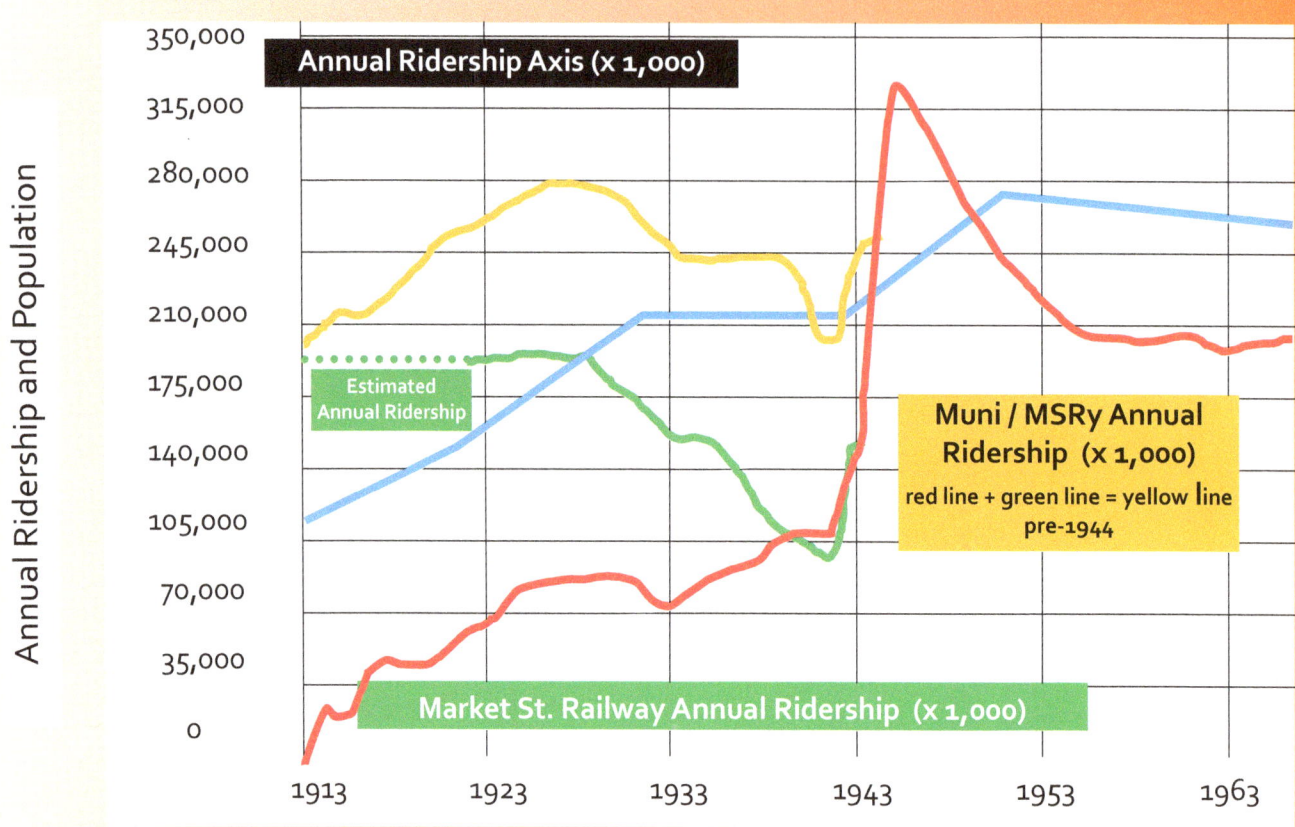

Notes

1) 1913-1928 - Population and ridership show steady increase - non-war peak reached in 1927-1928.
2) 1913-1944 - The yellow line is the combined total of the blue and green ridership lines of the Muni and MSRy from the inception of Muni 1912 to the merger of the two agencies in September 1944.
3) 1928-1933 - Population shows increase, but ridership shows decline - Depression and impact of increase in automobile ownership.
4) 1933-1941 - Population is stagnant - ridership shows increase - Continued service expansion and MSRy fare increase in 1938 are believed to be primary causes of increase.
5) 1941-1946 - World War II era record ridership (1946 = peak) - Gas rationing, S.F. population increase - unofficial - S.F. population reaches 800,000 by 1945 - merger with MSRy in September 1944.
6) 1950-1980 - Population and ridership show steady decrease - 1980 S.F. population 10% lower than 1950, suburbanization of Bay Area, road / freeway network heavy investment, transit receives lower investment, large drop in transit ridership 1968-1973, transit ridership gain 1974-1980.
7) 1980-1987 - Ridership data gap - data figures collected during this time shown to be inflated - new methodology adopted to improve accuracy.
8) 1990-2018 - Population increase - 2018 S.F. population 30% higher than 1980, significant increase in transit infrastructure (Muni Metro and BART) - ridership variable, but generally flat trendline since 1990.

A Fleet History of the San Francisco Municipal Railway
Section 7: Figures and Graphics

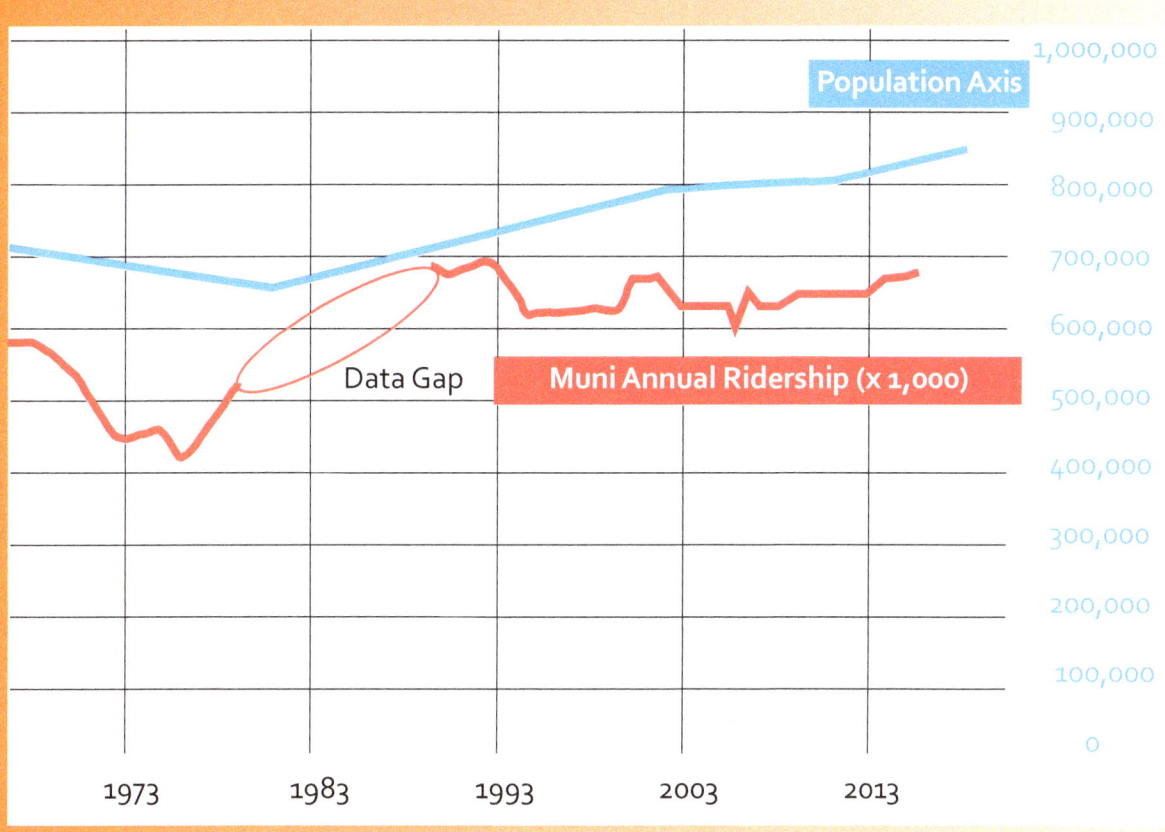

A Fleet History of the San Francisco Municipal Railway
Section 7: Figures and Graphics

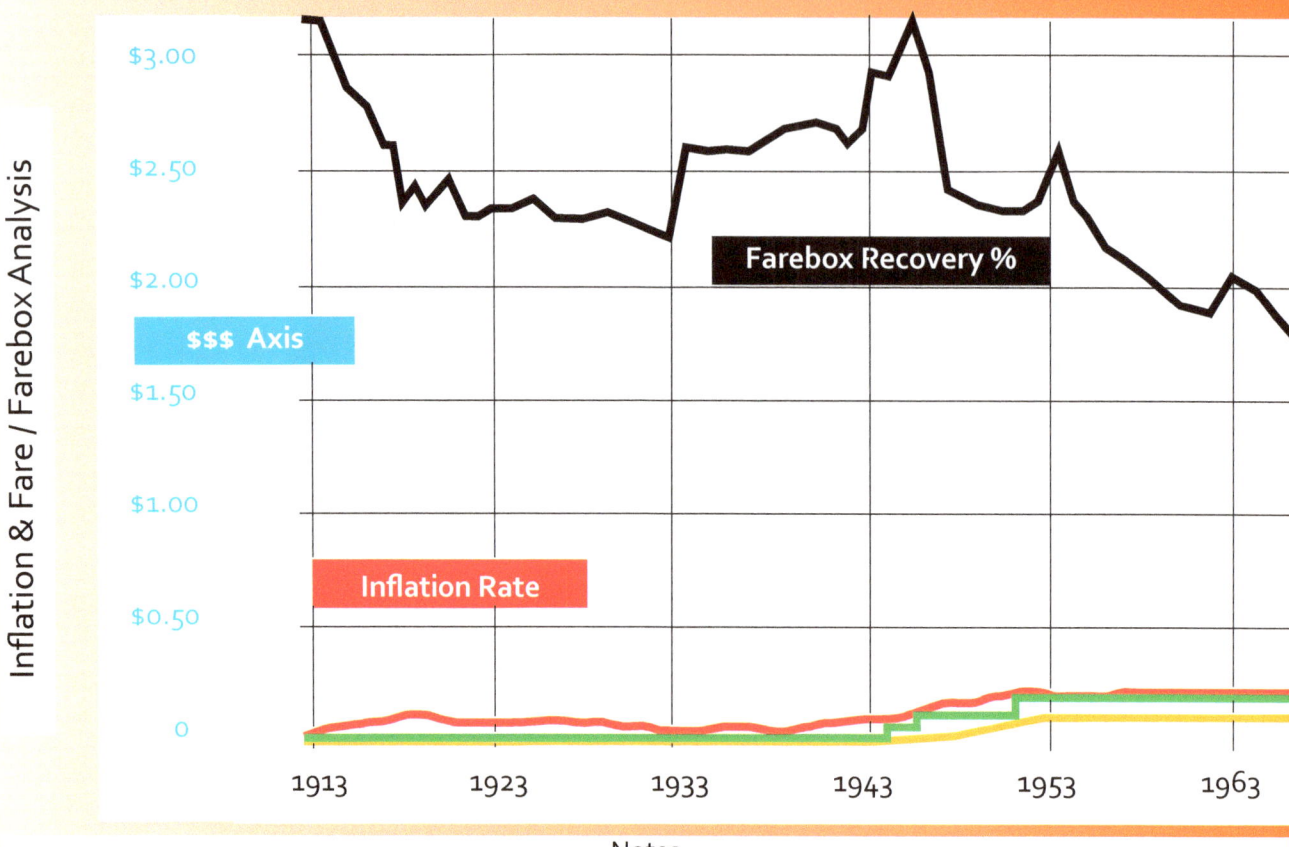

Notes

1) 1913-1943 - In the first 33 years of Muni operations, a 100% farebox recovery was achieved 50% of the time. A high point of a farebox recovery of 123% was achieved twice: 1913 and 1945.
2) 1944-1956 - As Muni transformed from a streetcar transit ageny with some buses to a bus and trolley bus agency with some streetcars, the decade after the merger and end of WWII showed generally declining ridership, but continued strong farebox recovery.
3) 1956-1973 - The fare increase to 15c lasted 17 years until 1969, but by 1973 the fare was raised twice to 25c. Average farebox recovery plummeted in this period from over 90% to less than 50% and ridership decreased by almost 25% in 7 years (1966-1973).
4) 1973-1989 - Inflation becomes a major factor in all types of transit performance analysis as the increase in this 15 year period equals the increase experienced in the 50 year period prior to 1973. Ridership increased by 33%-50% (data problems in 1980s impact this era), but farebox recovery contiued to decline, dropping by another 33%. By 1989 the adult cash fare is 85c. - more than triple the 1973 adult cash fare. The monthly fare "Fast Pass" is introduced in 1974. The disconnect between the adult cash fare (85c) and the average paid fare (30c) appears to increase and the Fast Pass is one reason for this change. Other reasons include signficant reduced senior, disabled and youth fares.

A Fleet History of the San Francisco Municipal Railway
Section 7: Figures and Graphics

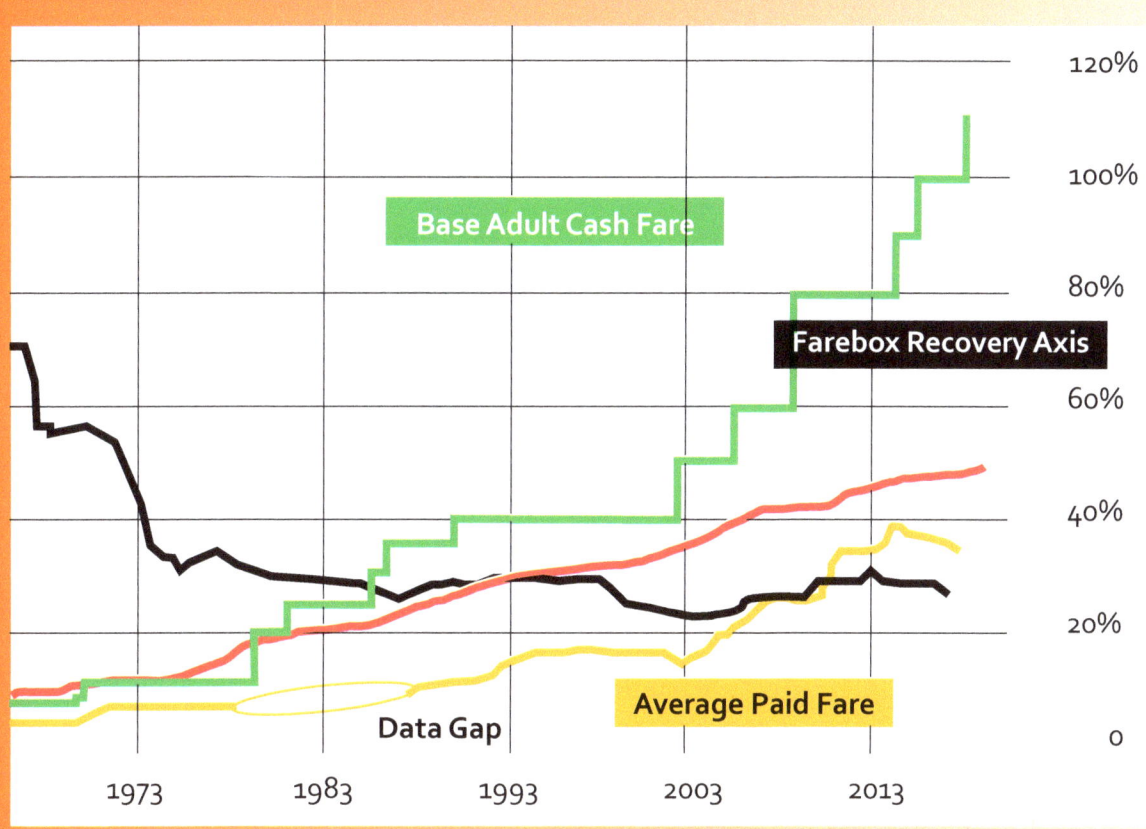

Notes

5) 1990-2016 - Inflation continues to increase, but at less than 50% of the rate in the previous era. The adult cash fare triples from 85c to $2.50, and the average paid fare more than triples from 30c to 98c. A greater variety of special passes are available than at any other time in Muni history. The regional stored value card, known as "Clipper" replaced the Fast Pass as the primary adult fare alternative to paying cash in 2011. Discounted tokens are also phased out by 2010. Farebox recovery declines slightly from the low-mid 30% range to mid-high 20% range. Most fares, including the basic adult cash fare, started to be indexed for future increases in 2011 via a formula determined by the Automatic Indexing Plan: a blended formula based on the Bay Area Labor Consumer Price Index for all urban consumers (CPI-U) and SFMTA labor costs".

6) 2016-2018 - Most U.S cities see transit ridership declines. San Francisco is an exception, at least through 2017, likley due to the ongoing population increase, positive service changes (Muni Forward program), and an influx of several hundred new transit vehicles of all types: buses, trolley buses and LRVs that have had a positive impact on vehicle availability and on-time performance. The average adult fare paid peaked at 98c in 2013, but since declined to 89c in 2016. Farebox recovery was 25.7% in 2016. After assessment for inflation, the original 5c cash fare of 1913 would be a $1.25 cash fare in 2018.

A Fleet History of the San Francisco Municipal Railway
Section 7: Figures and Graphics

MUNI AND SFMTA LEADERSHIP

S.F. Department of Public Works - S.F City Engineer
- 1912-1932   M.M. O'Shaughnessy

S.F. Municipal Railway - General Manager
- 1912-1918   Thomas J. Cashin
- 1918-1932   Frederick Boeken

The passage of a new City Charter in the election of March 26, 1931 included a provision to create a Public Utilities Commission to manage the city-owned public utilities: Airport, Hetch Hetchy Water Works, and the S.F. Municipal Railway. The action transferred power held by the Department of Public Works, led by M.M. O'Shaughnessy, to the new commission, which included an executive team led by an agency director.

S.F. Public Utilities Commission - Director
- 1932-1945   Edward G. Cahill
- 1945-1956   James H. Turner
- 1956-1958   T.N. Bland
- 1959-1964   Robert C. Kirkwood
- 1964-1970   James K. Carr
- 1970-1976   John O. Crowley
- 1977-1979   John B. Wentz
- 1979-1983   Richard Sklar
- 1983-1986   Rudolph Nothenberg
- 1986-1988   Rudolf J. Birrer
- 1988-1989   Dean W. Coffey
- 1989-1993   Thomas J. Elzey
- 1993-1994   Anson B. Moran

S.F. Muncipal Railway - General Manager
- 1932-1940   Frederick Boeken
- 1940-1951   William L. Scott
- 1951-1960   Charles F. Miller
- 1960-1968   Vernon W. Anderson
- 1968-1974   John M. Woods
- 1974-1982   Curtis E. Green
- 1982-1985   Harold H. Geissenheimer
- 1985-1990   William G. Stead
- 1990-1993   Johnny B. Stein

The passage of Proposition M on November 2, 1993 created the independent S.F. Public Transportation Commission: a board of five members with direct oversight of the S.F. Municipal Railway.

S.F. Public Transportation Commission - Director / General Manager
- 1993-1994   Johnny B. Stein
- 1994-1996   Philip Adams
- 1996-1998   Emilio J. Cruz
- 1998-1999   Michael T. Burns

The passage of Proposition E on November 2, 1999 approved the merger of the S.F. Municipal Railway and the S.F. Department of Parking and Traffic into one agency to be known as the S.F. Municipal Transportation Agency: controlled by a board of five members. The existing Public Transportation Commission was abolished.

S.F. Municipal Transportation Agency (SFMTA)
General Manager / Chief Executive Officer / Director of Transportation
- 1999-2005   Michael T. Burns
- 2006-2011   Nathaniel P. Ford
- 2011-   Edward D. Reiskin

A Fleet History of the San Francisco Municipal Railway
Photo Credits & Bibliography

A Fleet History of the San Francisco Municipal Railway
Photo Credits & Bibliography

A Fleet History of the San Francisco Municipal Railway
Photo Credits & Bibliography

PHOTO CREDITS AND BIBLIOGRAPHY

The photos used in this book came from several diferent photographers. They are listed below in page order as shown in the book. The most important photographers or sources were the San Francisco Municipal Transportation Agency (SFMTA) photo archives and a multiple individuals, who along with the author, provided the photos used in this book.

Many different sources of information were used to create this book. They are listed below in alphabetical order by author or source name. The most important sources were the 1981 publications *Inside Muni* and *The People's Railway* by John McKane and Anthony Perles, but over three dozen sources provided information used in this book.

Page ID	Photo	Author/Source	Page ID	Photo	Author/Source	Page ID	Photo	Author/Source
12-01	W01323	SFMTA	26-01	PC142	SFMTA	38-01	KM-1	Kevin Mueller
12-02	X48881	SFMTA	26-02	U06245	SFMTA	38-02	ML_6470	Matt Lee
12-03	X7510_1	SFMTA	27-01	U08370p	SFMTA	38-03	SL-1	ShoreLine Museum
13-01	PBFH-01	Paul Bignardi	27-02	X2020	SFMTA	39-01	PBFH-13	Paul Bignardi
13-02	056	SFMTA	28-01	X3815-6N_2	SFMTA	39-02	PBFH-14	Paul Bignardi
14-01	W07371	SFMTA	28-02	PBFH-09	SFMTA	39-03	PBFH-15	Paul Bignardi
14-02	A0286	SFMTA	28-03	X7173_4	SFMTA	40-01	PBFH-16	Paul Bignardi
15-01	D4754_3	SFMTA	28-04	X7173_1	SFMTA	40-02	PBFH-17	Paul Bignardi
15-02	PBFH-02	Paul Bignardi	29-01	X7400	SFMTA	41-01	MSRyMus-1	MSRy Museum
15-03	20664661	SFMTA	29-02	M1694_1	SFMTA	41-02	PBFH-18	Paul Bignardi
15-04	PBFH-03	Paul Bignardi	29-03	M1694_3	SFMTA	41-03	PBFH-19	Paul Bignardi
16-01	D4728C	SFMTA	30-01	AB1950_770	SFMTA	41-04	PBFH-20	Paul Bignardi
16-02	D4728A	SFMTA	30-02	ab1518	SFMTA	42-01	Graphic	MSRy Museum
17-01	D5313	SFMTA	30-03	910627_26	SFMTA	42-02	PBFH-21	Paul Bignardi
17-02	A6589	SFMTA	31-01	160322_32	SFMTA	42-03	PBFH-22	Paul Bignardi
18-01	PBFH-04	Paul Bignardi	31-02	160322_40	SFMTA	42-04	PBFH-23	Paul Bignardi
18-02	A6787	SFMTA	32-01	PBFH-10	Paul Bignardi	43-01	PBFH-24	Paul Bignardi
19-01	D4367A	SFMTA	32-02	PBFH-11	Paul Bignardi	43-02	Graphic	MSRy Museum
19-02	PBFH-05	Paul Bignardi	32-03	2018LRV4-3	SFMTA	43-03	PBFH-25	Paul Bignardi
20-01	PC106	SFMTA	33-01	ML_71110	Matt Lee	43-04	PBFH-26	Paul Bignardi
20-02	X2017	SFMTA	33-02	ML_0671	Matt Lee	44-01	Graphic	MSRy Museum
21-01	X2090A	SFMTA	33-03	ML_50507	Matt Lee	44-02	PBFH-27	Paul Bignardi
22-01	U18029	SFMTA	34-01	ML_4694	Matt Lee	44-03	ML_0466	Matt Lee
22-02	X14101D	SFMTA	34-02	ML_0315	Matt Lee	44-04	PBFH-28	Paul Bignardi
23-01	Graphic	MSRy Museum	35-01	ML_9962	Matt Lee	45-01	ML_952	Matt Lee
23-02	PBFH-06	Paul Bignardi	35-02	ML_0650	Matt Lee	45-02	PBFH-29	Paul Bignardi
24-01	PBFH-07	Paul Bignardi	35-03	120823_1006	SFMTA	45-03	PBFH-30	Paul Bignardi
24-02	PBFH-08	Paul Bignardi	36-01	ML_0537	Matt Lee	45-04	Graphic	MSRy Museum
24-03	WPN27.6327	SFMTA	36-02	ML_0653	Matt Lee	45-05	PBFH-31	Paul Bignardi
25-01	D4843	SFMTA	37-01	ML_8691	Matt Lee	46-01	Graphic	MSRy Museum
25-02	X1872	SFMTA	37-02	PBFH-12	Paul Bignardi	46-02	PBFH-32	Paul Bignardi
25-03	X1873	SFMTA	37-03	ML_3331	Matt Lee	49-01	W04246p	SFMTA

A Fleet History of the San Francisco Municipal Railway
Photo Credits & Bibliography

Page ID	Photo	Author/Source	Page ID	Photo	Author/Source	Page ID	Photo	Author/Source
49-01	Graphic	SFMTA	69-02		Val Lupiz	88-01	M2161_7	SFMTA
50-01	W09722	SFMTA	70-01	961011_1	SFMTA	88-02	PBFH-54	Paul Bignardi
51-01	Misc_0052	SFMTA	70-02	PBFH-41	Paul Bignardi	89-01	M0277_1	SFMTA
51-02	A4924	SFMTA	71-01	840206_16	SFMTA	89-02	M1412_1	SFMTA
52-01	A0111	SFMTA	71-02	891129_16	SFMTA	89-03	M1412_3	SFMTA
53-01	A4924	SFMTA	71-03	PBFH-42	Paul Bignardi	90-01	M2132_1	SFMTA
54-01	X0097_4	SFMTA	72-01	881005_19	SFMTA	90-02	910720_13	SFMTA
55-01	M0071	SFMTA	72-02	PBFH-43	Paul Bignardi	90-03	PBFH-55	Paul Bignardi
55-02	D4418	SFMTA	72-03	PBFH-44	Paul Bignardi	91-01	ML_92706	Matt Lee
55-03	M0339_2	SFMTA	73-01	900235_30	SFMTA	91-02	PBFH-56	Paul Bignardi
55-04	M0278_2	SFMTA	73-02	PBFH-45	Paul Bignardi	91-03	ML_81604	Matt Lee
56-01	PBFH-33	Paul Bignardi	73-03	ML_52911	Matt Lee	92-01	ML_81904	Matt Lee
56-02	PBFH-34	Paul Bignardi	73-04	ML_10607	Matt Lee	92-02	ML_52711	Matt Lee
56-03	A7020	SFMTA	74-01		Ron Downing	92-03	PBFH-57	Paul Bignardi
57-01	D4629	SFMTA	74-02	ML_20909	Matt Lee	92-04	ML_52607	Matt Lee
57-02	U09830p	SFMTA	74-03	ML_810088	Matt Lee	92-05	ML_111310	Matt Lee
58-01	U20408	SFMTA	75-01	PBFH-46	Paul Bignardi	93-01	ML_2429	Matt Lee
58-02	U17038-1	SFMTA	75-02	PBFH-47	Paul Bignardi	93-02	ML_90206	Matt Lee
59-01	U18048A_2	SFMTA	75-03	ML_3347	Matt Lee	93-03	ML_5485	Matt Lee
59-02	U18396	SFMTA	75-04	PBFH-48	Paul Bignardi	93-04	ML_5551	Matt Lee
60-01	M19389	SFMTA	76-01	ML_2516	Matt Lee	94-01	PBFH-58	Paul Bignardi
60-02	No #	SFMTA	76-02	ML_81010	Matt Lee	94-02	PBFH-59	Paul Bignardi
60-03	M-18794-1	SFMTA	76-03	ML_0308	Matt Lee	99-01	971207-17	SFMTA
61-01	U18802_3	SFMTA	77-01	ML_51806	Matt Lee	99-02	Graphic	MSRy. Museum
61-02	M-19484	SFMTA	77-02	ML_3262	Matt Lee	100-01	20304068_33	SFMTA
62-01	31701	SFMTA	77-03	ML_4957	Matt Lee	100-02	Graphic	MSRy. Museum
62-02	D5045	SFMTA	78-01	ML_8611	Matt Lee	100-03	M1883_13	SFMTA
63-01	X2023	SFMTA	78-02	ML_60106	Matt Lee	100-04	PBFH-60	Paul Bignardi
63-02	PBFH-35	Paul Bignardi	78-03	ML_42409	Matt Lee	100-05	Graphic	MSRy. Museum
64-01	X7172_3	SFMTA	78-04	ML_6810	Matt Lee	101-01	PBFH-61	Paul Bignardi
64-02	X2022	SFMTA	79-01	ML_9849	Matt Lee	101-02	PBFH-62	Paul Bignardi
64-03	PBFH-36	Paul Bignardi	79-02	ML_6036	Matt Lee	101-03	950318A_22	SFMTA
64-04	PBFH-37	Paul Bignardi	79-03	PBFH-49	Paul Bignardi	102-01	M1135	SFMTA
65-01	X7133_1	SFMTA	80-01	ML_2310	Matt Lee	102-02	90311_25	SFMTA
65-02	X8382_1	SFMTA	80-02	ML_9014	Matt Lee	102-01	2000415B_10	SFMTA
65-03	X7509_1	SFMTA	80-03	ML_8966	Matt Lee	102-02	Graphic	MSRy. Museum
65-04	PBFH-38	Paul Bignardi	81-01	D4632	SFMTA	103-03		Val Lupiz
66-01	M0674_11_1	SFMTA	84-01	PBFH-50	Paul Bignardi	103-04	Graphic	MSRy. Museum
66-02	M0674_7	SFMTA	84-02	PBFH-51	Paul Bignardi	103-05	PBFH-63	Paul Bignardi
66-03	831006_11	SFMTA	85-01	U15472c_980	SFMTA	103-06	Graphic	MSRy. Museum
67-01	PBFH-39	Paul Bignardi	85-02	PBFH-52	Paul Bignardi	104-01	ML_3717	Matt Lee
67-02	M0749_5	SFMTA	85-03	X1460	SFMTA	104-02	Graphic	MSRy. Museum
67-03	PBFH-40	Paul Bignardi	86-01	X1701	SFMTA	104-03	X2012	SFMTA
68-01	M2022_28	SFMTA	86-02	X7833_3	SFMTA	105-01	120507	SFMTA
68-02	ML_101406	Matt Lee	86-03	PBFH-53	Paul Bignardi	105-02	Graphic	MSRy. Museum
68-03	800507_09	SFMTA	87-01	M0799	SFMTA	105-03	X2998A_2	SFMTA
68-04	800501_01	SFMTA	87-02	X3554_2	SFMTA	105-04	Graphic	WSRy. Museum
69-01		Val Lupiz	87-03	D5997	SFMTA	106-01	X9812_4	SFMTA

A Fleet History of the San Francisco Municipal Railway
Photo Credits & Bibliography

Page ID	Photo	Author/Source	Page ID	Photo	Author/Source	Page ID	Photo	Author/Source
106-02	PBFH-64	Paul Bignardi	122-02		Seashore Museum	141-03	X9024_2	SFMTA
106-03	X1226c	SFMTA	123-01	PBFH-79	Paul Bignardi	141-04	PBFH-93	Paul Bignardi
107-01	PBFH-65	Paul Bignardi	123-02	X5352	SFMTA	142-01	A7295	SFMTA
107-02	X2354_2	SFMTA	123-03	PBFH-80	Paul Bignardi	142-02	PBFH-94	Paul Bignardi
107-03		Val Lupiz	124-01	AAC-8063	SF Pub. Library	143-01	PC043-55	SFMTA
107-04	M1603_8	SFMTA	124-02	PBFH-81	Paul Bignardi	143-02	PBFH-95	Paul Bignardi
107-05	20842027	SFMTA	124-03		Steve Graves	143-03	W07194	SFMTA
107-06		Val Lupiz	124-04	PBFH-82	Paul Bignardi	143-04	X1749	SFMTA
108-01	X2011_1	SFMTA	125-01	PBFH-83	Paul Bignardi	143-05	PBFH-96	Paul Bignardi
108-02	X2011_2	SFMTA	125-02	X5354	SFMTA	144-01	PCO43-55	SFMTA
108-03	PBFH-66	Paul Bignardi	126-01	X3062	SFMTA	144-02	PBFH-97	Paul Bignardi
108-04	M2333_7	SFMTA	126-02	X4087	SFMTA	144-03	PBFH-98	Paul Bignardi
108-05	Graphic	MSRy. Museum	126-03	PBFH-84	Paul Bignardi	144-04	A7312	SFMTA
109-01	PBFH-67	Paul Bignardi	127-01	PBFH-85	Paul Bignardi	144-05	PBFH-99	Paul Bignardi
109-02	Graphic	MSRy. Museum	127-02	PBFH-86	Paul Bignardi	145-01	U01090	SFMTA
109-03	617ZaQHN-et	Houghton-Mifflin	127-03		Oakwood Sr. Care	145-02	PCO64	SFMTA
109-04	X2632	SFMTA	128-01		Jack Demnyan	145-03	A7319	SFMTA
109-05	PBFH-68	Paul Bignardi	128-02	M2204_2	SFMTA	146-01	A7321	SFMTA
111-01	X2815A_1	SFMTA	129-01	X2249	SFMTA	146-02	Mo232_16	SFMTA
111-02	AAB-2846	SF Pub. Library	129-02	PBFH-87	Paul Bignardi	146-03	M1068_1	SFMTA
112-01	U06468	SFMTA	130-01	X4912	SFMTA	146-04	M2370_2	SFMTA
112-02	PBFH-69	Paul Bignardi	130-02	X4959	SFMTA	147-01	U00151_152	SFMTA
112-03	PBFH-70	Paul Bignardi	130-03		Osaka Museum	147-02	D5135	SFMTA
113-01	PBFH-71	Paul Bignardi	130-04		Osaka Inst. of Tech.	147-03	X3037	SFMTA
113-02	PBFH-72	Paul Bignardi	130-05		Osaka Inst. of Tech.	147-04	X3587	SFMTA
113-03	PBFH-73	Paul Bignardi	131-01	AAC-8015	SF Pub. Library	148-01	U00138_1	SFMTA
114-01	U07168	SFMTA	131-02	X3432_2	SFMTA	148-02	X3791	SFMTA
114-02	X5481	SFMTA	131-03	PBFH-88	Paul Bignardi	148-03	W07219	SFMTA
114-03	PBFH-74	Paul Bignardi	131-04	PBFH-89	Paul Bignardi	148-04	X9338_1	SFMTA
115-01		Bonham's Auctions	132-01	U60239	SFMTA	149-01	831220A_0	SFMTA
116-01		Eric Walls	132-02		Unknown	149-02	160924_MH	SFMTA
116-02		Poway Museum	133-01		Erie Co. Fair	149-03	D5459	SFMTA
117-01	PBFH-75	Paul Bignardi	133-02		Erie Co. Fair	149-04	M2063_11	SFMTA
117-02	PBFH-76	Paul Bignardi	133-03	AAC-7864	SF Pub. Library	150-01	X2497	SFMTA
117-03	PBFH-77	Paul Bignardi	133-04	X9848_2	SFMTA	150-02	150128	SFMTA
118-01		Ely Museum	133-05	PBFH-90	Paul Bignardi	150-03	D5361	SFMTA
118-02		Ely Museum	137-01	W00691	SFMTA	150-04	PBFH-100	Paul Bignardi
118-03	AAC-8019	SF Pub. Library	137-02	W08636	SFMTA	151-01	M1797	SFMTA
119-01	U02137	SFMTA	138-01	X1875	SFMTA	151-02	M2093_3	SFMTA
119-02		MSRy. Museum	138-02	X4283	SFMTA	152-01	PBFH-101	Paul Bignardi
119-03	930804_01	SFMTA	139-01	W07115	SFMTA	152-02	PBFH-102	Paul Bignardi
120-01		Val Lupiz	139-02	W10351	SFMTA	152-03	PBFH-103	Paul Bignardi
120-02	U03656	SFMTA	139-03	D4672	SFMTA	152-04	M2013_3	SFMTA
120-03		Orange Emp. Mus.	140-01	PBFH-91	Paul Bignardi	153-01	M2122_8	SFMTA
121-01	AAC-8110	SF Pub. Library	140-02	W00555	SFMTA	153-02	AB1520	SFMTA
121-02	AAC-8109	SF Pub. Library	140-03	PBFH-92	Paul Bignardi	153-03	PBFH-104	Paul Bignardi
121-03	PBFH-78	Paul Bignardi	141-01	U00154	SFMTA	153-04	PBFH-105	Paul Bignardi
122-01		Pioneer Museum	141-02	D4978A	SFMTA	153-05	PBFH-106	Paul Bignardi

A Fleet History of the San Francisco Municipal Railway
Photo Credits & Bibliography

Page ID	Photo	Author/Source	Page ID	Photo	Author/Source	Page ID	Photo	Author/Source
154-01	850916_09	SFMTA	156-01	6736470-et.	SFMTA	158-02	120530_196	SFMTA
154-02	PBFH-107	Paul Bignardi	156-02	3abacbcaf-et	SFMTA	158-03	X1882	SFMTA
154-03	M2382_4	SFMTA	156-03	170113_is_ck	SFMTA	158-04	140603_009	SFMTA
154-04	PBFH-108	Paul Bignardi	156-04	PBFH-112	Paul Bignardi	158-05	X3510_6	SFMTA
155-01	PBFH-109	Paul Bignardi	157-01	X1437(1)	SFMTA	158-06	PBFH-113	Paul Bignardi
155-02	PBFH-110	Paul Bignardi	157-02	A0288	SFMTA	206-01	PBFH-114	Paul Bignardi
155-03	PBFH-111	Paul Bignardi	158-01	W03035	SFMTA			

A Fleet History of the San Francisco Municipal Railway
Photo Credits & Bibliography

Callwell, Robert, Walter E Rice, PhD: *Of Cables and Grips: The Cable Cars of San Francisco*, Friends of the Cable Car Museum, San Francisco, CA, 2000, (unpublished 2005)

Cox, Harold E.: *PCC Cars of North America*, Lakewood, OH, Community Press, 1963

Ehrlich, Peter: *San Francisco's F-Line,* Bloomington, IN, Trafford Publishing, 2012

Hilton, George W.: *The Cable Car in America,* Stanford, CA, Stanford University Press, 1997

Jenkins, Arthur C.: *A Report On Economic and Organizational Features of The Municipal Railway of San Francisco,* San Francisco, CA, 1949

McKane, John, Anthony Perles: *Inside Muni,* Glendale, CA, Interurban Press, 1982

Newton, Leonard V.: *Postwar Transit Plan for Municipal Railway City and County of San Francisco.* Report to Public Utilities Commission, 1945

Perles, Anthony, John McKane, Tom Matoff, Peter Straus: *The People's Railway*, Glendale, CA, Interurban Press, 1981

Smallwood, Charles A: *The White Front Cars of San Francisco*, Glendale, CA, Interurban, Press, 1971, 1978

Stindt, Fred A.: *San Francisco's Century of Street Cars,* Kelseyville, CA , Fred A. Stindt, 1990

Ute, Grant, Phllip Hoffman, Cameron Beach, Robert Townley, Walter Vielbaum: *San Francisco's Municipal Railway: Muni*, Charleston, SC, Arcadia Press, 2011

_____: San Francisco Municipal Railway, A*nnual Reports: 1942, 1943, 1944, et al-1972*, San Francisco, CA

_____: San Francisco Municipal Railway, *Record of Rolling Stock Municipal Railway of San Francisco, - Fiscal Year Ending 1944, 1947, 1951, 1954,* San Francisco, CA

_____: San Francisco Municipal Railway, *Five-Year Plan: 1979-1984, 1981-1986, et al -1988-1993,* San Francisco, CA

_____: San Francisco Municipal Railway, *Short Range Transit Plan: 1984-1989, 1985-1990, et al - 2008-2027*, San Francisco, CA

_____: San Francisco Municipal Railway, *Mini Short Range Transit Plan: 2009-2028, 2017-2030*, San Francisco, CA

A Fleet History of the San Francisco Municipal Railway
Photo Credits & Bibliography

_____: San Francisco Municipal Railway, *Short Range Transit Plans and Capital Improvement Program: 1993-2002*, San Francisco, CA

_____: San Francisco Municipal Transportation Agency (SFMTA), *Annual Report 2001, 2002, et al -2017*, San Francisco, CA

_____:San Francisco Municipal Railway (Muni), *The Data Guide, 1990-1991*, San Francisco, CA

_____: San Francisco Municipal Transportation Agency, *Minutes of Board Meetings;2001-2017 (Selected)*, San Francisco, CA

_____: San Francisco Public Utilities Commission, *Minutes of Board Meetings,1932-1997 (Selected)*, San Francisco, CA

_____: San Francisco Public Transportation Commission, *Minutes of Board Meetings, 1997-2001 (Selected)*, San Francisco, CA

Market Street Railway (non-profit), *Inside Track 2015-2018*, San Francisco, CA

Copied list of notes: Cable Car and Streetcar Dispositions , 1982 (partial revised 1995); Anthony Marquardt

Rannells, Jackson, "An OK for Bus Linking Union Square, Wharf." San Francisco Chronicle, 12, April 1983

Oral interview: Anthony Marquardt; Muni Transit Operator and historian, May 18, 2017, February 15, 2019

Oral interview: Lionel Chartrand; Former Maintenance Manager, Ride the Ducks, May 29, 2017.

Oral interview: Phillip Wright; son of Arnold Gridley, current owner of five motorized former California Street Cable RR Cable Cars: #7, #17, #46, #52 and Jones Street Shuttle #60; also owner of non-motorized Sacramento-Clay Cable Car #18; October 13, 2018.

Oral interview: Brett Folena; owner of former motorized California Street Cable Car #49, January 19, 2019

Oral interview: Marty Biniasz, Erie County NY Fair; owner of motorized Sacramento-Clay Cable Car #17, February 15, 2019

Flanders, Steven, Owner S & S Shortline RR, Farmington, UT, Re. Inquiry about California Street Cable Car #44, October 27, 2017: Email

Bunker, K.V., Curator, South Pacific Coast RR (The Railroad Museum at Ardenwood), Newark, CA, Re. Inquiry about Powell Street Cable Car #13, January 15, 2018: Email

A Fleet History of the San Francisco Municipal Railway
Photo Credits & Bibliography

Holmgren, Don, President, Friends of the Cable Car Museum, San Francisco, CA, Re. Muni Cable Car Query, February 12, 2018: Email

Market Street Railway, 2000-2018
https://www.streetcar.org
Web, 2016, 2017, 2018
Website of non-profit group focused on preservation of San Francisco Municipal Railway historic streetcars and cable cars, and historic transit vehicles from all over the world

The Cable Car Home Page, Joe Thompson, 1996-2018
http://www.the-cable-car-guy.com
Web, 2016, 2017, 2018
Website with extensive information on the San Francisco Municipal Railway Cable Car system

San Francisco Cable Car Museum.org, Friends of the Cable Car Museum, 2004-2017
http://www.cablecarmuseum.org/
Web, 2016, 2017
Official website of the San Francisco Cable Car Museum located in the Cable Car Barn at Washington and Mason Streets in San Francisco, CA

North American Bus and Bus Body Builders, Coachbuilt.com, 2004-2017
https://http://www.coachbuilt.com/bus/
Web, 2016, 2017, 2018
Website with multiple pages of extensive information on North American bus manufacturers

San Francisco Municipal Railway, Canadian Public Transit Discussion Board (CPTDB), 2017
https://cptdb.ca/wiki/index.php/San_Francisco_Municipal_Railway
Web, 2016, 2017
Website with extensive information on San Francisco Municipal Railway fleet vehicles, both past and present.

A Fleet History of the San Francisco Municipal Railway
Photo Credits & Bibliography

ABOUT THE AUTHOR - PAUL BIGNARDI

I was born in San Francisco and grew up in South San Francisco, San Bruno and Daly City. I had a large extended family in San Francisco, and spent a lot of time in The City while growing up, including some time riding all types of Muni transit vehicles. I graduated from San Francisco State Unversity and University of California - Hastings College of Law. At the time of the completion of this book, I've worked for over 20 years in Transit Planning with time at AC Transit, the National Park Service and over a dozen years at the San Francisco Municipal Transportation Agency (SFMTA). I've also worked for five years as a driver for Hornblower Classic Cable Cars (previously Classic Cable Car Charters). Currently I live in San Mateo, CA.

My favorite Muni and former Muni vehicles are: California line cable car #58 (used as a backdrop for wedding photos with my wife and the rest of the wedding party), historic streetcar #578, Baby White bus #42, soon to be restored historic streetcar #798, the three Jones Street Shuttle cable cars, #60, 61 and 62, and former California cable car #4 (now ownedy by Hornblower), on which I have had the pleasure to drive people all over San Francisco and other parts of the Bay Area on charters, tours, weddings and other special events.

Photo taken while portraying a Muni cable car operator, but actually driving the Hornblower "movie cable car" during a filming of "Birth of the Dragon" in S.F. in January 2016. Sadly, no cable car scenes appeared in the finished movie, but it was a great and memorable experience.